Swami Abhedananda

SWAMI ABHEDANANDA'S
JOURNEY INTO KASHMIR AND TIBET

(With the life of Jesus by Nicolas Notovitch)

Rendered into English

By

Ansupati Dasgupta

And

Kunja Bihari Kundu

RAMAKRISHNA VEDANTA MATH
19 A & B, RAJA RAJKRISHNA STREET
KOLKATA-700 006, INDIA

Published by
Swami Satyakamananda
Ramakrishna Vedanta Math,
19 A & B, Raja Rajkrishna street, Kolkata-700 006
E-mail : ramakrishnavedantamath@gmail.com
Website : www.ramakrishnavedantamath.org

First Published May 1987
Second Reprint May 2001
Third Edition November 2014

ISBN 978-93-80568-36-2

Printed at
Pelican Press
85 Bepin Behari Ganguly Street
Kolkata 700 012

CONTENTS

CONTENTS

PREFACE

In 1922 Swami Abhedananda, the author of this book, undertook a long and strenuous journey across a highly difficult terrain from the plains of India to snow-capped Tibet. It is not necessary here to make any detailed observation on the nature of this journey. A perusal of the pages that follow will make it clear to the reader.

It was the policy and effort of the British Government to promote commerce between India on the one hand and Tibet and Sikkim on the other. The result was the discovery of a few routes leading to Tibet unknown till then to most people.

When Lofd Dufferin was the Governor General of India (1884—1888) British merchants felt tempted to undertake an expedition through the unknown territory of Ladakh to initiate trade in wool wth that country. They had already informed the British Government of their purpose in view and it came to be decided that a mission led by Lord Macaulay should be sent to Tibet. But the Chinese authorities lodged a vehement protest against this move. The British, too, had their doubts as to the wisdom in sending such a mission. None-the-less they

felt it necessary to come to an understanding with Kashmir and Tibet. It was decided, however, to postpone sending the mission in view of the Chinese intransigence and other political reasons. But the veteran diplomat-cum-explorer, Prejevalsky, decided on undertaking a tour of Tibet with a view to promoting Russia's interest. This move engendered a feeling of suspicion in the mind of Lord Curzon who apprehended a Russian incursion into that country. As a result the British thenceforward concentrated their attention on Tibet. They felt that strong action was necessary and decided on a military solution to the problem at hand. Accordingly British troops were despatched to Tibet under the command of Colonel Francis Younghusband and Mr. Ramsay Macdonald. The King of Bhutan acted as an ally of the British in this expedition and guided them on their way to Tibet. The British Government was thus enabled to extend their rule over that country. In 1904 the British Government and the Government of Tibet entered into a peace treaty and trade pact. These developments contributed largely to the discovery of more than one route from India to Tibet.

One may approach Tibet either via Kalimpong or via Darjeeling. The first takes one from Kalimpong to Pedi in fifteen days across Pedong, Gangtok, Yatung Farijang (14200 ft.), Syamada, Rangilo, Giangsi or Jnanatse and Kalsa. One can also reach Yatung from Darjeeling by taking a different route along eighty-three miles which takes five days to cover on foot. To do this one treks from Darjeeling to Jeleppa Pass from where a zig-zag road leads to Yatung on the border of the Chumbi Valley. From Yatung one has to go to Giangsi and from there to Lhasa covering a distance of two hundred seventy-four miles. From Yatung there is again a two-hundred-fifty mile trade route called Khongmar extending upto Lhasa. The entire distance from Kalimpong to Lhasa on the back of a mule can be covered in three weeks' time.

Besides these there are three trade routes, each two hundred fifty miles long, from Sikkim to Tibet. These routes are called 'Lantok-Nathula', 'Jeleppa-la', and 'Kangra-lama' or 'Lochen'. Mules are the only means of conveyance along these routes. The trade link between India and Tibet is maintained only through these routes across Sikkim. Travellers from India can use these routes to reach Ladakh and Tibet.

Swami Abhedananda went first to Kashmir and then to Tibet. His journey through Kashmir over, he started for Tibet along the bank of the Indus. The story of the Swami's travels is both interesting and full of historical references. The book is replete with detailed information regarding the spread of Buddhism in Tibet, China, Japan and Korea. It also gives us a vivid picture of the life, manners, customs and social as well as monastic habits of the lamas. Along with these details the book covers themes like games and sports and also medical treatment as prevalent at that time in Tibet. The work has been further enriched by the inclusion of the unknown life of Jesus Christ in India hitherto unpublished.

Jesus Christ, when thirty-three, was accused of heresy by the Jews in Jerusalem and capital punishment was meted out to him by the Roman ruler, Pontius Pilate. He was crucified along with two other culprits. Christians believe that Jesus Christ died on the cross. But according to some historians and archaeologists Jesus did not die as a result of crucifixion.

THE ROUTE ADOPTED BY SWAMI ABHEDANANDA FOR HIS JOURNEY TO TIBET FROM KASHMIR

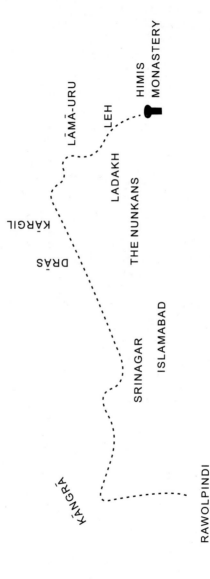

THE ROUTE ADOPTED BY SWAMI ABHEDANANDA FOR HIS
JOURNEY TO TIBET FROM KASHMIR

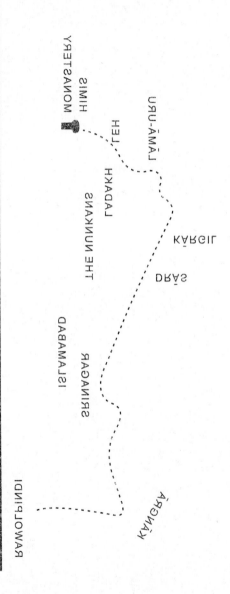

Some of his devoted disciples rescued him from the cross in a state of unconsciousness and restored him to life through nursing and attendance. His wounds were healed through application of juice from some medicinal herbs. Accounts of these startling facts are to be found in the now-rarely available book, *The Crucifixion by An Eye-witness*, the manuscript of which was found in Alexandria. Many, however, hold that the facts narrated in the book are not historically correct. But there are western scholars who believe that Jesus survived his ordeal on the cross, came to India and was kept in hiding to prevent his arrest by those opposed to him. Weighty arguments are not lacking in support of this view.

In May 1893 an article was published in *The Statesman*, an English daily. This article says that there is a tomb and altar believed to have been set up by St Thomas in a suburban locality, a few miles away from Karachi. Some people there still take pride in introducing themselves as Christians whose forefathers had been converted by St Thomas himself. They further claim that Christ lies buried beneath the said tomb. Every Sunday they make floral offerings to the tomb, light lamps and burn incense before it in the evening and hold a special prayer service at the end of which they dance and clap their hands. While doing so they repeatedly say, ''Victory to Jesus Christ'' The fact that Jesus Christ had not really been done to death through crucifixion and that he came to India after his recovery from the injuries therefrom finds its most eloquent corroboration in the following words in the speech delivered by the great saint, Swami Ramatirtha, under the caption *The Spiritual Power that Wins* :

''Now, Christ regained this union with the spirit before his death. You know that Christ did not die when he was crucified. This is a fact which may be proved. He was in a state called *samadhi*, a state where all life-functions stop, where the pulse beats not, where the blood apparently leaves the veins, where all signs of life are no more, where the body is, as it were, crucified. Christ threw himself into that state for three days and like a Yogi came to life again; made his escape and came back to live in Kashmir. Rama (Swami Ramatirtha) had been there and found many signs of Christ having lived there. Up to that time there was no Christian sect in Kashmir. There were many places called by his name, where Christians never came. Cities were called by the same names as many of the cities of Jerusalam through which Christ passed. There is standing a grave of nearly 2000 years. It is held very sacred and called the 'Grave of Eash'(Isha), which is the name of Christ in Hindusthani language, and 'Eash' means 'prince'. So there are many reasons to prove that He (Jesus) came to India, the same India where he learned his teaching.

"Again the people of India have a kind of magic ointment which is called the 'Christ Ointment' (Malam-i-Isha), and the story which the people, who prepare this ointment, tell is that this ointment Christ used to heal his wounds after he came to life and that ointment really heals all sorts of wounds miraculously."

There is a second book called *The Unknown Life of Jesus Christ* by Nicolas Notovitch which also contains some startling facts about Christ's life. It was written out of the authoritative manuscripts preserved in the Himis monastery in Tibet. We have it from Notovitch that Jesus Christ left Jerusalem and came to Sindh in India on foot in the company of some professional traders while he was only fourteen years old. As Notovitch writes :

"When Issa had attained the age of thirteen, when an Israelite should take a wife, the house, in which his parents dwelt and earned their livelihood in modest labour, became a meeting place for the rich and the noble, who desired to gain for a son-in-law, the young Issa, already celebrated for his edifying discourses in the name of the Almighty.

"It was then that Issa clandestinely left his father's house, went out of Jerusalem, and, in company with some merchants, travelled toward Sindh. ✱✱✱

"In the course of his fourteenth year, young Issa, blessed by God, journeyed beyond the Sindh and settled among the Aryas in the beloved country of God."

The reasons and proofs advanced by Notovitch in support of his contention are to be found in the appendix at the end of this book. Swami Abhedananda, like the Russian traveller Notovitch, discovered an ancient manuscript in Tibetan language in the Himis monastery. This manuscript unravels an unknown chapter in the life-story of Jesus. The Swami, with the help of a local lama interpreter, had it translated in part which has been inserted in Chapters 12 and 15 of this book. He also discovered a tomb dedicated to the memory of Jesus Christ at a place called Khana-yari in Kashmir. This fact together with a photo of the tomb has been incorporated in the book.

Swami Abhedananda's book *Journey into Kashmir and Tibet,* though primarily an account of his travels, offers many historical facts of inestimable value to seekers of truth. The Swami came to Belur Math (the world famous Ramakrishna Mission Monastery) on his return from America towards the end of 1921. On 14th July, 1922 he went first to Benares with a view to proceeding on a tour of Kashmir and Tibet. While at Benares he put up at Sri Ramakrishna Sevashram where the revered Hari Maharaj (Swami Turiananda) was then confined to bed with a carbuncle. The two were meeting after a gap of twenty-five years. It was a sad meeting no doubt, actually their last meeting, for Hari Maharaj did not long survive the surgical operation on his carbuncle made soon afterwards. With a heavy heart the Swami took leave of Hari Maharaj and left Benares on his way to Lahore.

Swami Abhedananda made it a rule to jot down in his diary the details of all that happened in course of his journey in Kashmir and Tibet. On completion of his travels he returned to Belur Math on 11th December, 1922. Brahmachari Bhairab Chaitanya accompanied him as his constant attendant. The Swami asked him to prepare the draft of a manuscript giving the story of his travels in Kashmir and Tibet. The Brahmachari wrote a long account of the travels on the basis of the diary written by the Swami. While doing this he also consulted, whenever necessary, *Rajatarangini, Tourists' Guide to Kashmir* and some other books on Kashmir and Tibet. Due to various preoccupations Swami Abhedananda did not get any opportunity to go through the manuscript as prepared by the Brahmachari. Afterwards he chose Calcutta as the centre of his activities. He first set up his Ramakrishna Vedanta Samity at Mechuabazar, Calcutta. Subsequently it was shifted to 11, Eden Hospital Road. In May, 1927 (Baisakh, 1334 B.S.) *Visvavani,* a monthly, acting as the mouth-piece of Ramakrishna Vedanta Samity came out for the first time. The account of the Swami's travels in Kashmir and Tibet as written by the Brahmachari started getting serially published in this journal. Later when Swami Abhedananda was requested to bring out the account in the form of a book he set about making changes and corrections in the travelogue as serialised in *Visvavani*. While doing this he consulted his diary and various other writings on travels in Kashmir and Tibet. The matters incorporated in the book, both cultural and historical, relating to countries like China, Japan, Korea etc were additions made by the Swami himself. The improved and enlarged manuscript thus prepared by the Swami came out in book-form in its first edition with the title *Paribrajak Swami Abhedananda* in the month of Bhadra, 1336 B.S. The title of the book was later changed to *Kashmir-O-Tibbate* (Bengali). Nearly about twenty-four years after this the second edition of the book came out in a more modified and enlarged form. Although the first edition of the book had been exhausted long ago, for various reasons there was much delay before the second edition could be published. We are now bringing out the fifth edition of the book, thanks to the interest shown by scholars and admirers and their goodwill. A new appendix has been added with extracts from *The Unknown Life of Jesus Christ* by Nicolas Notovitch, the Russian traveller. These extracts corroborate the account given by Swami Abhedananda.

We are now indeed very happy to bring out a new English edition of the Bengali book under the caption *Journey into Kashmir and Tibet* with the intention to extend the scope of its study by the English-speaking people all over the world. Let us hope readers will find the book to be of interest and value.

A few words about the translators. Shri Ansupati Dasgupta is at present Head of the Department of English, Surendranath College (formerly Ripon College). Shri Kunjabihari Kundu teaches at the same institution and belongs to its Department of Economics. Their work has been a labour of love undertaken at my request. I am more than happy to be able to put on record here my deep appreciation of the sincere task done by them amidst heavy preoccupations.

Ramakrishna Vedanta Math   Swami Prajnanananda.
Calcutta
October 1, 1986

CHAPTER — I

For long ten years from 1886 to 1896 Swami Abhedananda, before leaving for the West, lived the life of a wandering monk with no other possession except a staff and a begging bowl. He had visited the chief holy sites of India while practising religious austerities and meditation. But he had not had the opportunity of paying his respectful homage to the holy sanctuary of Lord Amarnath in Kashmir. While staying in America his desire to visit the shrine remained ever alive in his mind and became all the stronger after his return to India in 1921. After spending two summer months on the Shillong hills he came back to Belur Math and left for Kashmir on July 14, 1922, by the Punjab Mail.

Next day at 10-30 A.M. the Swami arrived at the monastery called Shri Ramkrishna Sevashram at Benares (also called Kashidham). There the revered Swami Turiananda lay bedridden with a carbuncle. Together they had preached the Vedantic philosophy in America and now after a long period of twenty years they were meeting each other again. It was a happy encounter no doubt and the hearts of both were filled with joy unspeakable. And yet who could imagine that this joy would be washed away by the tears of everlasting separation due to the demise of Swami Turiananda within a day or two?

The Swami took rest at the monastery for a day. After this he visited the famous Buddhist shrine, Sarnath (at Deer Park, Mrigadab) seven miles west of Benares. It was to this holy site that the Buddha, after having achieved enlightenment at Bodh Gaya, came to preach before a group of five disciples his first sermon on the Middle Path along which release from the problems and constraints of mortal existence might be gained. When one visits the archaelogical museum at Sarnath and the other age-old relics found on the site one can hardly help feeling grateful to Lord Curzon who, by his Act of 1904, sought to ensure the protection and preservation of India's ancient monuments and historic remains.

The most remarkable place of interest in modern Benares is the Hindu University founded by Pandit Malaviya as a centre of education in Indian art, culture and music and for the study of Sanskrit. The wide-ranging efforts in this institution to propagate learning and culture will certainly inspire every Indian with a sense of hope and pride. At the same time one must hold in high esteem the memory of that great lady, Dr.Annie Basant who first dreamt of the magnificent scheme that lies behind this University bearing eloquent testimony to modern India's bold step toward educational reforms and advancement.

Mr.King, the principal of the Engineering Department of the University, was a highly sociable person. He had a special affection for the Indian students for whose upliftment he was doing his utmost. He accorded a cordial welcome to the Swami and showed us various notable sites within the University. Pandit Madanmohan Malaviya told the Swami, ''Your highness stayed in America for twenty five years. I would request you to stay at Benares for at least twenty-five days so that we may be benefited by your Vedantic teachings.'' But the Swami expressed his desire to proceed to Kashmir immediately, for otherwise his pilgrimage to Amarnath would be unduly delayed. He took leave of Malaviyaji after assuring him that he would revisit the University for a longer stay on some other occasion.

On our way back to the monastery the Swami pointed out to us a garden near Durgabari where nearly thirty years ago he, as he told us, together with Saradananda, Sachchidananda, and Yogananda used to sit in religious prayer and meditation and lived on alms. Could anybody foresee at that time that the God-like Sri Ramakrishna was getting them trained through such austerities for the noble mission of bringing the message of Vedanta to millions of western people athirst for true spiritual knowledge ?

After a stay of three days at Benares the Swami started for Lahore by the up Punjab Mail from Mugalsarai Station. We awoke abruptly at dead of night to find that the train had stopped at Aligarh. A loud and confusing noise had broken our sleep. Five or six milk-vendors had entered our compartment and were making a terrific noise, asking people to buy from them. They had succeeded in breaking the sleep of the Swami too. Aligarh is known for its many milk-churning factories for the manufacture of butter. In this place whole milk is a rarity while skimmed milk is available in plenty. None in our compartment was however found interested in purchasing milk at such an odd hour.

At 5 in the morning our train reached Ambala Cantonment. From this place we had to board another train bound for Lahore ready to start after some time. After putting our luggages into a compartment we went round the place in search of food, but nothing of the kind was available there. Two persons were selling something on the platform. One of them was shouting his ware with cries of 'Hindu anda' (Hindu eggs) while the other was doing the same with cries of 'Muslim anda' (Muslim eggs). The entire station vibrated with their hollering. A Sikh passenger in front of our compartment purchased one Hindu anda. Out of curiosity we looked through our window and found that it was just a duck-egg seasoned with salt and black pepper dust. Obviously, the 'Muslim andas' were eggs of hens.

At nearly 12 noon our train reached Lahore. Knowing beforehand that Swami Abhedananda was coming there, some distinguished local Bengalees had come to the station with a view to according him a cordial welcome. The railway station of Lahore is quite large. One arrangement here was to the Swami's liking. It is simply this : Nearly 100 yards away from the station there is a depot of motor cars, horse-drawn carriages, and tongas[1]. If any passenger wants to hire one, it will be at once available to him simply at the blow of a whistle by an attending policeman. The fare is fixed and there is no need for higgling. That this arrangement is highly satisfactory will be readily appreciated by those who have the bitter experience of hiring a taxi in Calcutta.

At Lahore the Swami resided at the place of Sushil Kumar Chatterjee, a local advocate, whose earnest attention and warm geniality we shall never forget. It was then extremely hot at Lahore. News reached us that two ponies had died of sunstroke. One who has never visited the place will hardly understand how unbearably hot its climate can be. Exposed to this terrific heat we suffered unspeakable agony. So after visiting just a few sites of interest like Sahadara, Jumma Mosque,

---

[1]A tonga is a light two-wheeled carriage drawn by a pony.

Salimar Bag, Thandi Sarak and the like we left for Rawalpindi next day. The Swami said, "Let the weather cool down a little and we shall make a long stay at Lahore on our return from Kashmir."

It is a rewarding experience to travel along the North Western Railway. No other railway brings to view such charming mountain sights. We passed many a fountain and many a vale and many a tunnel and at last reached Rawalpindi at about 10 a.m. The transport hub of the city is located near the railway station which serves as the starting point for trips to Srinagar and other places of Kashmir by buses, motor cars, tongas or dandies. It takes seven hours to reach Srinagar from here by a car. For four passengers with only light luggages the journey costs Rs. 100/-. Heavy luggages can be put on a bus which usually reaches Srinagar after three days. A luggage-carrying truck takes three days and a tonga six days to reach Srinagar. Sometimes if there is a heavy rush or if the road condition is quite bad many travellers are compelled to be detained at Rawalpindi for three or four days. But our luck favoured us and we were spared this inconvenience. No sooner had we got down from the train than we found to our relief a passenger bus bound for Srinagar. After some argument with the bus-agent over the fare, the Swami paid up the entire amount in advance. Each seat within the interior of our bus cost FRs. 15, while for the front seat the fare was   Rs. 22.   The fare was rather high because of the heavy rush of pilgrims for Amarnath, the usual fare in the off-season not exceeding Rs. 8 or 10. A passenger was allowed to take with him a luggage of half a maund free of cost. Any amount above this would cost Rs. 8 per maund.

We placed our luggages inside the bus and then repaired to a nearby shop for some refreshment. Procuring food poses no problem here. There is a big market with hotels and refreshment rooms. There is also the Kalibari where one can go to partake of the food offered to the ruling deity. On return after a while we found that the bus-agent who had taken advance payment of Rs. 22 from the Swami for a seat at the front had reserved the same seat for Rs. 35 in favour of an Englishman named Major Skinner. This gentleman, however, proved to be a sport. On being informed of the whole affair, he gave the bus-agent a piece of his mind for his dishonesty and moved to another seat. Though scheduled to leave at twelve noon, the bus started actually at 4 p.m. in the afternoon. In this respect the practice followed in this province does not differ much from that followed in Bengal. In our bus there were twenty mendicants, indifferent and callous, who made it an occasion for smoking hemp continuously and for loudly shouting the name of Lord Hari repeatedly. The resulting noise, intense and riotous, startled even the people passing by who must have thought that something strange and unusual was taking place inside the bus.

The distance between Barkao and Rawalpindi is thirteen miles and a half. It is a good road stretching across a level surface. But we reached an acclivity near the village Chattar and after crossing the bridge in the village Saila found ourselves on an uneven road in a state of disrepair. In Chattar the bus was halted by Government officials who asked each one of us to pay a road cess of five annas. The path then moved upward through forest glades. It brought to view mountainous scenes of unforgettable beauty and loveliness. At a village called Traite the engine of our bus had to be fed with cold water because the strenuous upward ascent had made it too hot. A little after evening we arrived at a hill-town called Mari (or Kumari) — a village thirty-seven miles north of Rawalpindi — where we had to halt for the night. By night no vehicle, except bullock-carts, are allowed to traverse this road. During daytime, however, the rule is reversed. Here we felt extreme cold since Mari is 7000 feet above the sea-ievel. Its market is located at an altitude of 6050 feet. The place is used as a summer resort by numerous white people. So Mari can be called the Darjeeling of Northern India. We spent the night in the marketplace at the shop of a Marwari gentleman.

After breakfast in the morning we resumed our journey. We crossed many rivers, passed through numerous forests, touched many plateaus and valleys and finally at 1 p.m. reached Kohala, the frontier province of British India. Situated at an altitude of one thousand eight hundred and eighty feet above the sea level it is twenty-nine miles north of Mari. During summer the place becomes unbearably hot when the temperature sometimes shoots up to 115°. Here we found the river Vitasta (the Jhelum) flowing with a strong current. This we crossed along a hanging iron bridge. The old bridge had been destroy-

ed by the violent flood of 1893; the present one was built by
the Maharaja of Kashmir. On the opposite bank there is a
check-point where traffic is halted for inspection. When we
reached there we were subjected to a thorough police check-
ing. Our names and addresses, the purpose of our visiting
Srinagar, the duration of our stay—all these were recorded
by the police officials. The latter also examined our luggages
and collected a road cess of five annas from each passenger.
The amount thus realised goes to the treasury of the Kashmir
government.

We found here a small market mostly run by Muslims and a
big dak bungalow with good lodging facilities. Nowhere else
along this road so big a rest house for travellers is to be found.
Here we rested for an hour after lunch but found the place
unusually hot. Only when the bus started moving again we felt
somewhat refreshed by the cold air. Of course such comfort
could be enjoyed only by those occupying front seats of the
bus; those in the interior had to endure extreme discomfort
caused by dust, heat and constant jolting. All around the lofty
mountains enfolded in thick forests made an exquisite picture
of beauty and mystery and lifted our heart with a sense of
delight. From the village Chattar onwards we made a continuous
descent along a zig-zag course. The road along our journey
presented nowhere else so great a declivity as this. The bus
driver here stopped the engine and the vehicle glided downwards
of its own accord, causing thereby some saving of petrol. A
distance of seven miles was covered in this way when at last
we reached a fine bridge across a big river. This place called
Dulai is at an altitude of 2023 ft. above the sea level. Here
there is a nice dak bungalow for travellers. From this place
runs all along through mountains a rock-hewn road with scars
of occasional land-slides that take place during the rainy
season. Near Majfarabad we sighted a snow-capped mountain
peak glowing in bright loveliness. 1400 ft. in height it is called
Karnal. The sight of accumulated snows on the mountain top
and the fact of our being so near it thrilled the Swami with
immense delight. At a distance of nine miles and a half from
Dulai is a place called Domel which we reached at 4-30 p.m. in
the afternoon. Because our bus had traversed so many miles at
a stretch its engine grew once again extremely hot. It was
therefore brought to a halt in front of a government dak
bungalow where the driver got busy refilling the engine with

cold water. Meanwhile most of the passengers hurried to the nearby marketplace to get some refreshments. The Swami also, after taking a cup of tea, went for a quiet leisurely stroll. This spot, located at a height of 2171 ft., has to its credit a post office, a charitable dispensary and a market. Not far off is the confluence of the Krishnaganga and the Vitasta. This accounts for the name 'Domel', meaning a place where two rivers unite. From here the Vitasta flows eastward.

About half an hour later we started again. We covered a distance of one mile and a half when we came upon the view of an old fortress once held by the Sikhs and the temple of Majfarabad. The Sikhs had taken possession of the region in Kashmir called Sopor and were here in strength during the early years of this century. The local hill tribes, the Bombases and others tried hard to drive the Sikhs out of the region, but all their efforts went in vain.

It is at this spot that the road from Mari joins that to Abotabad. The latter road was pointed out to us by the Swami from our bus. This road, running all along leisurely by the side of the mountains, is at a height of 1500 ft. from the river bank. When seen from the bus it looked like so many cracks and fissures at different spots on the high mountain range. During winter nearly all roads in this area save this one get blocked by heavy snow-fall

Our bus was running at a speed of twelve miles per hour. As we proceeded, the valley in front revealed to us one beautiful scenery after another. At first sight it appeared to be quite narrow but as we drew near it opened an extensive vista before us. There was now quite a chill in the air and we had an unpleasant feeling of extreme cold. Very soon our bus had to negotiate a difficult bend. As it came round the corner, it faced another bus coming from the opposite direction. It was on its way from Srinagar to Rawalpindi and was almost upon us when our driver, by sounding his horn, gave it a signal to stop. But because the brake of the other bus was out of order it could not come to a halt and collided with our vehicle. Fortunately it entailed no loss of life, though it did great damage to our bus. The other bus, suffering only minor damage left for its destination but not before some hot exchange of words had taken place between the two drivers. Finding no way out our bus remained there at a stand-still. Our driver requisitioned the service of some local mechanics and with their help started repairing the bus. It is happy to note that in most villages and markets along this road car mechanics and artisans are easily available. After taking their meals in the marketplace: the passengers took rest for the night. Some lay down for sleep within the bus, some on its roof, some by the roadside while some others managed to procure shelter in nearby shops. We had already made arrangements to stay at the dak bungalow. Taking with us only a few blankets and bed-sheets we went there to spend the night.

All roads in this region are alike in having high-peaked mountains on one side and deep ravines on the other. Number-less trucks and motor cars have perished in these ravines due to careless driving. Accidents frequently take place while negotiating the hair-pin bends along these mountain roads. For these reasons one is advised to constantly sound the horn, never to allow an inexperienced man at the wheel and never to ride a vehicle with a faulty brake along these roads. Be that as it may, we soon reached the dak bungalow at the village of Gari and after taking our meals went to bed. The distance between Domel and Gari is 14 miles (height 2628 ft). The night proved to be extremely chilly. During summer mosquitoes multiply here in huge numbers and malaria takes a heavy toll.

We started again next morning after taking tea. The road we took was running along the river bank so far. But we left the river bank after crossing a distance of two miles and drove along by the side of a hill. After some more distance we found ourselves once again by the river-side. This spot is 3000 ft. above sea level.

Next to come was the village Hatian and we found enormous chunks of stone precariously hanging on the hillside. They have been hanging like this for a long time. The hills we came across so far were made of clay and stone; but the hills that confronted us hereafter were hard and rocky with pebbles of different sizes strewn all around. The road to Karnal valley now lay ahead of us and we could see a beautiful hanging bridge at a short distance. Pine trees abound at this spot with their long tapering leaves. On the other side of the river can be seen the ruins of a fortress once belonging to the Sikhs. The hill tribes mentioned earlier succeeded in administering a signal defeat on the Sikhs in a fierce battle here. At dead of night men of these tribes rolled down huge stones from the top of the hill and afterwards attacked the Sikhs sword in hand. Hundreds of Sikhs lost their lives in this battle.

The small marketplace of Chenary is situated at a small distance from here. Another mile and we were in front of a beautiful mountain cascade. Landslides often take place at this spot. Here once stood the Chakoti dak bungalow which came to be completely gutted by fire in 1914. The place is 3693 ft. above sea level. There is a hanging bridge on the river made of birch and ropes. There is plain land spread over a very small area near the bridge, a very rare sight in this mountainous region. The scenery around was a feast to the eyes.

The village of Chenary is situated at a distance of 16 miles front Gari. On our way we crossed quite a number of waterfalls. But from this point onwards the road ahead no longer obliged us with such pretty scenes save high mountains on one side and deep ravines on the other. Our vehicle took many a zig-zag turn and continued moving onwards. From our high altitude the river Vitasta looked like a very thin thread lying far below. The road here has been built by hewing large stones and sometimes by blowing up the same with dynamite; many spots singed by the latter are still visible. To build this road many a' labourer had to lay down his life. A big iron bridge stands a little distance away from this spot. It should be mentioned that all bridges on this route were formerly made of wood but now they have all been rebuilt with iron. At a place called Barambhat we saw debris caused by land-slides at different spots. During rains huge stones come hurtling down from above and block the roads, making journey along them almost impossible. A small field near Uri situated at a height of 300 ft. above the river bank spreads adorned with a fortress and presents a mountain view which is simply wonderful. A Muslim king who held the honorific title of Uri once reigned here and the place derives its name from him. There is a small hanging bridge near the fortress. All around the road we saw small fields clinging to the hills on one side while on the other side lay slopes going down to the ravines. It is a place infested with bears. A ditch runs nearby where beasts locally known as 'Markhar' are found in large numbers. Many Englishmen come here for 'shikar'. It took us two hours to cross the eighteen miles that stretch between Chenary and Uri. From the top of a hill called Hajipir the road running through Poonch presents a very beautiful sight. But it is too narrow to be motorable and one has to traverse it on ponies.

Gradually the valley spread in front got narrower and narrower. On both sides of us we saw hills made of limestone and chalkstone. Some of them were made of stones yellow and violet in colour. The road passing through the forest of Pirpanjal sloped further and further as we moved ahead. Ruins of a number of ancient temples met our eyes as we entered the village of Brankutri. The scenery here is simply captivating. It seemed to us that Nature bedecked with flowers of different hues was offering all her charms as homage to the mountain-god. Trees in full blossom, cascading fountains, the dense forests and snow-clad peaks—all combined to make this place a wonderful beauty spot. Adjacent to the place there is a power house which supplies electricity to the whole of Kashmir. There are eight turbines here constantly revolving under the pressure of water. It is definitely a spot worth visiting. Few countries can boast of having hydraulic power of such huge dimensions. Sombre-looking mountains stand nearby with their peaks aspiring as it were to touch the very heavens. Beyond this at a short distance is situated Rampur 'basti' - a colony of local people. The place is very beautiful and has a salubrious climate. It is situated at a height of 4842 ft. above sea level and is at a distance of 13 miles from Uri. After this the road passes through a region comparatively level. A mile away from Rampur we found ourselves crossing a river called Vaniar. After this came a saw-mill and a small market place. While crossing another bend we almost came to a collision with a motor car coming from the opposite direction but succeeded in narrowly averting an accident. The man at the wheel in the motor car had made a timely move to the left and had applied the brake. Had he failed to do so, a collision was inevitable as the road there was extremely narrow. Engineers engaged in the repair of this road had their branch office and rest house near the market place. Debris caused by landslides could be seen strewn all around. Hill tops under massive pressure of glaciers often break into pieces and cause these enormous landslides. We moved onwards and soon came upon a very beautiful ancient temple called Vaniar. It was renovated a few years ago under the patronage of Dewan Kriparam. This serves as a model of how the ancient Hindus raised their temples. A little further from here stands the ancient fortress of Nawshera at the centre of a village with the same name. The tremendous earthquake that took place on the 30th May of 1885 caused heavy damage to this village. The valley of Vitasta gets wide once again after this and we felt giddy as we looked down the ravines. The trees far below looked like tiny bushes. We began to move up an ascent after this and the valley spread before our eyes presented a beautiful sight. The pine forests on the hills grew more and more dense. Interspersed among them we saw tiny hamlets, fields and fountains. Hill after hill seemed to close around us and we could hardly make out how we had made our way into them and how we were ever to be out of their clutches. Far in the north stand the snow-clad peaks and in the midst of the valley surrounded by hills lies Srinagar, the capital of Kashmir. Our anxiety grew as we approached the town. The Nanga Parvat and the Harmukh stood before our eyes resplendent in their snow-white garbs. The sky-scraping mountains of Gulmarg stood full of pride and self-assurance in the south. The Kolahai mountain looked like an enormous lion in repose with a tiny lamb placed within easy reach of its mouth.

Gradually we reached the town of Baramula and our vehicle stopped there for a while. We got down from it for a little rest. It is 16 miles away from Rampur and situated at a height of 5193 ft. above sea level. The Swami sat down in front of a Roman Catholic Mission School to enjoy the beauty of the place to his heart's content. A road runs nearby to the town of Gulmarg. Among our fellow passengers there were two young men belonging to the Sikh community on their way to Gulmarg. They had boarded the bus at Rawalpindi and were occupying the two seats just in front of us. Soon we came to be on friendly terms with them. They struck up an engaging conversation with the Swami. One of them was named Kalowant Singh and he hailed from Lahore. His brother-in-law worked in the forest department. The two youngmen were on their way to his place. They got down from the bus at Baramula. Before taking leave of us they requested the Swami over and over again to visit them at Gulmarg. The Swami accepted their invitation. Gulmarg is only 18 miles from Baramula. One can easily hire a pony or a tonga to go there. One can also halt a car on its way to Baramula and request a ride to the place.

The name 'Baramula' is derived from 'Varaha-Mul'. The Hindus of Kashmir believe that it was at this spot that God Vishnu incarnated himself as a boar(Varaha). The town is situated at the bank of Vitasta and is the chief city of the district of Baramula. The *Rajatarangini* states that Sri Suyya, the chief engineer of king Avantivarman, saved the city from a calamitous flood by building an embankment on the Vitasta. The terrible earthquake of 1885 had almost destroyed the city. Yet it is highly rewarding to visit its two sites of interest that still remain, — an old caravanserai of the Mughal soldiers and the ruins of an old fortress built during the reign of the Sikhs. Two springs of sulphureous water, an ancient temple dedicated to Siva, the relics of an age-old city-gate—all these remind us of the lost glory of this city of great antiquity. The things of interest of modern Baramula city that deserve mention are one dak bungalow, several rest houses for the local officials, an English school, a marketplace : and a wood factory. This place abounds with charm and beauty and is regarded by many as superior to any other spot in Kashmir in point of natural scenic grandeur. The large number of plain and rounded pebbles to be seen around the city and all over the place suggest their having been eroded by gushing waters. This proves that in some remote past the entire region was under water with tumultuous waves rushing over the area. Later perhaps due to earthquake or some such natural cause all these mountains and plains rose to the surface and in course of time all water evaporated. The Swami said, "Those Kashmiri Aryans who happened to witness this natural occurrence recorded it in their religious books in the form of the story of Vishnu's Varaha incarnation"[2].

Baramula is somewhat less cold as it is situated 1000 ft. below Srinagar and this explains why during winter many people come from Srinagar and Gulmarg to stay here. It is from this place that the road from Rawalpindi to Srinagar is ranged on both sides with attractive rows of poplars for 34½ miles at a stretch. An avenue so long as this is rarely to be seen

---

[2]Reference is to the Hindu mythology according to which Vishnu took the form of a boar, a water-loving creature, in order to create the world out of cosmic waters.

anywhere else. At present a huge machine operated by electricity has been installed here with a view to excavating a canal to the Vitasta. From this place numerous cargo-laden boats go daily to Srinagar via Ular Lake and Sadipur.

We had to make haste since we were rather anxious to reach Srinagar before evening. We boarded the bus again and it started at once. For some distance our road lay by the side of the hills and then it ran across the middle of a plateau. Moving eastward for 14 miles we reached a village called Patan where we saw many small fields and numerous *chenar* trees. The village is situated at a height of 5220 ft. from the sea level. From this place the sight of Nanga Parvat became clearer than before. We were yet to cover 18 miles to reach Srinagar. Since we could afford no delay our bus quickened its speed. The road hereafter is level all along; it is full of charming mountain sights and is decked with numerous poplar trees standing in rows on either side. On reaching the plain near Srinagar the bus started running at a high speed. From now on there was no hill on our way. So long our road ran through hills only and this made things rather monotonous for us.

On reaching the level ground we heaved a sigh of relief. Near the fourteenth milestone we had to cross a canal built in 1904. There are small fields and pools in the place called Mirgund which came next. Around them we saw tents for soldiers of the Dogra Regiment entrusted with the responsibility of defending the frontiers of Kashmir. Another route to Gulmarg starts from a point one mile from this place. By and by we could see Srinagar hailing to us from a distance and in no time we found ourselves at the heart of the city.

———————

The long route from Rawalpindi to Srinagar stretches across one hundred and ninety-eight miles. Few places in the world can boast of such a motorable mountain road. The road from Rawalpindi to Baramula was constructed in 1880 and that from Barmula to Srinagar in 1890. Maharaja Pratap Singh Bahadur was the first man to cover the distance from Srinagar to Rawalpindi in a motor car. After doing this he declared the road open to traffic. To beautify this road and to make it easily negotiable the Maharaja had to incur heavy expenditure and many labourers lost their lives while its construction was in progress. Huge landslides took place during the heavy flood of 1893 and most of the bridges on the route came to be seriously damaged. Once again the Maharaja had to spend millions for necessary repairs.

Our bus wended its way through the marketplace and crossed the Amira Kadal (the first bridge) and came to a halt on the western bank of the Vitasta in front of the office of the Punjab Motor Company. And at once about a score of temple touts surrounded us and started bombarding us with questions as to our names, caste, native place, parentage and so on and so forth. Among them we could spot Sudama, the temple tout attached to Belur Math. With his help we could find our way to the Bengalee school founded by the Late Dr. A. Mitra. We put up there with our luggages. Upen Babu, a teacher of this school, made all necessary arrangements for us. The widow of Dr. A. Mitra, the famous Bengalee physician of Srinagar, had fixed this place for us even before we arrived there. We knew Upen Babu since the days when he used to stay in the office of Udbodhan at Bagbazar, Calcutta. Meeting him among so many strangers in far away Kashmir was a great pleasure. We found venerable Rasik Ranjan Ghosh living with his family in a house by the side of the school. In this house he runs a shop named The Kashmir Trading Syndicate whose wares consist of shawls and woolen wrappers. Rasik Babu arranged our meal at his place. On taking it we retired for rest after our long and hard journey. But rest was made impossible throughout the night because of bed-bugs. They are so minute in size that they find no difficulty in getting through the mosquito nets. They are so quick in their movements that it is almost impossible to kill them. In appearance they are like lice but their colour is red. Wooden floors and furniture are their usual habitat. In Kashmir most of the houses are made of wood and that is why these insects are so abundant there.

Maharaja Jai Singh of Alwar, a great friend of Swami Abhedananda, had sent a telegram to the Maharaja of Kashmir informing him of the Swami's journey to Amarnath. He was requested by him to see that the government of Kashmir made all possible arrangements for the comfort of Swamiji while on his pilgrimage. On coming to know that the Swami had arrived at Srinagar, Maharaja Pratap Singh of Kashmir expressed his desire to see him and sent him his car. It is the custom in Kashmir to wear a turban while going to visit royalty. The Swami was an adept in the art of winding a turban round the head in a trice. So he had no difficulty in donning one in no time. Soon he was out in an orange-coloured robe cap-a-pie and we all boarded the car. On crossing the Vitasta the car passed through the market place and halted in front of the royal palace. On entering it we were guided through the parlour and the accounts office and were finally brought to the carpeted balcony on the first floor overlooking the Vitasta. Arrangements had been made for the Swami to take his seat there. Pandit Sri Jagat Ram Zoo, the state secretary of Kashmir, Mutamind Durbar Roy Bahadur, Pandit Sri Manamohan Lall Langer and other high officials came and sat by us. The Maharaja also arrived shortly afterwards. Somewhat dark in complexion and short and lean in stature, he was dressed in white trousers and a very huge turban. Two young aides-de-camp attended the King. The Maharaja is profoundly religious by temperament. He patronises various charitable institutions in different places of Kashmir and everyday he worships his household deity with one thousand and eight lotus-blooms. On his worship being over, the flowers are offered to the river. Throughout the day they float on its bosom, — a wonderful sight for all to see.

His Majesty then entered into a long conversation with the Swami about religion, the missionary activities of Swami Vivekananda, the various beneficial operations of Belur Math and Ramakrishna Mission and different other subjects. Then he added; "Long ago Swami Vivekananda accompanied by Nivedita came to my place. I had the good fortune of having my palm read by him." They conversed for an hour when the Maharaja requested the Swami to become his honoured guest for the period he intended to stay in Kashmir. The Swami gave his consent whereupon the Maharaja ordered the state secretary to treat the Swami as a state guest and to make all necessary arrangements for his journey to Amarnath. After this we took leave of him and returned to our quarters.

Four days still remained before the commencement of our journey and as all arrangements were being made at the government level the Swami in a relaxed mood began touring the suburbs to his heart's content.

People usually mean Srinagar when they refer to Kashmir. In ancient times the capital of Kashmir was Puranadhisthana, now called Pandrethan, situated at a distance of three miles to the south of Srinagar. The *Rajatarangini* mentions that in 50 B.C. two temples of Siva, called Bhim Swamina and Vardhamanesa were built in this place. This undoubtedly testifies to the antiquity of the town. A Siva temple in this ancient town made of very antique stones is the only historic relic here that has survived from the past. The stones are found placed side by side without any use of mortar. The temple was built sometime between 913 and 921 A.D. by Partha, the then king of Kashmir and its ruling deity Siva was called Meru-Vardhan Swami after the name of the king's Chief Minister. The capital stood on the left bank of the river at the beginning of the reign of king Pravarsena II who later shifted the same to the south of the Vitasta. According to Kalhan, it was Emperor Ashoka who in 300 B.C. built the city of Srinagar which later on came to be the country's capital during the reign of king Abhimanyu who assumed power in 960 A.D. The ruins of Pandrethan are still to be seen. The Srinagar of Ashoka stood on the eastern part of the present Srinagar and is now called Gape (Aiteganj). King Pravarsena II founded the new capital Pravarpur near Hari Parvat. He built the first bridge of boats across the Vitasta and also many temples and palaces. In the sixth century A.D. king Gopaditya had his capital in Gopakar, a name which derives from Gopagriha. This is now the abode of many English people. Here are now found many vinyards and distilleries catering for the English.

The names and activities of the following kings are usually found in the ancient history of Kashmir :

Period	Names of Kings	Activities
Third Century B.C.	Emperor Ashoka	He built the city of Srinagar and spread Buddhism.
Second Century B.C.	Hushka, Jushka and Kanishka	All three Kushan rulers embraced Buddhism.
Sixth Century A.D.	Mihirgula	He was a Hun king. His suzerainty extended even to Central Asia. He favoured the Brahmins in various ways.
Sixth Century A.D.	Gopaditya	He built many temples and monasteries in Gopagriha and on the mountain called Sankaracarya.
Sixth Century A.D.	Matrigupta	During his time Kashmir came under the domination of the kingdom of Ujjain.
Sixth Century A.D.	Pravarsena II	He founded the new capital near Hari parvat.
Seventh Century A.D.	Durlabhvardhan	He conquered the whole of the Punjab. It was during his reign that the famous Chinese traveller Huen-Tsang visited Kashmir.

Period	Names of Kings	Activities
699—735 A.D.	Lalitaditya	He defeated the Turks and drove the Tibetans out of Baltistan. He founded the city called Martanda and built the pillars of the Sun temple there. He also excavated a canal there and had the city of Jaipur established by a ruler named Jaipid.
855—883 A.D.	Avantivarman	He constructed an embankment on the Vitasta and built a large number of mansions.
883—903A.D.	Shankarvarman	He made an attempt to recover his lost kingdom.
928—937 A.D.	Chakravarman	The landlords under his sway rose in revolt against him.
950—1003 A.D.	Queen Dinda (or Diksha)	She married a farmer of low origin. This gave rise to a new royal dynasty.
1089—1101 A.D.	Harsha	A man with many parts but a tyrant none-the-less. He was killed for his misdeeds.
1139 A.D.	Shahmir	He was the first Muslim ruler of Kashmir. During his reign Sikandar Butsikast destroyed many Hindu and Buddhist temples.

Period	Names of Kings	Activities
1420—1470 A.D.	Zain-ul-Abidin	He patronised learning. His period of reign was one of prosperity. Many Hindus were rehabilitated in Kashmir during his reign.
1540 A.D.	Mirza Haidar	He entered Kashmir from the north and conquered it.
1586 A.D.	Emperor Akbar	He conquered Kashmir.
1600 A.D.	Emperor Jahangir	He spent millions to beautify Kashmir. The famous Achhibal, Verinag, Salimarbag, Chashmashahi, etc all bear testimony to his aesthetic and lavish temperament. He was a great builder of mansions and garden houses. Asaf Khan, his chief minister and father-in-law, built the famous Nishatbag.
1752 A.D.	Reign of the Pathans	Kashmir came under the sway of Kabul.
1819 A.D.	Dewan Chand	The Sikhs captured the Kashmir valley.
1833 A.D.	Colonel Mian Singh	He worked for the state's prosperity.
1843 A.D.	Gulab Singh	He was the late grandfather of the present king of Kashmir. He came to be the ruler of Kashmir by entering into a treaty with the English. He conquered Western Tibet.

Srinagar is the prime city of Kashmir described as the heaven on earth by poets in one voice. So it goes without saying that the city possesses great charm and beauty. There is no second place like this in point of its attractiveness and charm. At the heart of the city flows the lazy winding Vitasta. There are seven bridges in all across the river within the city's boundary. The first two are modern while the rest are built in the old Kashmiri style. In Kashmir a bridge is called 'Kadal'. The names of the seven bridges can be cited seriatim: Amira or Pratap Singh Kadal, Hawah Kadal, Fateh Kadal, Zina Kadal, Ali Kadal, Naya Kadal, and Saffar Kadal.

The spot between the first and the second bridge is the best part of the city since it cradles in its fold the royal palace, the market, the museum, the hospital, the post and telegraph office, the law court etc. The locality between the second and the fourth bridge is not very smart and posh while the area between the fourth and the seventh bridge is certainly the worst part of the city. Local people mostly live in the area between the third and the fifth bridge wherein also are located the manufactories of shawls and woolen wrappers. The extent onwards from the sixth bridge is scantily populated and is not of much importance.

In the vicinity of the first bridge lies a big ground called Huzuribagh where every afternoon boys from schools and colleges gather to play football. Many a gentleman takes his constitutional on this ground. Public lectures take place almost everyday. Nearby is the office of the Arya Samaj. From Huzuribagh one gets a pleasing panoramic view of the high-peaked mountains of Gulmarg. Just by the side of this playground is the government hospital. There are two other hospitals in the city—one called Mission Hospital near Munsibag and the other at Maharaj Ganj near the fourth bridge at the centre of the city. The postal service in Kashmir is run by two separate administrations, - one under the English Government and the other under the Government of Kashmir. The postal service run by the latter is restricted within the boundary of Kashmir; it has no jurisdiction outside the state. On the other bank of the Vitasta there is a college named after Pratap Singh facing the general post office under the English Government. This is the largest institution for higher education in Kashmir. Within a stone's throw of this place stands the best hotel of Kashmir—

Nedou and Sons. It is the most favourite resort of Europeans. Near it sprawls the beautiful polo ground of Kashmir.

On the eastern side of the city is a conspicuous mountain which is called Takht-i-Sulaiman, 6200 ft. high. It is also called Sankaracarya because on its summit survives a monastery founded by Sankaracarya himself. No hermit lives in that monastery permanently. Stone steps lead one to the top of the mountain within half an hour. From there one gets a panoramic view of extraordinary beauty. On this mountain a Buddhist temple was built by Jalaka, a son of Emperor Ashoka, in 200 B.C. In the sixth century A.D. king Gopaditya converted it into a temple of Siva and also built a separate temple here. The ruins of the latter are yet to be seen. Below this rise like waves hill after hill. The names of these hills are Sonarbag, Munsibag, Kuthibag, Hari Singh and Sekhbag. Shops and establishments of English factors are to be seen in large numbers at Munsibag where one can buy various types of wares, both indigenous and foreign. Opposite to Sekhbag on the other side of the Vitasta is to be seen a quay called Lallmundi near which stands the museum of Srinagar. In it are to be seen shawls and woolen wrappers of antiquity, icons both Hindu and Buddhist, ancient coins, and weapons in use long ago. The mansion for housing state guests is situated near the museum. Shri Sadilall, the Chief Justice of Lahore, was enjoying the hospitality of the Government of Kashmir at that time. The huge silk factory owned by Prince Hari Singh is situated in the locality of Shupian in the sourthern part of the city. It is the biggest silk factory in India. No one in Kashmir is allowed to trade in silk and the Prince enjoys full monopoly. Nearly four thousand men and women are employed in his factory. Their daily wages vary from four annas to eight annas. Nearly a hundred and fifty thousand men, women and children are engaged in various jobs like breeding cocoons and collecting them from the valleys of Kashmir. At a small distance from this factory stands the mausoleum of Maharaja Gulab Singh of the Dogra clan. Near this place is situated the 'Narayan Math' of Swami Brahmananda, a Bengalee monk, who purchased two bighas of land in Kashmir and founded the monastery twenty-two years ago. A large number of monks reside here. The garden belonging to the monastery is lush with foliage and fruits of all kinds. We visited the monastery and enjoyed the many types of delicious fruits in this garden.

The city of Srinagar is at a height of 5200 ft above sea level. It is very hot here during July and August. But during spring and late autumn its climate is temperate and very inviting on that account. Nearly a hundred and twenty thousand people live here seventy-five percent of whom are Muslims. About thirteen years ago a large part of the city was destroyed by fire. The old palace came to be entirely gutted. The Vitasta flows with a gentle rhythm just below the palace where the present Maharaja resides. It is very pleasant to move along the Vitasta in a 'Shikara' (a flat-bottomed boat). The Swami hired one for a ride along the river on both sides of which stand wooden houses presenting a beautiful sight. It is the custom among the Kashmiris to grow grass and flower plants on roofs and terraces of their houses. We saw many people, — men, women, and children, — bathing in the river. The white robe (ferang) worn by both the sexes is of Aryan origin. Near the second bridge once stood the temple called Tard-Manesh founded by king Samadhmat in 50 B.C.; nearby are a crematorium and quite a big island called Mayasum. The latter serves now as a locality of English people. The place now called Drogjan was known as Durgagalika. The ancient name of Bochwara was Bhukarsibatika. It was at Durgagalika that the blind king Yudhisthira of Kashmir was kept confined in prison. On the bank of the river stands the beautiful mosque of Shah-Hamadan all made of wood and with wonderful engravings on it. Nearby stands another beautiful mosque made entirely of stone and therefore called Pathar Musjid. It was founded by Empress Nurmahal. Near the fourth bridge is situated the famous mausoleum of Zain-ul-Abidin. On a block of stone in it there is an inscription in Pali. To Reverend Dr. Abbott, the famous traveller, goes the credit of discovering this inscription. Near this is the market place of Maharajganj. It is the only marketplace in Srinagar where fish is bought and sold. Within a very short distance stands the famous Zumma Musjid. Between the third and the fourth bridge are to be found a large number of shops whose chief wares consist of papier-mache, chappals, shoes, shawls, woolen wrappers and various other products of Kashmiri craft. While going down the river we saw huge hoardings with advertisements on both sides. Further south there is a beautiful temple founded by Pandit Ramjash of Srinagar. The scenery of the river is most exquisite near the sixth bridge. There are majestic hills on all sides. In front lies a prayer ground for Muslims and by its side can be seen the Dufferin Hospital and a serai for people coming from and going to Yarkand. In late autumn people from Yarkand in Central Asia come across the Karakoram on yaks with their merchandise to Srinagar. During their stay in the city they put in serais of this type. They return when winter is over and the mountain routes open after the snows have melted. The road from Srinagar to Rawalpindi is not far from here and we could see it from our boat as we were cruising along the Vitasta. A canal from the Vitasta winds through Gaukadal and Chenarbag and finally flows into the Dal Lake. Both European and Indian tourists hire houseboats on this canal and make them their residence during summer. On all sides are to be seen numberless *chenars.* The place is comfortable and protected from heat but not very congenial from the hygienic point of view because of its being infested with mosquitoes. There is a sluice-gate erected by Maharaja Gulab Singh at the junction of this canal and the Dal Lake known as the Dal Darwaja. The waters of the lake cannot enter the canal if this gate is kept closed. Sluice-gates of this kind are to be seen in different places of Srinagar. The floods of 1893 and 1903 caused great damage to the city. So such gates were erected to prevent recurrence of such damage. There is another canal coming from the direction of Sankaracárya hill and flowing into the Dal Lake. This is known as Markhal. The point from which this canal starts is known as Dildar Khanbag. There is a government school there. The canal is spanned by a number of bridges and studded with numerous bathing-ghats. Its water, however, is awfully unclean. The place where the canal flows into the Dal Lake is known as Anchar. From here there is a water route to the Indus and Gandharbal. This route proceeds through the Dal Lake choked with water hyacinth. There is one maidan nearby. On the other side of it there is a beautiful mosque built in the fifteenth century known as Ali Musjid.

Nearby stands the Hari Parvat. On its top there is an ancient fortress and at its base is to be seen the Zumma Musjid. The mosque is quite adjacent to the fourth bridge known as Zina Kadal. It was built in 1388 by a Muslim ruler called Sultan Sikandar Shah. Destroyed by fire in 1473, it was rebuilt by Sultan Muhammad Shah. But it was destroyed by fire once again in 1665 and this time it was the Mughal Emperor Aurangzeb who had it repaired. All the Muslim rulers of Kashmir looked after this mosque with great veneration and care. Emperor

Akbar tried to build a city near this place. History tells us that very near the site of this mosque there once stood a temple dedicated to Mahadeva. The temple was built by king Pravarsena II who also built a township here. At that time the area was known as Sharitak. To the north of this place was a temple dedicated to Durga while to the south there was another dedicated to Ganesa. There was yet another temple in the south-west corner whose deity was Vishnuran Swami. The temple mentioned last was built by king Ramaditya. The ruins of these temples are yet to be seen. The various objects of importance excavated in this area include an inscription in Brahmi-script discovered by Dr. Abbott. The date of this inscription is 150 B.C. They also include coins of the time of king Pravarsena II and of that of king Avanti-varman. They have been preserved in the museum of Srinagar.

To visit the fortress on the top of Hari Parvat one has to secure permission from the relevant authorities. It is situated at a height of 400 ft above the base of the hill. In ancient times it was a monastery of the Buddhists. Later it was converted into a fortress by Emperor Akbar. At present one finds there only a few guns and a handful of soldiers in the employ of the Maharaja of Kashmir.

On descending from the top of Hari Parvat the Swami went to visit the tomb of Jesus Christ which is situated in a locality called Khana-yari. Local Muslims believe that to save himself from the clutches of his enemies the Prophet Issa had to flee his own country and stay here in secret along with a few companions till the last day of his life. He died a natural death and his disciples buried him at this spot. The tomb has a sacred atmosphere. A fine fragrance comes out of a hollow in the wall of the tomb which, according to many, is an indication of the prophet's miraculous power. Many come to the place for cure of their illness. It is said that the tank with whose water Jesus performed his ablutions while on his way from Kabul to Kashmir is still in existence. The keepers of the tomb told us that the matter has been described in an ancient book of the Arabs called the *Tarikh-i-Azham*. The tank is referred to as Yusuf Talao. The various stories in circulation about Jesus Christ's arrival at the Himis Monastery in Western Tibet in his youth and his study of the *Vedas* under the Brahmins at Puri all seemed to be true to us while moving around this place. In his famous book called *The Unknown Life of Jesus Christ* Dr. Nicolas Notovitch has discussed Christ's sojourn in Tibet with convincing arguments. But it is a matter of regret that this book came to be proscribed by the government. The Swami commented, "If proper research is conducted in India, the gaps in the life story of Christ can be suitably filled in." After taking a few snaps of the place the Swami left the precincts of the tomb and made for the library named after Vivekananda in the locality called Ranabari.

Dr. Sriram and members of the library accorded to us a hearty reception. The reading room is quite spacious. Almost all the books by Swami Vivekananda are to be found in this library. Portraits of Sri Ramakrishna, Swami Vivekananda and other holy men adorn the wall. Boys from local schools and colleges get together here every afternoon and lectures take place on Saturdays and Sundays. Dr. Sriram takes a leading part in all the functions arranged by the library and heads a band·of boy-scouts always ready to do his bidding. The gentleman hails from the Punjab. He lives at Srinagar with his family and works as a sub-assistant surgeon at the Dufferin Hospital. Already familiar with his books, members of the library were all keen to see Swami Abhedananda. At their request the Swami delivered a neat speech on 'Duty of the Student life'. The students requested the Swami to send a dedicated worker to the place so that they might be benefited by his guidance and teaching. The Swami assured them that he would try to do so. We then left the place and mounted our 'Shikara' for other destinations.

At a short distance from this place is a locality called Kranial where there is a mosque belonging to the Muslims of the 'Shia' sect. In it are to be seen mementos of the fierce revolt of 1874. To the north of this mosque stands the prison house of Srinagar. One can buy paper made by the prisoners and carpets.woven by them. Near it is situated a lepers' asylum run by the government containing 120 beds. The bathing ghat in front of this is named Kujiarball. We went ahead a little from here and reached the famous Dal Lake.

The Dal Lake stretches five miles from north to south and two miles from east to west. We found large parts of the lake choked with water hyacinth, algae, and lichen moss with small stretches of water here and there both transparent and deep. Behind the lake stands a row of mountains and in it there are innumerable floating gardens—a speciality of Kashmir. These floating gardens are made by putting the algae and the moss tightly within frames made of bamboos and by covering them with earth. In these gardens are grown water melons of various kinds and different vegetables. These gardens can be taken from place to place, if necessary, by fastening them behind boats in motion.At other times they are kept fastened to willows on the bank. One of the most prosperous trades in Kashmir is that of sports goods. Her willow trees are of great use in this trade because from them are made cricket bats.

The huge mosque of Hazaratball is situated by the lake. A tuft of hair collected from the holy head of Hazarat Muhammad is kept preserved here along with utensils made of stone of the shape of swans, snakes, fish etc. During Id festival a big fair takes place here. Nearly half the population of Srinagar assemble here during the prayers of Id. At a short distance from it there is a beautiful garden built by Emperor Akbar known as Nasimbag. The lordly *chenars* in this garden present a wonderful sight.

The beautiful island of Swarnalanka is situated at the heart of the lake not far from here. After this should be mentioned the famous Shalimarbag, a mile-long imperial garden. We went there and found it situated on a slope at the base of a row of mountains. In this garden there are nearly one hundred spouts. The engineering skill displayed in these water spouts deserves high praise. Huge torrents of water are found here descending along giant steps to the lake. One can come to this spot in a car or tonga. There are flowers and fruits of various kinds in the field. At the centre there is a rest house entirely made of black marble stones with various kinds of engravings on them. Inside this there is a separate chamber (Zenana) specially meant for ladies. In 1619 Emperor Jahangir built this pleasure garden for Nurjahan, his queen. One cannot but admit that the beauty of Kashmir found its best appreciation from the Mughal emperors without whose efforts the place would not have been what it is to-day, a veritable piece of heaven on earth.

There is another garden very near this place testifying to the love the Mughal emperors had for nature's beauty. Named

Nishatbag, it was built by Asaf Khan, Emperor Jahangir's father-in-law and chief minister. It is in no way inferior to Shalimarbag. We found a number of men and women enjoying picnic at this spot. Would they have dared to indulge in this sacrilege had the Mughal Empire been in existence now ? The glories of the great Mughal Empire are a very distant memory now and much change has been wrought by the inexorable passage of time. We thought of this as we sat in the garden surrounded by the memory of its golden past.

Another island called Rupalanka is situated very near. Not far from this island are the localities of Gopakar and Parimahal. In 1450 Muslims of the 'Sufi' sect made this place the chief centre of studies in astronomy. Ruins of ancient mansions can be seen here. The beautiful garden called Chashmasahi built by Jahangir is situated not far from this place. The meaning of Chashma in Kashmiri is a water cascade. Attracted by the beauty of this place many people have settled down in the area.

After spending three days in Kashmir the Swami directed us on the fourth day to get ready to leave for Amarnath. Some Bengalee pilgrims on their way from Calcutta to Amarnath had come to Srinagar at the time. They were putting up in the outhouse of Rasik Babu. Among them we knew one Atul Krishna Das hailing from Bowbazar, Calcutta. He was a great devotee of Sri Ramakrishna Dev and often visited Belur Math and the office of Udbodhan. He sought permission to serve the Swami which the latter granted. It was decided that he would accompany us during our journey to Amarnath. In the evening the Maharaja sent us guides, horses, cooks, food, warm clothings, a dandi, a motor car and various accessories. The official who brought them to us gave us all necessary instructions and left for the bazar to bring some other things which he thought we needed.

Next morning we were to start on our journey. With great joy and satisfaction in our hearts we made all preparations till far into the night.

CHAPTER—3

Next day it was the first of August. At eight in the morning Atulbabu and Sudama left Srinagar for Martanda with a group of pilgrims in two government tongas. They took the Swami's luggages with them. Martanda is nearly sixty miles away from Srinagar. It is there that pilgrims spend their first night on their way to Amarnath.

The following day the Swami, accompanied by the government care-taker, Prasad Zoo, started for Aishmokam in an official car. On our way we alighted at Avantipur where we visited the ruins of many temples. Situated just by the side of our road, the place is nearly eighteen miles from Srinagar. It was the capital of king Avantivarman who reigned from 855 to 883 A.D. He built here two temples, Avantiswar and Avantiswami, consecrated to Siva. Excavations at this place brought to light the ruins of these two temples and various other antiquities, thanks to the scholarly efforts of Mr. Jagadish Chandra Chatterjee, the great archaeologist, under whose direction the excavation work was still in progress. Ruins of the ancient capital buried deep in earth have been found in the site and are being preserved here with care. Many of these historic remains are stored in the museum of Srinagar.

At nearly 2 p.m. we reached Aishmokam where, after leaving Srinagar, the pilgrims for Amarnath spend their second night. This place is situated at a distance of fourteen miles from Martands. Much before our arrival at Aishmokam the pilgrims including Atulbabu had already reached there. Kashiram Zoo, the Director of the Department for Religious Activities under the Government of Kashmir, had in the meantime rigged up on a very good site two tents for us and made all other necessary arrangements for our stay. Drinking water had to be brought from a nearby paddy field under water since water of the village stream was found to be polluted. In the past Kashmir had often been scourged by the outbreak of cholera resulting from water pollution. More than six thousand people had died of this fatal disease. At this the authorities became alert and sunk many tubewells in the city of Srinagar. Even then the disease swept through the city in 1900, 1907 and again in 1915 but each time with less virulence than before.

Every year the government of Kashmir donates nearly Rs.12,000/— to its Department of Religious Activities for making all necessary arrangements for the Amarnath festival. The said department spends this sum on various activities with an eye to making the pilgrimage to Amarnath as comfortable as possible. These activities include building roads and bridges, ensuring medical aid, engaging volunteers etc. and also making charitable gifts of food and winter garments to the poor and the monks. In many places along this road milk, fuel, coolies and ponies are hard to procure. By making them easily available to the pilgrims the members of the said department earn, as it were, the blessings of God.

We found pilgrims putting up in nearly two hundred tents pitched on a field on the bank of a small river at Aishmokam. In each tent was ablaze an oven emitting smoke. Nearly five hundred pilgrims were on their way to Amarnath this year. In previous years there was no such tremendous rush of pilgrims. A small barge with passengers was also sailing in the direction of the holy place. The sky was overcast with clouds. For the last two days there had been constant rain. It had just stopped in the morning on the day we arrived there. But the possibility of its onset again could not be ruled out. It may be mentioned that along this road pilgrims suffer terribly if they are caught in rain. Fuel, clothings, luggages all get soaked and the wet tents become so heavy that they cannot be easily transported from one place to another. The road from Srinagar upto this point is pretty wide. But owing to rain for the last two days it became slimy and slippery and several parts of it had turned into veritable puddles of slush both big and small. Much effort and patience were required on the part of the pilgrims to cross these places with their luggages on ponies. Our car also came to a standstill whenever its wheels got stuck in the mud. It could be made to move only with the aid of the porters who gave the necessary push to the car whenever required.

The high-peaked mountains all around, the river flowing far below, the plains carpeted with green grass all created a scene of incomparable beauty before us and we felt that the place was rightly called 'Aishmokam' meaning an 'abode of rest'. Drinking deep in the beauty of the place the Swami told us, "To call Kashmir just a piece of heaven on earth is to belittle it. It is in fact the sum total of many heavens."

Aishmokam is a small hamlet with inhabitants mostly Muslim. Made of wood, the houses here are often two-storeyed. Adjoining almost every house is a kitchen-garden fenced all around and richly laden with greens and vegetables of various kinds. Many villagers came to see the pilgrims and to sell them milk, apples, pears and other fruits. The Swami went for a visit to the village. There in a mosque we saw a school for children in session. It was an age-old mosque. A long time ago some Zainuddin, a disciple of Nuruddin, the famous Muslim prophet of Kashmir, used to live in this village. It is said that he possessed some miraculous powers. His body, so the saying goes, could not be traced after his death. Later his disciples while asleep at night had received a divine command in a dream to erect a mosque at the place where his stick would be found in the morning. The mosque came to be built accordingly. At a little distance from this place is the site called Hapatnag where there is a copper mine. After a visit to it the Swami returned to the tent. There was a heavy downpour of rain at night. Those who had with them one-roofed tents got all their belongings thoroughly drenched. Our two tents were double-roofed and so rain could not do us much harm.

In the morning the rain ceased. The Swami left the car and mounted a 'jhampan' while others took ponies. Sudama and Prasad Zoo went along with our porters and horses carrying our loads. Atulbabu was not used to riding ponies. So his syce took hold of the reins and dragged the pony onwards slowly. Gradually he fell far behind us.

That day our destination was Pahalgam at a distance of twelve miles from Aishmokam. It is the custom here to decide beforehand what distance to cover each day while on a journey. All pilgrims should go together and must always follow the party preceding them. This leading party, usually consisting of several monks equipped with maces and other weapons, starts before all others in the small hours of the morning. This rule has been followed through ages in this region. With great joy in our hearts we proceeded along the mountain road lush with green forest foliage, now moving up a steep ascent and then going down a declining slope.

By and by we covered six miles from Aishmokam when Batakot, a small hamlet lying on both sides of the road, came into view. We found it quite neat and clean and encircled by rows of mountains. The road from Srinagar upto this place is motorable but henceforward it presents mild slopes, now upward and then downward, making it impossible for cars or tongas to pass. But we saw road construction going on in full swing and nearing completion. So one can expect that in very near future the road up to Pahalgam will be easily negotiable by cars and tongas. At a short distance from this place we moved up an ascent and then arrived at a holy site called Ganesaball. Here all pilgrims performed their ablutions and made devotional offerings to Lord Ganesa. Sudama, the temple tout, commented, "Without offering worship to Ganesji one can hardly expect to derive full benefit from the pilgrimage to Amarnath." So we went to pay our respects to Ganesji. Far below the road on the other side of the river we saw a block of stone smeared with oil and vermilion representing the image of Ganesa. From this spot onward the valley gets wider and wider. We saw the twin peaks of Kolahai clad in snow dazzling in sunlight. Gradually we reached Pahalgam around two in the afternoon.

Pahalgam is very hot in summer in spite of its height of 7200 ft above sea level. Gulmarg enjoys plenty of rains but the case with Pahalgam is different; its climate is dry. English people are very fond of the natural beauty of Pahalgam. There is a big departmental store in this place along with a dak bungalow, a bazar, and a post office. The place is open to traffic for eight months in the year. For the remaining four months roads leading to it are blocked with snow. It is so cold then that one can hardly stay there. Far below the town flows the Nilganga on the banks of which there are stretches of green fields dotted with tents of pilgrims. Innumerable fish could be seen gliding along the surface of the clean and transparent waters of the Nilganga.

Shortly the sky began to be overcast with clouds. Everything was sure to get drenched soon with heavy rains. It was already biting cold. Rains would make it colder still. But nobody seemed to bother much about this. The beauty of the place had so enchanted our companions that we found all of them moving about with a carefree attitude. The Swami left the tent to have a good look at the town of Pahalgam.

According to many Pahalgam offers the most beautiful scenic beauty in Kashmir. From here roads lead to Sonasar, Sheshnag, Amarnath, Harnag, Lidderboth and the Kolahoi glacier. The Swami returned to the tent after having visited the ruins of an ancient Hindu temple at Mamar which is not very far from Pahalgam.

It started raining cats and dogs at dead of night. Six pilgrims from a tent nearby came to take shelter with us since their tent had been thoroughly drenched.

Next day the Swami got ready to start again after taking his morning coffee. Incessant rains had made the hilly tracks extremely slippery. So pilgrims had been warned by the authorities to be very careful while climbing ascents on horseback and to get down from their horses while negotiating descents. We were also asked not to overload our horses. At different bends along the route arrangements had been made to see if these warnings were paid due heed to by the pilgrims.

Our destination now was Chandanbari or Tanin (9500ft high). This place is situated at a distance of nine miles from Pahalgam. Our path now lay along the hill-side with the Nilganga to keep company with us. We saw the river rushing forward through dense forests and receiving the torrential flow of waterfalls here and there cascading into it with a terrific roar. Our joy knew no bounds at the sight of the natural beauty that greeted our eyes all through the journey from now on. After covering four miles from Pahalgam we arrived at a village called Presslang. It is a small village with less than ten families inhabiting it. They are all Muslims. The houses in this village are all two-storeyed and made of wood. Almost every house has a garden with a fencing around it and a haystack within. We found a grocery and a tailoring shop on the ground floor of these houses. The villagers are all handsome to look at and sturdy in build. Like all other Kashmiris they have aquiline noses. Both men and women wear a loose robe called *ferang*. The women cover their heads with handkerchiefs and wear a number of pigtails. They do not use any ornaments. As we approached the village all its inhabitants came out of their houses to have a look at us. After this our route lay through deep forests.

Around two in the afternoon we reached Chandanbari. The sky was overclouded and rain was about to set in. Quickly we pitched our tents and placed our luggages inside. Already nearly 100 tents stood at the spot. Gradually more and more pilgrims started arriving in large numbers. Upenbabu arrived long after his other companions. It was because he had selected for himself a very old horse lest he fell down from the back of a young and spirited one. One of the legs of his horse was somewhat longer in size than the other three. Later he had this horse changed.

Very near our tent there was huge accumulation of snow at the foot of a hill. At this sight the pilgrims made a rush towards the same. They had heard that it snows on the Himalayan ranges but had never seen it snowing. That day they were over-joyed and started putting handfuls of snow greedily into their mouth. The Swami also partook of a little snow and then said, "To do this is to invite hill diarrhoea and goitre. So let us stop this madness."

We were now in the midst of a very wide valley surrounded by hills and forests. A mountain river could be seen rushing headlong from above on the rocks below. Our guide warned, "Beasts of prey prowl around this spot at night."

After spending the night at Chandanbari we started for Vayubyajan next morning. On our way we had to negotiate 1500 ft along a very steep ascent known as 'Pishu'. 'Pishu' is a kind of louse. Whether the name of this ascent derives from this or from 'Pisar' is not quite certain. 'Pisar' in Kashmiri means 'slippery'. The ascent has the shape of the last letter in the English alphabet. To mount this ascent on horseback or in a 'jhampan' is impossible. One has to negotiate this ascent simply on foot. It is advisable not to lag behind others during this ascent because if by accident a horse slips or a heavy luggage hurtles down, those behind will be inevitably crushed It is also advisable to finish crossing this ascent before the sun gets unbearable. Its scorching rays make the ascent a terrific ordeal for pilgrims. One must not sit down to rest while covering this part of the route even though one might feel awfully exhausted. Once you sit down, you will find your thighs too heavy to lift. So it is better to keep standing while taking rest. One has to carry dry grapes, pomegranates, lemons etc which one should take instead of water to quench thirst while making the ascent. One must not climb hills with an empty stomach for that would result in cramp in the intestines. One must also make it a point not to get lost in absorption at a scenery however beautiful, for this might result in a fatal slip.

Soon we reached the topmost point on the ascent. From here the pilgrims below looked like rows of tiny ants. The road to Amarnath was to be seen far above our route along a high plateau. The sylvan beauty of the place is simply charming. The air full of ozone here took away our exertion in no time and we felt very much enervated. The pilgrims stopped here for rest. The horses were set free for a while and some of our companions sat down to light refreshments. The Punjabi ladies with babies in their arms proved to be as hardy as their menfolk. They trudged along with us or rode bravely with beaming faces indicating great enthusiasm and energy. They provided a sharp contrast to ladies hailing from Bengal. Of course, there were three Bengalee ladies with us who bore all hazards of the journey with remarkable calm and fortitude.

At two in the afternoon we were at Vayubyajan. A fierce gale constantly blows here. The pilgrims here started making preparations for cooking. Juniper trees serve as good fuel. In the evening it started drizzling and soon we were in the midst of a terrific storm. It was indescribably cold at night.

From Chandanbari to Jojpal it was only five miles. The latter is at a height of 11300 ft. A thousand feet below the same there is a mountain rivulet with green fields on both sides. A little distance away within a forest we saw huts of the Gujars, a hill tribe, whose chief occupation is tending cows. On climbing another 800 ft of steep ascent one reaches the beautiful lake of Sonasar which receives glaciers gliding into it.

From Jojpal to Sheshnag it is four miles to the east. The height of the latter is 12000 ft. Sheshnag is a lake of the size of Hedua (Cornwallis Square, now Azad Hind Bag) of Calcutta. On both sides of the lake stand mountains clad in snow that never melts. The glaciers to be seen on these mountains offer a breath-taking sight. The dazzling green hue of the lake's surface lends to the place the charm of a fairyland. Some of the pilgrims took a holy dip in the lake and performed sacred ablutions. It is generally believed that a bath in this lake is a cure to various diseases. While looking at the lake the Swami said, "Do you see how glaciers here come down from the mountains all around? It is this that made our ancestors conjure the picture of Siva; the snow-clad peak represents his head and the glaciers his matted locks." To the south of this lake behind a row of mountain peaks stands the widely known Kohinoor Parvat.

Next day we started with the resolve to cover eleven miles and reach Panchatarani (the land of five rivers). On our way we had to negotiate a mountain pass at a height of 14000 ft. It is a highly inaccessible route which remains deserted almost all the year round. Only when pilgrims come to visit Amarnath on the full-moon day of the month of Shravan, the government tries to make some arrangements for them to use it. But who can relieve the distress involved in climbing dizzy ascents? The snow-clad peaks become dazzlingly white with the scorching rays of the sun on them and cause great harm to the eyes of pilgrims. One is advised to use coloured glasses (preferably green) while journeying in this region. We saw season flowers of various hues and shapes on the hill-side. It is beyond the power of man to describe how beautiful they are. The hills seem to be entirely covered with flowers and look like a panoramic embroidery work of various colours. We collected some flower plants with the idea of taking them home. The Swami, however, said, "It is useless to take the trouble of taking them to our place. They grow only along the snowline and would not survive for a moment in the plains." Sudama said, "Some of these flowers are poisonous. Blown by the wind their pollens sometimes brush against the faces of pilgrms and blacken them beyond recognition. This results in deadly ulcers on the cheek or the nose that refuse to get healed easily. So one is advised to wash the face and hands with warm water and carbolic soap on reaching the destination after the day's journey." On hearing this the Swami added, "On top of this one has a feeling of nausea because of the dizzy altitude and the skin gets cracked because of extreme cold resulting in ugly sores."

On our way we found a pilgrim, sick and vomiting, being nursed by some volunteers. A medical officer came and examined him. He was sent back to Pahalgam in a 'jhampan' under the care of some volunteers.

We reached the peak and sat down to rest. The Swami took a few snaps. From this high altitude the clouds seemed to be very close to us and the sun looked dim. All the mountains surrounding us except a few at some distance appeared to be very small. The Swami said, "Many people at a height like this suffer from nausea and giddiness. This makes them vomit and drop down in exhaustion. This is popularly called mountain-sickness. I had once an experience of this at the top of the Kedarnath (11700 ft high). Oxygen is insufficient in the rarefied air at such a height; Hence breathing becomes difficult and the journey fatiguing. Going a little uphill is as tiring as walking four miles on plain land."

From here the mountain Amarnath appeared to be at a hailing distance. It seemed that we might run up there at once. We saw a large number of waterfalls. Some of them find their way to the river Amaravati while the others are received by the river Indus.

We gradually came down in the opposite direction and then began to move towards Panchatarani through a beautiful table-land. While proceeding on we found many stones, big and small, dislodged from the adjacent mountains and lying scattered on the road. One after another we crossed the five branches of the river Panchatarani and came upon a meadow not very large at the foot of the Bhairab Ghat mountain, also known as the Bairagi Ghat mountain. This place is called Panchatarani because to come to this spot one has to cross the same river five times. The water in two of the five streams is less than knee-deep; but in the others it is very deep and swift-flowing. Over the latter ones light bridges have been constructed by the department concerned. The spot earmarked for the pilgrims is on a higher level, a little above the river. The junipers are the only available fuel here for no other plants grow in this area.

If one proceeds nine miles along the bank of the river Amaravati towards the west, one reaches the village of Baltal on the frontier between India and Tibet. The route is a difficult one and most people find it utterly impossible to negotiate.

Only few tourists are found brave enough to undertake a journey along this difficult route.

Next day we got up very early in the morning to start for Amarnath betimes, as otherwise our return could be very much delayed. We set out at once leaving the government porters in charge of our tents and belongings. Our path lay along the side of sky-scraping mountains. The river Amaravati kept company with us all along the route. On our way we came across many waterfalls of great beauty. There was no trace of any trees or plants on the mountain. It was a dreary picture of barrenness all around. Besides that a sort of solemn serenity and sombre silence reigned supreme there. The place may undoubtedly claim to be a centre of everlasting attraction for poets, painters and travellers.

We left our horses and 'jhampans' at a place called Gugam and proceeded on foot because the path was extremely narrow and unsuitable for all kinds of conveyances. This time we began to climb a hill of worn-out stones. This journey uphill was soon followed by a sharp descent and after some time we reached the perpetually snow-covered bank of the river Amaravati. At the distance of a furlong from that place the river Amaravati could be seen under a snow-bridge rushing foward with a mighty roar. While crossing the river over the snow-bridge one must put on hob-nailed shoes and use a stick. Otherwise there is a sure chance of losing one's balance and slipping. For the convenience of travelling many among the pilgrims had brought with them straw-made 'chappals' bought at Srinagar. At the end of the snowy path we reached at long last the famous cave of Amarnath.

Cascades big and small had frozen here and there inside the cave into heaps of snow. The largest among them was the sacred ice *lingam* of Amarnath. It was cylindrical in shape with a circumference of about six cubits and a height of three cubits. On every heap of snow water from the roof of the cave was dribbling. The pilgrims' guide, Sudama said, "The *Linga* of Lord Siva waxes and wanes along with the waxing and waning of the moon. To-day it being the full-moon day in the Bengali month of Shravana, the *Linga* has assumed full size." In the cave a few Muslims could be seen selling chalk-dust which they claimed to be the ashes of Siva. The Muslims too have a right to this cave because about a hundred years ago a Muslim shepherd discovered the place for the first time and gave the information to the Hindus. The hills here are mostly made of chalk-stone. The Swami said, "This gypsum, if burnt and then powdered into dust, becomes plaster of Paris." Situated at a height of 13000 ft from the sea level and nestled in the bosom of a perpetually snow-covered mountain 18000 ft high, it is a natural cave with a dimension of 150 cubic feet. In this cave we found several titmice flying about much to the annoyance of the pilgrims. While we were looking on, two black pigeons came out of the cave and flew away. According to the 'pandas' these two black pigeons serve as guards to the deity inside the cave. In one corner of the cave could be seen two clods of snow. One of them, we were told, represented Parvati and the other Lord Ganesa. There is no temple inside the cave.

Just below the cave flows the river Amaravati. The river here is called Dudh-Ganga because of its whitish colour, — carrying as it does alluvium from the chalk-cliffs. The pilgrims bathed in the river and offered oblations of water to their dead ancestors and gods. It was in fact a sort of ancestor-worship called *Tarpan*. After their bath the pilgrims with wet clothes on gathered flowers growing on the hill-sides and offered them in worship to Lord Siva. In their zeal they touched and embraced and went round and round the *Lingam*. At the time of ablution and worship the 'pandas' (pilgrim-guides) recited sacred hymns and the pilgrims repeated after them the same.

Just in front of the cave stands the mountain called Bhairav Ghati or Bairagi Ghat. It rises up to a height of 18000 ft. A path over this mountain extends up to the cave of Amarnath. But it is a perilous path and very few except veteran and painstaking travellers or saints dare using this route.

Having seen and worshipped Amarnath we came back to Panchatarani at about 2 p.m. Water was kept boiling on a primus. After finishing our bath we ate our simple meal of rice and curry and then took rest for the day. Our journey from Panchatarani to the cave of Amarnath tired us much. This long rest after so many days of strenuous labour was very sweet and pleasant. Some among the pilgrims decided, however, on going back to Pahalgam at once. To do this they had to ride twenty-nine miles from Panchatarani to Pahalgam at a high speed involving great danger for them.

The Swami said, "On coming here I am reminded of an incident in America. There my friend Professor Parker and myself once scaled the Canadian Alps. The height of that mountain is also 18000 ft. There are glaciers all around the top. We broke our own records by trekking forty-eight miles over hills that day. Ordinarily people cover this distance on horseback in three days. There is a lake in that region. People call it the Emerald Lake. A hotel is situated near it. With the shades of the evening lengthening around us, we decided to pass the night there. Two roads lay before us. By taking one of them we could reach the hotel in fifteen minutes. But Mr. Parker decided on taking the other one and we trudged on endlessly as it were. Soon it was night. We came to a jungle infested with bears and wolves and got lost in it. There were hills on every side and we got bogged down in slush and mire. At last we caught sight of a drain-like passage through which water from the lake flowed out. Just over that water-passage we found a path. But in spite of our best efforts we failed to cross the drain and, to make things worse, Mr. Parker fell into it. There was neck-deep water in the drain and it was terribly cold. Somehow I managed to drag him out of the drain. The poor fellow was thoroughly drenched and shivering with cold. What could I do? Groping in the darkness I collected some pieces of wet wood and tried to ignite them. There was only one stick in the match-box, that too was half-soaked in water and could not be lighted. I could not, therefore, make any fire. There was water all around and we could not find any dry spot where we could sit. At last we somehow came upon the half-rotten trunk of a tree on which we two sat. He was still then shivering with cold. I hugged him close to my bosom to warm him up. Thus we spent the night with our limbs all frozen and the fear of our being attacked with pneumonia haunted us. At early dawn we took to the road again, dead tired, hungry and thirsty. The waters of the lake were putrid and undrinkable. On our way back we drank from the springs wherever we came across them and thus reached the hotel after a tiresome walk of ten miles."

At night 'pandaji' (the pilgrims' guide) read out to us the sacred book called *Amara Purana* depicting the glory of Lord Amarnath and then realised from us the dues for his priestly service.

The following day in the morning the Swami returned from Panchatarani. Our next destination was Asthanmarg situated at a distance of eleven miles from this place. We covered nearly two miles from Panchatarani and reached a place called Khelnur. After reaching this point we left the road we had so long been following and took a different route leading to the right. The permanent glaciers on the high mountain ranges and their peaks were now very near us. It was clear that we were moving on very high altitude. We came across grasses clinging to hillsides here and there — a new sight in this region — and many small unknown lakes with frozen waters along their borders.

By and by we reached a mountain pass, 1400 ft high, called Sachkati. From this height the scenery around looked highly pleasing to the eye. We were now to descend two miles downward to the plains below and just to form an idea of this distance we cast our eyes downwards. How terrific the descent appeared to be! We felt dizzy and choked. The place is rightly called Sachkati, since a look downwards from this place takes one's breath away.

Seen from this high altitude the mounds and the depressions lying far below seem all alike. Nor from this distance can one distinguish a pony from a cow if these creatures are not moving. Also children, youths and old people at the foot of the descent are indistinguishable from each other if viewed from this high point. Very cautiously the pilgrims began to negotiate the descent with the name of Amarnathji on their lips.

They were helped in their journey downward by the volunteers who were stationed at different watch-posts. Along the road sloping down there were big chunks of stone scattered loosely here and there. There is always the danger of losing one's balance while treading over them. At some places the stones look arranged like so many steps while at others they just lie strewn around. It is a desolate place with no trace of vegetation anywhere. While descending it appeared to us as if we were coming down to the earth from the realm of clouds overhead At various places the road lay submerged in water gushing from nearby springs. With their lives hanging perilously on a thread, as it were, the pilgrims managed somehow to descend the road very slowly and cautiously. But the coolies, the ponies and the dandi-bearers were having a far worse time. If by chance any of them slipped, it would mean for him a headlong fall for straight two miles downwards. His body would be lost completely with no trace of it anywhere. Negotiating the descent from Sachkati seemed to us to be more arduous than climbing the ascent of 'Pishu'. Had the slope been less steep and a little more winding our journey would have been less painful and less strenuous.

The Swami was going down the slope like one well accustomed to this kind of trial. Seeing this the pilgrims commented, "Who is this strong Bengali fellow striding along the road like a tiger? He must be a prince of some state."

It took two hours to get out of this dangerous mountain gorge and at last we found ourselves at a safe place below. Our heart was still beating very fast at an irregular pace. For the last time we turned our gaze to the mountain peak high above so as to assess the length of the incline just traversed by us. But no longer could we descry the same, since a gigantic piece of cloud had enveloped it completely.

When the pilgrims had all descended one by one we proceeded northward and soon reached our destination. Here we found plots of land with lush greenery and huts of the Gujars, the local inhabitants. There is no other locality or village in the vicinity. All around prevailed a great calm punctuated only by the ripple of water flowing from a nearby fountain. A route from Asthanmarg leads to Haranag mountain the top of which can be reached only after trailing along an ice-covered ascent of 2000 ft for five hours.

We spent the night at Asthanmarg. Next day at dawn we left for Pahalgam situated at a distance of 15 miles from Asthanmarg. The road lay through deep forests. Near Chandanbari we had to make another arduous descent from a steep mountain surrounded by dense forest foliage. Often our passage was blocked by trees, plants and creepers. We had to push these aside to find our way and this considerably slackened our pace. Immediately after coming down from this forest-covered mountain we found ourselves at the very spot in Chandanbari where we had spent the night in our earlier journey. But this time we did not stay there. Instead we took our old familiar road once again and proceeded toward Pahalgam. We reached the place at nearly three in the afternoon.

Next day in the morning we left Pahalgam and started for Aishmokam. There we passed the night on the same field where we had stayed in our earlier journey. Next day we reached Martanda where we left the company of our co-pilgrims and decided to stay for a few days at the residence of Sudama with a view to visiting some of the beauty spots of Kashmir such as Bhaban, Islamabad, Achchibal etc. The leave sanctioned to Atulbabu by his office was coming to an end. He therefore took leave of us and started for Srinagar so as to reach Calcutta as early as possible.

Kashiram Zoo, the superintendent of the Department of Religious Activities, met us here. The Swami intimated to him his intention of staying at the place for a few days. He then asked him to take back to Srinagar the tents and articles no longer necessary and to send after four days a barge to the quay at Khanabal so that we might return to Srinagar by water.

It is not too much to say that Martanda is the Gaya of Kashmir, Gaya being the place where the Hindus offer oblations to their departed ancestors. It is at Martanda that the Hindus of Kashmir perform these funeral obsequies. Here there is a temple dedicated to the deity Martanda from whom the name of the place derives. The temple was built by king Lalitaditya (699—735 AD). But according to the *Rajatarangini* the said temple was founded by king Ramaditya and the adjoining temples by his queen Amritaprabha. The natural beauty of the place is unique and without parallel. All inhabitants of Martanda are Brahmins. Kashmir can boast of no other place having so many members of this caste. All touts of Amarnath live here. Kashmir has lost the glory of her ancient lore. And yet if there be any place retaining some semblance of the early Aryan Brahminism, then it will be found here and among these people. One can hardly dispute the truth of this assertion after one has come in contact with the Kashmiri Brahmins of this place.

People of different castes live in all provinces of India. Kashmir is an exception. There only Brahmins (Kashmiri Pundits) and Muslims reside. The Brahmins employ Muslim servants, Hindu menials being rare. The water fetched by the Muslim servants is used by the Brahmins for their daily religious services and for cooking, bathing and drinking purposes but this does not make them lose their caste.

The Kashmiris like the Bengalees take rice twice a day. The Hindus and the Muslims are all non-vegetarians. But the Muslims are not allowed to slaughter cow or to take beef. Any Muslim transgressing this injunction receives special punishment which may extend to imprisonment and a fine of rupees fifty. The Kashmiris, like East Bengal people, use too much chillies in cooking. Their favourite curry is a special kind of soup the chief ingredients of which are turnip leaves mixed with a paste of chillies and oil or butter. They take this soup with rice. We also tasted it at the house of Sudama; it gave a stinging pungent sensation to our throat and tongue causing much inconvenience. The Bengalees will learn to their astonishment that the Kashmiri Hindus take meat of various fowls, chicken and wild pigs and in keeping with the practice of ancient Aryans offer as oblations twelve different kinds of meat while performing *Sraddha* rites.

Two miles to the north of Martanda lies the village called Bhaban. Half a mile away from this are several hills near a place called Bumju where we went for a visit to some caves. The largest of these is nearly 200 ft. in length. Its inside is steeped in darkness. We lighted match-sticks while finding our way into it. For some distance we walked with slow steps but then we could proceed further only by crawling. The far end of the cave, though well-lighted, could not however, be reached owing to a blockade created by boulders dislodged from above. Some monk kept himself immersed in religious practices in this cave. Very recently he breathed his last while in a trance. His bones were still lying at the spot where he used to sit in meditation. We felt ourselves blessed at the sight of his bodily remains.

We came out of this cave and proceeded to visit another in the vicinity. There is a beautiful holy shrine in it with nicely carved images of some deities on its rocky walls.

Islamabad is four miles and a half from Bhaban. We went there for a visit. Next to Srinagar it is the largest town in Kashmir. Its population is 20,000. From this place a road comes out leading to the state of Jammu. Quite a number of cloth-dealers reside in this town. Their perfect embroidery-work on shawls, woolen wrappers, table-cloths, valances, screens and various other trimmings are simply incomparable as products of art. Outside the city precincts is a hospital for ladies called Zenana Church Mission Hospital conducted by Christian missionaries. Environed by mountains, enriched with myriads of trees and plants bearing loads of fruits and flowers and studded with so many rivulets, this beautiful city offers breath-taking natural views all around. At one place two exquisite cascades could be seen gushing out of a mountain and falling into two different ponds. Nearby lies the beautiful garden-house of the Maharaja of Kashmir with a temple standing not far off. The town can boast of many other water cascades, one of them being sulphureous and another showing above it a fine-looking mosque built with artistic skill. Islamabad offers you roads to various places of interest such as Phulgam, Dandamarg, Mangjam, Haribal, Kangbattan, Kangsarnag, Shupian and Verinag.

Quite a number of waterfalls are to be seen in Verinag. It was at this place that Emperor Jahangir had a charming garden and a royal palace built for him. He loved the place so much that on the eve of his death he asked to be brought here.

After spending three days at Martanda we started for Achchibal. It is situated at a distance of ten miles from Martanda. We went beyond Islamabad and on crossing a river called the Arpat moved south-west. On our way we saw numerous paddy-fields. As in Bengal, paddy grows abundantly in Kashmir. Now and then we found rows of willows on both sides of the road. There were still six miles to go before we could reach Achchibal but in no time we covered the distance.

Nature has adorned this place with matchless beauty and charm. At the foot of a mountain there is a wonderful pleasure garden belonging to the period of the Nawabs. In it are to be found numerous trees which, bending as it were under the burden of countless delicious fruits, add to the loveliness of the surroundings. In the garden house lives the holy personage who is the preceptor of the Maharaja of Kashmir. We went there to visit the holy man but could not find him as he was away on a visit elsewhere. The lake within the garden serves as a centre of pisciculture run by the government. Many officials are engaged in this job. All fish here are of the trout variety. They resemble more or less a particular species called *Mrigel* in Bengal.

Achchibal is the favourite summer resort of many Europeans and local aristocrats. A gentleman of distinction hailing from Naushera in Sialkot was then putting up there in a tent. He came to recognise the Swami and invited him to spend some time with him. He offered us sumptuous Kashmiri dishes along with delicious eatables of the Sikhs. We took them to our heart's content. The sister of Pandit Motilal Nehru was then spending her summer recess at Achchibal. She sent to the Swami a gift consisting of different local fruits of royal quality and a bouquet of flowers.

The Swami began his journey again in the afternoon. A little distance away from Achchibal we reached the village of Khanabal passing through which we reached the bank of the Vitasta. It is at Khanabal that three separate rivulets, the Arpat, the Bring and the Sandrine join to give rise to the river Vitasta. At the landing place here a government barge bound for Srinagar was waiting to receive us. Leaving our coolies and horses here we boarded it at once. Moving with the current, the barge had a smooth sailing with a woman at the helm. Thickets of hemp on both banks of the Vitasta, the far-off mountain ranges, many hamlets large and small, temples in ruins, mosques thatched with hay and various other sights came upon our view as we sailed onwards. By and by we reached Srinagar after a journey that lasted a day and a half. We alighted at the landing place called Lalmundi and found our lodging in a government house-boat which had been kept reserved for the Swami.

Two days later, at the request of the members of the local Arya Samaj the Swami delivered a speech in English at Huzuri-bagh. Nearly all citizens belonging to the said association attended the meeting. The subject of the speech was 'My Experience in America'.

After the meeting was over the members flocked round the Swami with various questions on religious matters. He answered them all and also spoke to them about Sri Ramakrishna. His religious discourse being over in an hour and a half, the Swami returned to the house-boat.t.

The Janmastami followed two days later. It is the hallowed birthday of Lord Krishna. At five in the afternoon the Swami delivered another lecture from a rostrum set up in a vast field near the marketplace The meeting was held under the auspices of the king of Kashmir, Maharaj Bahadur Pratap Singh, its subject being 'Lord Krishna, the World Teacher.' The Maharaja of Kashmir accompanied by the Prince of Poonch, his private and state secretaries, the Police Superintendent and other state officials and many distinguished and learned persons of the town were present at the meeting. For nearly two hours the Swami addressed his audience in words, vigorous and lively. All were enthralled by his speech and many of them later came regularly to the house-boat to have a talk with the Swami. As days passed the rush of visitors became so heavy that the Swami could hardly find time to perform his usual ablutions and take his meals.

At the time the queen of Baroda was living at the garden-house of Chashmasahi as a state guest of the Maharaja of Kashmir. She sent a car for the Swami so that he might come to see her. In 1906 she had been to America with her husband, Maharaj Sayaji Rao Gaikowad. The couple had been accorded a cordial reception by the Vedanta Society of New York. It was on that occasion that she came to be acquainted with the Swami and since then both their Majesties held the Swami in great reverence. The Maharani now requested the Swami to come to Baroda and found a school for girls. For this she promised to extend necessary financial assistance. She directed her private secretary to treat the Swami as a state guest and render him all necessary service during his stay at Baroda. After this interview with the Maharani the Swami came back to the house-boat.

CHAPTER — 5

Coming to know that the Swami had been to Amarnath and was back to Srinagar Kalowant Singh invited him to come to Gulmarg on a tour of the place. On receiving his invitation the Swami left Srinagar on 23rd April in a tonga for Gulmarg. It was a ride of only twenty-seven miles.

The tonga went along the Happy Valley Road. Our horse was a spirited animal. It trotted at a speed of ten miles an hour. To our right was to be seen the Vitasta gurgling along in its onward course. To our left we saw Kashmiri soldiers camping at the foot of the mountain nearby. These soldiers resembled men of Peshawar. But they were all Sikhs belonging to the Dogra community. After crossing eight miles from our starting point we reached a trijunction of roads and found a signboard indicating the direction to Gulmarg. A little ahead of this place was a bridge on the other side of which lay the village of Magam. The place is equidistant from Gulmarg and Srinagar. Government officials took down our names, address and the purpose of our visit here in accordance with the law of the land. They also examined our luggages. After resting for a while we started again. The Pir Panjal ranges stood in front of us. Cradled near the top of one of them lies the town of Gulmarg. It was a red gravelled path along which we rode. On one side of this path was to be seen a mountain river flowing fast while on the other side lay vast paddy fields. We saw Kashmiri women reaping the corn and singing in a tune of extremely sweet melody.

The Swami commented, "I have heard local songs in the hilly regions of Sweden, Austria, Switzerland and many other countries. Their tunes are all alike."

We saw most of the pilgrims on horseback on the way to Gulmarg. Kashmiri women, like their sisters hailing from the Punjab, are excellent riders. We had to cover four miles of steep ascent to Tanmarg and our tonga had to slacken its speed. We reached Tanmarg at nearly ten in the morning. We found Kalowant Singh, Teja Singh and some other Sikhs waiting to receive us there.

Situated atop a mountain, the town of Gulmarg is three miles away from Tanmarg. Motor cars and tongas cannot climb this steep height. The last lap of the ascent has to be covered either on foot or on horseback. So we got down from our carriage and proceeded on with two porters guiding us as we slowly rode on with great caution. Our path lay through pine forests. It was very cool with the shade of trees above us. On our way we could see the entire valley of Ḳashmir spread far below with the ranges of Nanga Parvat and Pir Panjal guarding the horizon. The Nanga Parvat is 27000 ft high and entirely covered with snow. It presents a sight more glorious than that of Kanchanjangha seen from Darjeeling. It remains unconquered up till now[1] In 1895 the famous mountaineer, Mr. Albert F. Mummery, ignorant of the real problems of Himalayan climbing, attempted to scale the height of Nanga Parvat. He was accompanied by two Nepalese guides. With pickaxe in their hands they carved a path through quite a long distance. But they all got buried under a roaring avalanche.

After covering half the distance to Gulmarg we sat down to rest for a while. We saw pine fruits scattered all around us. The Swami picked up one or two of them and said, "The English call them pine cones. You will find nuts within highly delicious to taste."

Around 1 p.m. we reached Gulmarg and made our way to the house of Royjada Hukma Singh, Deputy Forest Officer and uncle to Kalowant Singh. He was a man of kind disposition. We found that he had rigged up a beautiful tent for us in the garden attached to his house. Having spent so many days inside tents while on the way to Amarnath, the Swami had developed quite a liking for them. After a rest for the day the Swami went out next morning for a tour of the outskirts of Gulmarg in the company of Royjada, Kalowant Singh and others. The meaning of Gulmarg is a field full of roses. It is said that the name was given by Emperor Shah Jahan. The view of the place with a valley two miles in length and half a mile in breadth surrounded on all sides with houses made of wood and tin captures the fancy of all tourists. Golf links,

---

[1] Nanga Parvat is considered the most treacherous among the Himalayan peaks and many a mountaineer attempting to climb it has perished. It remained unconquered at the time when the Swami visited Kashmir. It was finally scaled in July 1953 by a German-Austrian expedition.

polo grounds and a race course are to be seen in this valley. The official bungalow of the English resident and the royal palace are situated near the post office and the marketplace. The big 'Naidu Hotel' of this town was gutted completely sometime ago and this has caused much inconvenience to foreigners and the rich local tourists. We heard that its owner Mr. Hari Naidu had decided to rebuild it soon. His name may mislead one to infer that he is a Hindu hailing from Madras. But he is no Hindu. Formerly a Christian he gave up his own religion to embrace Islam and marry a Muslim girl. He is now a devout Muslim doing his *namaj* regularly. Quite a large number of white people live in the town and at first sight it looks like a place in Europe. The town also serves as the summer residence of Hari Singh Bahadur, the Crown Prince of Kashmir.

The monsoon sets in at Gulmarg in June. By the end of September it starts snowing so much that the place becomes uninhabitable and continues to be so till May. The whole place gets covered with thick snow and the people of Gulmarg then go away to Baramula and Srinagar. It is only during summer that you can get a well-furnished bungalow at Gulmarg at a monthly rent of five or six hundred rupees. You need not bring any luggages or furniture with you, for everything is available in the bungalows.

Three miles to the north-east of Gulmarg there is the village of Babamarishi at a height of 7000 ft. It is said that during the Mughal reign there lived here a pious man named Baba Pamdin who had acquired great occult power through austere religious practices. The path to this village lies along a steep ascent. We passed by the side of cottages inhabited by people of local tribes and proceeded through a deep forest. On our way we found a 'dharmashala' and a big house where a large number of mendicants reside. The area is infested with wild bears. But still the natural beauty of the place is so attractive that many Europeans spend the summer here.

From Gulmarg the Swami went on a visit to the lake of Alpathar. One has to pass through a valley called Killenmarg to reach this lake. There is luxuriant growth of green grass in this place and shepherds come here with their flocks of sheep. The meaning of Killenmarg is a field for goats to graze on.

From Alpathar you can see the borders of Poonch. Royjada had arranged a picnic for us at Killenmarg. After having our picnic we returned to Gulmarg around evening. We were told that many an unfortunate man had been accosted by bears while going from Killenmarg to Gulmarg after sunset.

At this time Mrs Mitra had shifted to her bungalow at Gulmarg from Srinagar. On coming to know that the Swami had come to Gulmarg, she invited him to her place and arranged various kinds of dishes for him. Dr. A. Mitra was at one time the only Bengalee inhabitant of Srinagar. He had purchased two villas at Srinagar and Gulmarg on a permanent basis. Such purchase is no longer allowed now. No non-Kashmiri can purchase immovable property at Kashmir according to rules enacted of late.

Next morning Pandit Ajnaram and a young Sikh named Lala Chetram came to see the Swami. The latter had received training in paper manufacture in U.S.A. It is there that he had had the opportunity of getting acquainted with the Swami. They now took tea with him. After this the Swami went to the polo ground where a festival was going on. There we met Major Skinner, the man to whom the seat reserved for the Swami for Rs. 22 in the bus carrying us from Rawalpindi to Srinagar had been given by the bus-owner against Rs. 35. He received the Swami very warmly, took him to his bungalow and offered him tea and snacks. After a tete-a-tete with him we left for the bazar to buy photographs of the wonderful natural scenery of Kashmir. After visiting a few shops we came to an establishment run by an English lady. There we found the best collection of photographs.

At Gulmarg there is a palace belonging to the Maharaja of Kashmir. From there one can get the view of the entire city on one side and that of the peaks of Nanga Parvat clad eternally in snow on the other. The Swami went to the palace to get a view of these contrasting pictures and returned from there in a very happy mood. In the afternoon Chetram visited the Swami and had a long talk with him.

Next day Chetram took the Swami with him for a visit to Sardar Abdul Rahman Effendi, the Prince of Afganistan. The Effendi received the Swami with great honour. The latter returned to the camp after nearly an hour's talk with him.

Thus we spent a fortnight at Gulmarg enjoying heartily the beauty of nature that the place had to offer us. Then the Swami returned to the government house-boat at Srinagar Lala Chetram Kolay was also back from Gulmarg to Srinagar and he invited the Swami to supper at his place. This was followed by more invitations at different places. After thus spending a few days at Srinagar the Swami said, "Let us go to Kshirbhabani hallowed by the august visit of Swami Vivekananda."

The government house-boat being ugly and inconvenient, we procured with the help of Mr.Kolay another houseboat that served our purpose better. It was a well-furnished vessel provided with all amenities. It should be mentioned here that the boatmen are all Muslims. Every houseboat is accompanied by a small dinghy for going ashore and coming back whenever necessary. Such dinghies are called 'Shikaras' in Kashmir.

We started next day at eight in the morning and found ourselves nearing Sadipur around three in the afternoon. Our journey was very smooth up to this point because we were sailing with the current. At Sadipur we found high mountain peaks clad in snow dazzling with the sunlight on them while birds of a myriad variety flew overhead. The *chenars* with their leaves of various hues seemed to emit a wonderful light. By and by we came to a halt near a landing place.

The place is called Sadipur because the Indus and the Vitasta have their confluence here. It was known as Paritranpur in the days of yore. It was the capital of king Lalitaditya in the eighth century. Later the capital was shifted by king Shankarvarman to a place called Pattan. Ancient ruins are to be seen there.

Sadipur offers great scenic beauty to the visitor. The Swami spent a night here and next day went out on a round. There is a government rest-house near the landing place and one can stay there free of cost for three days at a stretch. Wide expanses of paddy fields greet the eyes as one enters Sadipur. The village is situated on both the banks of the river. Potatoes, fish, flour, rice, butter and other articles of daily use are available in the market adjoining the landing place. We found quite a number of Englishmen with their womenfolk in a houseboat near the other side of the river. The place is a favourite resort for Europeans during summer.

The Vitasta receives all the garbage and filth of Srinagar. Its water is therefore unsuitable for drinking purpose. But the water of the Indus is excellent. It is so clean and transparent that one can see tiny pebbles and fish very clearly even at a depth of seven or eight cubits. Mamdu, our boatman, soon impaled a number of trouts with his javelin. They are very tasty and soft when cooked. Limbs get numbed in the cold waters of the Indus if one takes even a moment's dip. The waters increase remarkably in volume towards afternoon because the snow that accumulates on the hills at night melts as the sun goes up in the sky.

From Sadipur we went to see a very beautiful lake called Manasball. To go there one has to proceed along a canal starting from a sprawling village called Sambal which we reached soon afterwards. On one side of this village stands a hill named Aahatej. Most of the inhabitants of the village are fishermen. The lordly *chenars* by the river present a wonderful sight.

The lake of Manasball is flanked by the hill known as Aahatej on one side and a high plateau on the other. The lake is very deep with its water clean and unpolluted. A branch of the Indus flows into the lake. From this point there is a seven-mile route leading to Gandharball. At a spot nearby there is a mausoleum and a cave. Near this we found the ruins of an ancient temple mostly submerged in the waters. The village of Kundaball lies at the base of the hill of Aahatej. Plenty of limestones is to be seen in this hill. Not very far from here lie the remains of Darogabagh, the famous pleasure-garden made at the behest of Jahangir. He made a gift of this garden to Empress Nurjahan. Numerous plots of land lying fallow are to be seen at the south-west corner of the lake. Travellers and hunters usually pitch their tents on these plots dotted with the ruins of ancient structures.

In the hills adjoining this place the Prince of Kashmir often comes on bear-hunting. No other man is allowed to undertake hunting expeditions in these hills without prior sanction from the government. One cannot even come to this lake or the canal leading to it for the purpose of angling. Nowhere in India will one find innumerable lotus blooms stretching for miles as they do in the lakes of Kashmir. One who has had the opportunity of seeing this heavenly sight will have no doubt in his mind as to the fact that Kashmir is a veritable paradise on earth. It has already been mentioned that the king of Kashmir worships everyday his household deity with one thousand and eight lotus blooms. They are mostly collected from these beautiful lakes by men specially drafted for the purpose. If a man tries to collect them for his own use he has to pay a fine as penalty. In the villages adjoining the lake one can buy lotus-honey in plenty.

Manasball is the smallest lake in Kashmir. According to geologists, the lakes scattered at and near Srinagar (Dal, Ular, Manasball etc) were once parts of a gigantic lake in the past, known as Sati-sagar. It dried up in course of time in many places and we have these lakes today separated by stretches of land.

After visiting the Dal lake and Manasball we now made for the Ular lake. In the evening our boat reached Ular which receives in its wide bosom the waters of the Vitasta.

———————

On the road from Srinagar to Bandipur one has to cross a river near Sambal. Two miles away from this place lies the lake of Manasball. Proceeding northwards by land along the shore of this lake one passes through several fields at the base of mountains in a row and then reaches the villages called Ajas and Sadarkot. At some distance from them lies the lake of Ular. In summer as well as in the rainy season the water of this lake increases so much in volume that the said villages get almost completely inundated. But with the coming of winter water subsides and the lake recedes many miles away from them. The water of this lake which comes entirely from the Vitasta is extremely polluted and not at all drinkable. During the rainy season its level rises so high that one fails to discern its shores and the vast expanse of water stretching for fifteen or sixteen miles rushes at a terrific speed washing the feet of so many mountains. To go for a cruise over it then in a houseboat or in a 'Shikara' is simply to invite disaster. Only in the small hours of the morning can one dare to steer a boat over this lake, for after 9 a.m. onwards a terrific gale sweeps over it for the rest of the day. At times sudden cyclonic storms blow from the nearby mountains, overturning boats and taking toll of many a life. It is generally assumed that these mighty storms blow from the valley of the Harmukh mountain.

A circular island of a diameter of nearly fifty cubits is situated in the lake on its eastern side not far off from where the Vitasta flows into it. During winter when the water of the lake sinks to a lower level revealing stretches of dry land here and there, it is possible to go to the island on foot. At other times, however, it can be reached only by a boat. All around the island known as Sonalanka is a forest of water-chestnut. One still finds here remains of four landing places of stone, a dilapidated temple dedicated to Siva and the ruins of a mosque. Remains of four houses are also to be seen at four corners of the island. Besides all these we saw ancient pillars, floors of rooms and various other relics of the past. They all clearly indicate that in some remote antiquity the place could boast of having nice buildings, beautiful bathing ghats and the like. It is now a deserted place with no human habitation anywhere.

The temple of Siva without any roof and without any deity inside appears to be much older than the mosque. Remnants of decorations can still be seen on its walls and also on the stairs leading to its entrance. Its arches resemble exactly those seen in Roman Catholic churches. Engravings on them still retain traces of the beauty they once had. A look at this temple on all sides of which broken walls exist even now will convince one that no mortar was used in its construction. Stones were placed on stones with great skill in raising the structure. Long ago a rather big stone of black colour lay in front of this temple. It was subsequently lifted from the spot under the direction of archaeologists to be preserved in the museum of Srinagar.

According to many the mosque here was erected by Zain ul-Abedin. It was then called Bardwari. Opposite to it stands a hill called Baba-Shukur-Uddin near which the lake's depth is the greatest. On the top of the hill is a tomb dedicated to a disciple of the famous Muslim saint named Nuruddin. Not far off bubbles can be seen continually rising to the surface of the lake. Scientists think that some natural spring lies below. The Kashmiris call it Nag-Devata (the god of serpents). The local Hindu villagers look upon it as the wheel wielded by God Vishnu and worship it as such.

To the north-western corner of the Lake stands the Harmukh mountain, its height being 16900 ft above the sea level. It has eight peaks each of which is ever clad in snow. The height of its lowest peak is 6000 ft. Dr. E. F. Neve and Mr. G. W. Millais were the first to scale in 1900 its highest peak. The city of Bandipur lying to the south of this mountain is used as a favourite summer resort by numerous Europeans living in houseboats. It is a small city but its exquisite natural scenery is a feast for the eyes. At the sight of the deep rolling waters below with their sublime appeal the enchanted viewer feels a deep yearning within himself to commune with the endless mystery of existence. We found quite a number of Europeans of both sexes taking fresh air while sauntering by the side of the lake. Guns in hand, their children were engaged in shooting birds. The loud report of their guns disturbed the solitude of the hills.

In Bandipur you will find one dak bungalow, a post office, a serai and a playground for the Europeans and several beautiful spots for camping. Since the town is situated very near the lake, fish is available there in plenty. While on the way to the city of Gilgit one has to pass through Bandipur. The distance between the two places is nearly two hundred miles. One can reach Gilgit from Bandipur within a fortnight or so if one can cover each day nearly fifteen miles at least either on foot or on horseback. At the end of each day's journey one finds a dak bungalow for rest. The road is as smooth as possible without any hard ascent or unsafe descent. There is, however, a continuous ascent only at one place along the route across a mountain nearly 10000 ft high called Tragball. Many people climb this mountain with the intention of getting a full view of the Ular lake and the scenery surrounding the same. From this high point the sight of the Pir Panjal Range and the Harmukh mountain is really enchanting.

During summer one is oppressed by heat while on the way to Gilgit, since the road for the most part runs at a height of four to five thousand feet only. Even in winter one does not experience much cold while journeying along this road. It is, however, highly dangerous to traverse it during winter, since there is always the possibility of an avalanche descending furiously at any moment. The great mass of snow and ice accumulated at a high altitude hurtles down the mountain-side with a terrific noise, often carrying with it at lightning speed thousands of tons of rocks and crushing in a trice numerous travellers in its downward course. This explains why travellers are rarely found on this road during winter.

To the east of Bandipur are spread several plateaus at a modest height, their names being Hap Killenmarg, Nagmarg etc. Beyond them there are rows of hills clad in permanent glaciers. They present a panoramic and enthralling view. Bandipur receives its water-supply from a spring on Hap Killenmarg.

In Kashmir one hears names of places like Gulmarg, Shonemarg, Killenmarg, Nagmarg, Tanmarg etc. The word 'Marg' in Kashmiri means 'tableland'. Besides these there are names like Sheshnag, Anantanag, Harnag, Verinag and various other names ending with the suffix 'Nag'. The word 'Nag' stands for 'snake'. The mass of snow on the mountain top increases in volume under terrific pressure and lengthens itself gradually downwards till it touches the level ground below. From a distance it looks like a gigantic white serpent coiling around the mountain side. This explains why such perpetually snow-clad mountains are given the title of 'snake' or 'Nag'. In the eyes of many these mountains resemble Lord Siva with his matted locks.

Soldiers of the kingdom of Kashmir are garrisoned in the town of Gilgit where cavalry and infantrymen receive their regular military training. It is the north-eastern frontier province of India. From this place one can easily go to Central Asia and Russian Turkestan. This is why the king of Kashmir has kept reserved here quite a large number of soldiers and various war materials for self defence against foreign aggression. Before 1845 Gilgit was no part of British India. On being attacked in that year by the chief of Yasin, the ruler of Gilgit sought the help of the Sikhs. Then Nathu Shah, the Sikh general, came over to Gilgit and conquered it. He also entered into polygamy with the three daughters of the rulers of the three provinces, Yasin, Hunza and Nagar. But in 1847 the ruler of Hunza attacked Gilgit and killed Nathu Shah. Later in 1852 the chief of Yasin attacked Gilgit once again and inflicted a crushing defeat upon the forces sent by the ruler of Astor to help the king of Hunza. Later the ruler of Astor himself faced a military debacle and lost his kingdom. In 1860 the Sikh leader, Devi Singh succeeded in asserting his sovereignty over Gilgit, Astor, Yasin and Hunza, all of which thenceforward formed parts of the kingdom of Kashmir.[1] But sporadic revolts and uprisings, a common feature in these regions, necessitated strong military measures. The Hunza-Nagar expedition of 1891 under Colonel A. Durand resulted in the assertion of British authority over the entire area and in marking the political boundary of Kashmir as extending to the plateau of Pamir and the Chinese frontier.

The state of Gilgit is extremely barren, so much so that the barley grown here hardly suffices to feed all its population.

---

[1]The two regions, Hunza and Nagar, lying encircled by high-peaked mountains and swift-flowing rivers, remained immune for a long time from sudden foreign incursions. Their inhabitants therefore lived in peace. The soil in these regions is highly fertile and one finds plots of land in which barley, wheat, maize, radish, etc grow in abundance. The inhabitants of Hunza belong to the 'Mulai' sect of the Muslims, while those of Nagar are 'Shia' Muslims.

Hence Gilgit has to depend permanently on Kashmir. The people are called Dards. Their faces and eyes bear Aryan stamp unlike that on the average mountain-bred peoples. In general appearance they look almost like Pathans but in temperament they are less arrogant and less revengeful than the latter. The inhabitants in this region are all Muslims belonging to the 'Shia' sect excepting those who live in Kafristan.

There is no other mountain pass in the Karakoram and the Hindukush Ranges at a level lower than the region of Gilgit. In the 14th century when Tamerlane invaded India he reached Chitral along this difficult route.

The river Vitasta issues from the south-west corner of the Ular lake. Not far from this spot lies a beautiful village called Shiupur. Situated on the shore of the lake at the foot of a mountain it offers an exquisite panoramic view. Many Europeans spend their summer recess in houseboats here. One can easily bring all necessary things from the city of Baramula which is very near this place.

After visiting the lake of Ular we returned to Sadipur again and started for Gandharball nearly seven miles away. The entire distance had to be covered by towing the boat against the current. The picturesque sight of the village of Gandharball seen from a distance reminded us of the breathtaking beauty and charm of the land of the Gandharvas described by romantic poets. Indeed the entire region with its treasures of beauty, matchless and incomparable, captures the mind of tourists in no time and takes away all their feelings of hardship encountered in journeying to such a distant place amidst alien surroundings. Gadharball is twelve miles and a half to the north of Srinagar and its height is greater by 1000 ft than that of the latter. That is why sailing from Gandharball to Srinagar requires towing the boat against the current of the river, though there is also a metalled road open to tongas and motor cars connecting the two places. There is yet another road to Gandharball via Marlala and the Lake of Anchar. Gandharball is bounded on the east, west and north by mountains and on the south by the river Indus. Across this river here lies an old-styled wide bridge which is accessible to tongas and other vehicles. It is entirely made of wood, including its supporting pillars going deep into the water. Bridges of this type are found only in

Kashmir. Gandharball enjoys the facility of a post and telegraph office, a dak bungalow and 'kutchari' and a small mart where more or less all articles of daily use are available.

From June to September the place remains fully crowded with people coming from various places in India and also from abroad. A large number of Europeans and affluent people from Srinagar come in their houseboats to this place and use it as their summer resort. During this period one witnesses hundreds of houseboats near the bank of the Indus and the place becomes reverberent with the neighing of horses, honks of motor-horns, and the hue and cry of servants and stewards. Filled with all the various articles of regular use by the Europeans the small marketplace expands like anything in summer. Chowkidars then attend to their duties day and night. Throughout this period vendors of fruits and bread and hawkers of newspapers come regularly to this place from Srinagar. For these few months only a government hospital is set up here. While the day temperature in Srinagar becomes rather high in summer, this place remains quite cool and soothing and the barometer here never registers a temperature above 80 degrees. The leaves of *chenars* here remain green even then and the snows on the mountain tops start melting.

Three miles to the north of Gandharball stands the temple dedicated to the goddess of Kshirbhabani. Considerably wide and running along a channel, the road is wide enough for tongas to ply smoothly and without difficulty. And as you go along the road, you feast your eyes on beautiful scenes of wild flowers blooming in millions on both sides and presenting a veritable carnival of colours, — red, yelow, blue, and green. Lordly *chenars* standing for ages fringe both sides of the road. Some of these are over two centuries old and are found simply standing on their rather thick barks with the wood and pulp inside rotten and discarded. The cavity thus formed can easily accommodate three or four persons within it. The *chenar* trees grow only in cold countries. Their leaves and fruits resemble those of *peepul* trees, — the fruits being of no use at all. A big *chenar* can attain a height of about 90 ft and its trunk is too thick to be hugged fully even by three or four persons together. During summer it develops fresh leaves which are of greenish colour. With the advent of winter the leaves gradually become yellow and crimson and finally scarlet when they drop off. The

Swami said, "The cold generated by the snows of November causes this change of colour. The leaves of maple trees in America also change colour like this". The sight of these trees is then really captivating and many people come to Kashmir simply to have their eyeful of this brilliant scene,—a scene ablaze with red and looking as if on fire. Leaves begin to drop in increasing numbers and soon the gardens and the roads are bestrewn with them. Villagers store them to make fire with during winter.

Three miles away from Gandharball is the village called Tulmul. On entering this, one is likely to err in taking it for a typical small village of Bengal. One finds drains overflowing with putrid water on both sides of the road, gardens converted into jungles, fences in ruins and houses in a state of disrepair. The houses here are all made of wood; on their roofs are grown grasses and flower plants. These roofs are constructed in a strange manner. Birch leaves are placed two or three cubits high and on them are laid small twigs of trees. Finally clay is spread thick over the whole thing. It does not rain here much and so it is not at all necessary to have roofs of concrete. The affluent at Srinagar, Gulmarg and other towns, however, build roofs for their houses in the modern fashion with bricks, lime, tin etc. But the practice has not as yet spread to villages. There houses stand open to the elements from all sides. One is simply amazed to see how they live in these houses entirely exposed to the terrible cold in winter. The people here are insufficiently protected against cold with only a thick robe as their chief wear. Very few people are seen with shoes on. Of course both the sexes wear wooden sandals. The typical outfit of a Kashmiri Brahmin consists of a white turban, a loose-fitting robe and wooden sandals. He wears a mark of saffron on his forehead. The Brahmins of Kashmir are called 'Pandits' while their women-folk are referred to as 'Panditanis'. The latter use nearly the same kind of outfit, the only difference being that they wear a wide handkerchief instead of a turban on the head with four or five tassels hanging from the same. The Muslims do not wear any mark on their foreheads. Their turbans are also worn in a style completely different from those of the 'pandits'. The language they use is similar in many, respects with Sanskrit. They say "Kutar gachcha"? when they mean to ask "Where are you going?" "Kutar gachcha" seems to be a near variant of

"Kutra Gachchati" in Sanskrit. The Sanskrit for 'toad' is 'Manduka'. The Kashmiris also use this word while speaking of toads.

All the Hindus of this region are Brahmins, other castes (Kshatriya, Vaishya and Sudra) being non-existent. All these Brahmins are of fair complexion. Nowhere will you find in Kashmir a single dark complexioned Brahmin. The Hindus form only three percent of the population, the rest being all Muslims. The ancestors of the latter were Hindus, later converted to Islam under the oppressive reign of the Muslim rulers. From the eleventh century onwards Islam began to be preached in this region. The initiative was taken by a Muslim ruler, Allauddin. The names of the Muslims of this region, in many cases, indicate their Hindu origin. We came to be acquainted here with a well-known dealer in shawls whose name was Pandit Amadulla.

Scantily protected against cold with their insufficient clothings, the Kashmiris all use *Kangris* to guard themselves from being frozen. A *Kangri* is a small earthen bowl with burning charcoal in it placed within a small basket of cane with a handle. Both men and women have these *Kangris* hanging from their necks and placed deftly inside their robes. They seldom get overturned causing burns.

Like the Bengalees, the Kashmiris take rice as their cheaf cereal. They rarely take bread. They prepare a soup with turnip leaves which is considered by them as a highly delicious preparation. Besides this, various other green vegetables are available in moderate quantities. They use much salt and chillies in preparing their soup and curry. Fresh vegetables are however not available during winter when the entire region lies under snow. People here then depend on dried vegetables which they begin to store with the coming of winter. All take tea regularly. They prepare tea in a pot made of brass and drink this from a small bowl made of the same metal. To eat anything directly by using hands goes against their custom. So they hold the bowl of tea with their hands concealed under long sleeves of their loose vests. Nor is it their practice to take food from a pot placed on the floor. Like the Punjabis at their meals they keep their pots and trays on a mat spread on it.

The temple dedicated to the Goddess Kshirbhabani is situated in the outskirts of the village of Tulmul. It is skirted by a swiftly-flowing canal on three sides whose waters are free of all impurities. The canal flows into the Indus three miles away from this place. Near the temple stand trees of various kinds. A few ancient shrines are to be seen nearby.

On returning to the houseboat from the temple of Kshirbhabani the Swami said, "The venerable Gangadhar Maharaj came back from Tibet along this route. I am also feeling an urge to take to it for a visit to Tibet."

Soon after this the Swami asked that all arrangements should be made for the said journey. A high official of the Government of Kashmir was in Gandharball at this time. He came to our boat for a meeting with the Swami. On learning from us that we were planning to visit Tibet he gave us the name of a trusted guide who could also act as our interpreter. He asked our boatman to take care of the things we were leaving behind in the boat. We got from him letters of introduction to the Wazier of Leh and the Tahasildar of Kargil.

We were overwhelmed with gratitude at all the kind arrangements he made for us for our journey. We started on foot along the bank of the Indus with our tent and other necessary things on the back of two load-carrying horses. The Swami said, "It is my intention to cross the Himalayas on foot. Let us see how far this is possible. If necessary, we shall hire horses later."

CHAPTER—7

Our next destination was the village of Kangan, situated at a distance of eleven miles and a half to the north-east of Gandharball. This distance would have to be covered in course of a single day because there is no resting place on the way. One can get horses both for riding and for carrying luggages with the help of local contractors. It is, however, advisable to examine the horses thoroughly before commencement of the journey and see that they are not old or lame or uncontrollable or pregnant.

Shortly after we started from Gandharball we had to cross a hanging bridge on the Indus on which cars are not allowed. We met two European hunters on our way. They had been to Drass and were on their way back. Like us they had deposited their luggages in their houseboat before undertaking their journey. We enquired of them whether the mountain roads they had traversed were in good shape. Soon it started drizzling and we put on our raincoats. The road ahead was quite broad and with a plain level. At a short distance could be seen lofty mountains on both sides of the road. Our route lay through a valley and by the side of the Indus. On both sides of the road lay fields of paddy, maize and wheat. Apple trees and vinyards richly laden with fruits also greeted our eyes as we wended our way towards our destination.

At a distance of four miles from Gandharball is the village of Nunnar. We found a large number of people picking fruits at an orchard. The Swami asked Gania, our guide, to get some fruits for us and gave him a two-anna bit[1] for the purpose. Great was our wonder when Gania brought heaps of fruits for us within a short while. We were overjoyed to get so much against so little a payment. Beyond the village there is a place called Wayle. There we crossed the Indus. After this we had to traverse two or three miles entirely barren and without trees. The soil beneath our feet consisting of sand and stone was extremely hot.

---

[1]According to the present currency system a two-anna piece amounts to twelve paise.

At four in the afternoon we reached the dak bungalow at Kangan. Situated near the bazar the bungalow is very neat and clean. The Swami had a chair brought to its verandah and stretched himself on it for rest. The chowkidar made himself very useful to us and helped us in all possible ways.

The Indus flows with speed very near this dak bungalow. It is not much wide here, but very deep. High mountains covered with dense forests overlook the river. About a hundred people live in this locality of whom the great majority are Muslims. Very few Hindu families live here, but all of them are Brahmins by caste.

From here many people go to visit the lake of Gangaball, nine miles to the west. One can start at dawn and return by evening if the weather holds. There are quite a number of lakes scattered on the Harmukh mountain. The largest among them is known as Gangaball. It is situated at a height of 1300 ft above sea level. Around this place are to be seen the ruins of ancient Buddhist temples. But the road leading to the spot is in such a bad shape that just a little rain renders it extremely slippery and unsafe. Many pilgrims have lost their lives or suffered grievous physical injury on this road during the rainy season. A fair is held every year in this place during August and pilgrims gather to make offerings to their dead ancestors, — a sacred custom among Hindus.

The village of Wanggat where one can go from Kangan is full of attractive mountain scenery. Situated at a height of 6800 ft the village is, to tourists, a favourite haunt. Three miles away from it stand the ruins of two ancient Buddhist temples. The umbrella-like arches of the temples are simply wonderful. The huge blocks of stone used in the construction of the temples fill one with amazement and it seems that superhuman beings were at work in building them. Near the site of these ruins are two water-springs called Nagball and Rajodyanball.

After leaving Kangan you will find apples and pears no more. So one is advised to make a stock of these fruits if one proposes going further north. It is not advisable to take water for the purpose of quenching thirst while journeying along mountain routes. Taking fruit-juice is better because of its enervating effect. Journey beyond Kangan is known as 'Sind valley Trip'.Before one undertakes this journey one should procure food and other necessaries from the market of Srinagar, for the more you move to the north the more you will find it difficult to procure them. After spending the night at the dak bungalow at Kangan we began making preparations for the commencement of our journey at early dawn. At this time the police came and started taking down our names, whereabouts and other particulars. When they were told that the Swami was a state guest in Kashmir, they treated him with great respect. They told us that the intelligence department of the Government had been alerted against Russian Bolsheviks who might try to enter India along this route. After they left us we hurried through our breakfast. Then with our lunch packets and luggages placed carefully on the back of our horses we set out for the day's journey.

It was twentieth September and the sky was clear, The rays of the sun were not yet unbearable. Our destination that day was Gunda, thirteen miles to the north-east of Kangan. The road was almost plain with only a few minor ascents and small descents. The hills on the way were full of pebbles and clay indicating that the entire area once lay in a submerged state. On our way we saw an old type of bridge across the Indus. It was a strange thing with a very thick rope above and two ropes below. A basket hangs from the thick rope above. One has to sit in this basket and cross the river by pulling with both hands the ropes below. Not far from the bridge lies a road leading to Srinagar via Shalemarbagh. The road proceeds in a zig-zag way across a high mountain on the other side of which lies the Dal Lake. Near it there is a small village called Hayan inhabited by about ten Muslim families. It has fields of maize and rye all around. In each cornfield there is a wooden platform. The owner of the field has to make a bed of hay on this platfrom and lie on it at night. In between snatches of sleep he has to make a sound by beating an empty tin container hanging from the platfrom. This sound is supposed to keep bears away. It is strictly forbidden to kill a bear on these hills without licence issued by the government. We found some villagers picking maize from the fields and some others collecting twigs from willow trees. It is the practice here to make huge bundles of maize, husks of rye, young twigs of willow trees and put them on tree-tops during summer. In winter when the whole place is under thick snow and food becomes scarce these bundles are used as cattle-fodder. On both sides of the road we saw rows of willow trees. Soon we reached a village called Mamur. The inhabitants of the place were all quite stout and fair-complexioned. They watched us with curious looks in their eyes. We found a small field near a grocery. Many a traveller is seen putting up in tents pitched on this field surrounded by mountains on all sides. The Indus flows swiftly by this field. We sat down beneath a tree for a little rest.

After covering a little distance we again sat down on the trunk of a huge tree felled sometime ago and took some light refreshments. A mile ahead and we were at a place called Ganjan. The scenic beauty of the place reminded us of the Eden Garden at Calcutta. We had to cross and recross the Indus in course of a very short distance and reached the village of Gunda around five in the evening. The small dak bungalow at Gunda stood invitingly by the roadside and a beautiful cascade could be seen gurgling along in the forest of willows nearby. The place is surrounded by hills all green with forests. A little below the dak bungalow could be seen the Indus whose waters looked bluish from above. The place is at a higher altitude than Gandharball and is therefore colder.

We entered the dak bungalow and found that the forest-ranger of the place had pitched his tent in its courtyard and been living there for some time. It should be mentioned that one is allowed to stay in the courtyard of a dak bungalow inside a tent on payment of a very meagre sum. Under this arrangement one should not expect the chowkidar to render one any service or assistance. The forest ranger, a Sikh, turned out to be quite a learned man when we opened conversation with him. The gentleman struck up a good friendship with the Swami in no time. He was surprised to learn that the Swami had undertaken his hard and perilous journey on foot and gave him letters of introduction to the collectors at Kargil and Leh. This unexpected help proffered by him seemed to us to be a gift of God. We took our meals and spent the night in the dak bungalow. Next day we started again at nine in the morning after breakfast. The forest ranger saw us off after accompanying the Swami and his party for a short distance.

Our next destination was the village of Shonmarg situated at a distance of a little over fourteen miles to the north-east of Gunda. We proceeded along a road hewn through the rocks and crossed the small villages of Rebil and Kulan. People of Shonmarg collect their food and other necessaries from these villages. We proceeded a mile and a half and crossed the Indus over a bridge built recently. We recrossed the river shortly after this and proceeded along a pastoral field with wild walnut trees on both sides of us. The hilly people of this place extract oil from these walnuts. After crossing seven miles we came to the small hamlet of Gagangir, a favourite haunt for many a hunter. The hills nearby are infested with bears. The valley along which we were moving towards our destination became narrower and narrower. On both sides of the road we found hills 9000 ft high standing erect and perpendicular-wise. At places we found gigantic stones perched precariously on hill tops that seemed ready to come down at any moment,—a fearful sight indeed. A beautiful waterfall could be seen cascading down from dizzy heights. The hillside is covered with raspberry trees. Clusters of ripe berries, red, yellow and pink in colour, seemed to shed enchanting light of a myriad hues all along the way. There were also innumerable walnut, maple and hazelnut trees.

Through this dense forest flows the Indus with a terrific speed. The river is not very wide here but quite considerably deep. Snow trouts are available here in abundance. Huge tree trunks in their thousands could be seen floating towards Srinagar. Sometimes they got stuck against boulders. There were officials engaged in the task of pushing these trunks into the current again with the help of big bamboo poles. In this way wood is transported to different places far away. By and by we came across three waterfalls and other excellent mountain scenery and in course of time reached the village of Shonmarg before it was evening.

Shonmarg is situated on the Indus at a distance of fifty miles from Srinagar. It is said that gold-dust could be found in the sands of the river Indus in the past. From the writings of Pliny and Herodotus we come to know that people of our country collected gold even from ant-hills and dug holes in the ground near them to preserve the same. Later on people delved into these holes and procured gold from there. According to these historians quite a large number of such holes containing gold were there in the sands of the Indus.

The village of Shonmarg with its exquisite mountain scenery lies cradled within a bend of the river Indus forming a semi-circle in the shape of a crescent moon. Shonmarg was the last beautiful place visited by us in course of our journey through Kashmir. After this there is no other valley containing so much of loveliness and charm. Many Europeans come here during the summer. The glacier valley of Shonmarg and the eternally snow-clad mountain-ranges of Thajbas and Jhabar have great appeal for tourists. The snow has remained in the same state for thousands of years and become so hard that it is impossible to melt it. Heated by fire it will crack but never melt. Crystal is made out of such immensely hard snow. Situated at a height of 9000 ft the place is terribly cold. It rains almost everyday during summer and the rainy season. Tourists are therefore advised to be equipped with tents which could come in handy if there was no accommodation in the dak bungalow or the serai. The local inhabitants are all Muslims and extremely poor. It is impossible to secure shelter in their houses. Along this road merchants come and go with their cargo placed on the backs of yaks and horses. They spend nights on the bare field by the side of the village and do not mind being soaked in ice-cold rains. Seldom do they catch cold or fall ill as a result of such hardship. If one desires to proceed further than Shonmarg one will have to carry food and other necessaries, for nothing except fuel is available in the village of Baltal, the stoppage next to Shonmarg.

In the morning we started getting ready after breakfast for our journey onwards. Our destination now was a place only nine miles from Shonmarg. So we proceeded in a somewhat leisurely manner. One of the two horses carrying our loads had developed a sore on one of its legs and so moved with great difficulty. We wanted to lessen its burden and began to look for another horse. The chowkidar of the dak bungalow and Gania, our guide, made a long search and finally succeeded in procuring one from a widow who lived nearby. Her son got ready to come along with us up to Drass, a distance of thirty-eight miles which would take three days to cover. The widow requested us with tears in her eyes to see that her son did not come to any harm during the journey with us. The Swami assured her that everything would be all right with her son and set forth with the name of Sri Durga on his lips.

Our route lay through a birch forest. We saw hill-people collecting barks for sale. After proceeding five miles we arrived at a place called Sirbal. We took rest here for a while and had our lunch. There is a road issuing from Sirbal leading to the famous glacier Kolohoi. As we were getting ready to start again, a rider halted near us and from him we learnt that the Wazier of Leh was on his way to Sirbal. There was a possibility that we might meet on the next day. The rider, a bailiff to the Wazier, was proceeding to Shonmarg on official duty.

Gradually the valley along which we were proceeding and the river Indus got narrower and narrower. The village of Baltal is situated at the foot of the sixteen-thousand feet-high mountain called Jojila. The region of Tibet lies at the other end of the Jojila Pass, a route that has been used since times immemorial by people of Central Asia while on their journey to India. Many a traveller comes to Baltal and stays there for a day or two with the intention of visiting Jojila Pass. It is a solitary and quiet region but one need not fear attack by wild beasts here.

From Baltal to the cave of Amarnath it is only a distance of nine miles. Not many people use the route we were following to reach Amarnath. It is a rather dangerous route for pilgrims and fit only for highly experienced mountaineers. You have to cross a bridge of snow as it were over a river. In summer the snow melts and the route also becomes unusable. The waters of a river called Amarganga flow into the Indus here. The hills in this region are of chalk-stone like the hill of Amarnath.

On reaching the dak bungalow at Baltal we found that a railway official was in occupation of both the rooms in it with his family. He turned down our request to be allowed to have one of these rooms. The Swami then came forward. After a talk with him the railway official agreed to let us occupy a room in the dak bungalow.

There is almost no man at Baltal, and almost nothing is available there. So when Sri Sadhu Singh, a Punjabi Sikh, offered the Swami a jug of milk we felt highly grateful. In the morning we made preparations for departure and set forth on our journey after signing the visitors' book, our destination now being a mountain called Mechohi.

Our route lay through Jojila Pass. On both sides of the pass we saw season flowers, edelweiss, forget-me-nots etc in profusion, — a veritable feast for the eyes. The Swami said, "Most of these flowers are not to be found anywhere except on the Alpine heights. Hence they are called Alpine flowers. The edelweiss blooms near the permanent glaciers on the Alps. To go to pick them is to invite great danger. White or green in colour they look like stars and are soft as velvet". The Swami further said, "The rich in Europe are more fond of edelweiss than of Persian rose. In Austria, Hungary and Tyrol soldiers are rewarded for valour with edelweiss-shaped medals."

The flowers we saw in the region were of numerous variety and in most cases we did not know their name. The dandelions were very soothing to the eye and we were told that yellow colour is extracted from them. The violet colour of the forget-me-nots is extremely pleasant to see.

But there was danger lurking behind all this beauty and enchantment. There was green grass all around that looked highly inviting but cattle die as soon as they start grazing on them. Our guides had a difficult time with the horses eager to browse upon them. On our way we found a majestic waterfall cascading straight from the mountain top into the Indus. We took a little rest near the waterfall and quenched our thirst from it.

All on a sudden two big stones came hurtling down from the hill-top. Our guides shouted warning to us and we had a narrow escape. This kind of experience is quite common in this region and yaks, horses and men are often hit by such falling stones that cause great injury or even death to them. The natural scenery around the place is, however, simply unforgettable. There is a narrow path just below the pass. It is used in winter when the pass gets entirely blocked with snow.

The height of the Jojila mountain is 11300 ft. The rivulets on its southern side flow towards Kashmir, while those on its northern side wind along towards Tibet. The mountain thus serves as a watershed as the Swami explained to us. Many people come on a visit to this place from Kashmir.

The road to Jojila is open to traffic only during the summer. It starts snowing from the middle of October and the whole region becomes impassable. Caravans of load-carrying horses start coming from June onwards. The telegraph wires sometimes get snapped under pressure of snow and telegraph posts get cracked and broken. During this period of highly inclement weather postal service remains almost completely suspended. Only a skeleton service is maintained in the temporary post offices set up at the foot of the mountains. One of them is at Baltal and the other at Mechohi.

The scenery all around gets completely transformed as one crosses the Jojila. The traveller will come to feel that he has been transported to a strange region the like of which he has never seen before. There is not a tree to be seen anywhere on the hills around. Their peaks are eternally clad in snow. Although they present an enchanting view to one, things get terrible at noontime. The rays of the sun are reflected on the snow-capped hills and eyes ache and get bloodshot at the sight. This may result in temporary blindness that might last even seven or eight days. This is called snow-blindness against which one is advised to use blue glasses. The Swami said, "I suffered from this kind of ailment once while mountaineering at Canada."

The Jojila once served as the frontier between Tibet and India. Maharaja Gulab Singh of Jammu sent Zorawar Singh, his brave general, with 10000 Dogra troops in 1834 to conquer the region. The general mounted his attack and in no time succeeded in annexing to Kashmir Skardu (Little Tibet), Kargil (Baltistan) and Ladakh (Western Tibet). Since then the territories of Kashmir have been considered to be extending up to the region of Manas Sarovar. We find in the *Rajatarangini* that Kanishka (2nd. Century B.C.), Mihirgula (6th Century A.D.) and also Lalitaditya reigned over these regions of Tibet.

Having lost these territories the Lama who previously had his sway over them appealed to the Raja of Kashmir for help in his distress. The Raja fixed an allowance of Rs 500 a year for the Lama and permitted the latter to live in peace in a village called Stog near Leh, the capital of Ladakh.

After having annexed Western Tibet Zorawar Singh led a
military expedition with the aim to conquer Lhasa. On his way
he destroyed many an ancient monastery, towns and villages.
But he suffered a smashing defeat in the hands of the Chinese
in a battle fought near Manas Sarovar. All his soldiers were put
to the sword and he himself was killed during a fight that took
place on the twelfth of December, 1849. Reinforcements were
sent from Kashmir and seven thousand Dogra troops came to
Ladakh and set up a garrison there. The Raja of Kashmir
entered into a treaty with Lhasa. According to its provisions he
started sending numerous costly gifts to Lhasa every three
years.

On crossing the Jojila we selected a good place for rest near
a spring and started making preparations for our lunch. All
around us there were unending stretches of snow without
even a blade of grass anywhere in sight. The Swami took his
seat on a big stone which also served as his dining table. The
thermosflask containing warm tea was placed on snow since
there was no room for it elsewhere. After a few minutes the
Swami lifted the thermosflask from where it had been placed
and started cracking jokes with Gania and other guides. He
said to them, "Isn't it miraculous that even though placed on
snow the tea inside the flask is still so hot that on opening the
lid we find steam coming out?" At his words the innocent
fellows looked with wide eyes at the thermosflask. And then
all on a sudden we could hear the clattering sound of horse-
hoofs. We looked in the direction from which the sound was
coming nearer and nearer and found horsemen bearing down
upon us with great speed.

CHAPTER—8

And in no time the Wazier of Leh with his entourage was upon us. He demanded to know who we were and what destination we were bound for. The Swami handed over to him the two letters of introduction we were carrying with us. On reading the letters the Wazier expressed great happiness and wrote down on the spot a general order to all whom it might concern to render the Swami all the assistance he might stand in need of. The Swami offered him sincere thanks. After paying his respects to the Swami the Wazier took leave of us.

After lunch we set forth on our journey again and reached the dak bungalow at Mechohi around five in the evening. Like Baltal Mechohi is also entirely uninhabited by men. But there is a post office and a serai there. You can procure only dry grass and faggots for fuel but nothing else from the chowkidar at the dak bungalow.

The dak bungalow at Mechohi is situated almost on the top of a hill near a permanent glacier. The place is terribly cold at night and there is a fierce gale cold as ice blowing constantly. Water gets frozen with the result that the container often cracks.

A terrific storm began to blow as soon as darkness descended on us and we shivered with biting cold. The Swami said that a blizzard was imminent. And soon it started snowing on all sides. The cold we felt is simply indescribable. Only those with similar experience would realise the intensity of our distress. We put piles and piles of logs in the fireplace and tried in vain to keep ourselves warm. It was freezing cold even two cubits away from the fire. We pulled our cot as near it as possible and yet failed to get even a wink of sleep because of the excruciating cold. It seemed that the fire had lost its power of generating heat. We even placed burning cinders on our palms but the moment we did so we found them extinguished and dead.

We set out next morning from Mechohi at half past nine with the intention to reach Drass in course of the day. The entire route before us which lay across a mountain was under snow. As soon as we started our trek we were overtaken by a spate of snowfall. The snow fell silently and inexorably all around. After trudging along six miles from Mechohi we arrived at a small village called Matayan. This is the first Tibetan village on the route leading from Kashmir to Tibet. There is a dak bungalow and a serai in this village. The population here is extremely small and nothing is available excepting milk and logs to make fire with. The place is almost as cold as Mechohi. Even in summer one has to take very good protection here against extreme cold. *Dhoti* is an absolutely unsuitable wear in the climate here. It is not safe to come to this region except in warm trousers. The village of Matayan is situated at the centre of a wide maidan. There are two or three springs near the village with their surface covered under a thick coating of snow which melts not before nine or ten in the morning. We went four miles ahead after this and arrived at another small village called Pan Das. There we got down from our horses for a while and took a little rest. Then we started again and reached the dak bungalow at Drass nearby at six in the evening.

Far beneath the village we could see a wide and green expanse with an old fortress which once belonged to the Sikhs. The soil here is extremely fertile. It is 10000 ft high and a non-stop freezing gale blows here. The inhabitants of this village are mostly Dards while a few are Baltiks. Buddhists here outnumber Muslims. The Muslims are referred to as Bhatias while the Buddhists are called Lamas. The Lamas are of two different varieties. Some of them are always in red uniform while the others are in yellow. This difference in dress indicates that they belong to two different sects. The Lamas are quite peaceable and quiet by temperament and wear shorn heads. Their caps are somewhat similar in appearance with those worn by the Vaishnavas in Bengal. A loose-fitting robe constitutes their chief article of dress. Their boots with woolen lining stretch up to the knees. Their soles are made of leather. Ladakhis do not use stockings. Instead of that they wear long bands of cloth wound round their legs from ankle to knee for protection against cold. Non-Muslims of Ladakh all wear long pigtails.

The women of this region hang strips of lambskin over their

ears. They also fasten on their heads a long strip of leather decorated with lapis-lazuli, crystals and other stones of various shades of colour. Another piece of lambskin with hair-lining is tied on their backs. From a distance it seems that two snakes are dangling from their heads with their hoods spread out. Boots worn by both sexes are similar in appearance. The women, however, do not don caps as men do. The chief articles of dress worn by the former consist of a long robe and a skirt. People of Ladakh all look jolly and stout. Their stature is short and their complexion midway between fair and dark.

We slept a sound sleep at the dak bungalow and woke up much refreshed. It is much less cold at Drass than at Mechohi or Matayan. In the morning we made preparations to start again.

We made full payment for the horses hired by us at Gandhar-ball and Shonmarg. We were thoroughly exhausted after our trek to Drass made entirely on foot and it was decided that we were to ride henceforth. So three horses were procured with the help of the local contractor. Our weary legs got a little respite as we rode on from Drass. It was a great relief to us, tired and footsore as we were.

We started from Drass at eight in the morning. Our destination next was Simse-Kharbu at a distance of twenty-one miles from Drass. The hilly track we had to follow was sufficiently broad to enable two horsemen to ride side by side. On our way we saw tradesmen from Yarkand proceeding to Kashmir with their merchandise placed on the back of yaks. We enquired of them whether the road before us was passable and safe.

Yarkand is a Muslim state situated amidst the mountains of Central Asia. To reach it you have to cross the Karakoram Ranges and then proceed on a journey lasting more than three weeks. Nothing is available on the way and one has to carry food, tent and all other necessaries.

It is best to make journey to Yarkand in summer. During other seasons the road remains blocked with thick snow for seven or eight months at a stretch. Horses, porters and yaks that may be needed for the journey are available at Drass in good number. The yaks can always find out the track to be followed even if the whole region comes to be buried under snow. For this reason a batch of yaks is sent as vanguard when traffic first opens after the snows have melted to a considerable extent. Horses and men follow their footprints and have no trouble in their onward progress. It is dangerous to set foot on snow that has not sufficiently hardened as yet and it is always advisable in course of journeys like ours to set foot on hard and solidified snow. The yaks can easily distinguish at sight between hard and soft snow.

On our way we came across hills dark in appearance and full of rocks extremely smooth. These rocks seem to be huge blocks of touchstone. The mountain rivers in their onward flow through untold centuries have carved out their own course as it were through layers and layers of rocks. Geologists can ascertain the age of these rivers by examining these layers.

After some distance we met a group of Lamas in a village called Dun-dul Thang. They were peripatetic preachers of Buddhism. Their group consisted of a woman and five men. The men all carried prayer-wheels which they refused to part with in spite of our request to be given at least one of them against whatever price they might demand.

These prayer-wheels consist of a round container made of copper, a handle half a cubit long with various decorations on it and wheels fastened to the handle. This handle is fixed at the centre of the container. Chained to the wheels are pellets of copper. Inside the container the incantation Om Manipadme Hum is written a hundred thousand times on paper made of cotton pulp.

One holds the handle around which one gently rotates the container over and over again. As one does so the incantation also rotates. At each revolution the incantation goes round a hundred thousand times, thus lessening the labour of repeating it orally again and again.

Shadows of the evening were lengthening as we reached Tasgam after a trek of fifteen miles. To reach Simse-Kharbu one has to cross the river Shingo from here. On reaching the dak bungalow at Simse-Kharbu we found it closed. Gania went in search of the chowkidar and found him in no time. The latter came and unlocked the door of the dak bungalow for us. Pilgrims on this route rarely put up at dak bungalows. They usually take shelter at humble serais called 'Chatti'. For this reason chowkidars present themselves at the dak bungalow in their charge only in the evening after spending the whole day in work in their fields. A little below the dak bungalow there is a small rivulet with a beautiful orchard on its other side. Simse-Kharbu is situated at a height of 8000 ft above sea level. Since we came there from much higher altitudes we found the place to be quite warm. The village is rather small and very sparsely populated. Bending downwards and without using their palms for the purpose the lamas here drink water directly through their mouth,—a rather curious sight for us. They carry a small wooden bowl inside their robes. This also is used by them for drinking. They prepare a kind of wine from barley and call it chhang'.

Most people here do not know how to read and write. The only language they speak is Ladakhi. We had brought with us an interpreter from Kashmir. Without him at our side we would have found ourselves in deep sea. Of course one should try to pick up a few words of everyday use instead of depending entirely on the service of the interpreter.

At night we burnt logs in the fireplace. We were horribly dirty with lice crawling all over our bodies. So we badly required a bath. It was also essential to wash our clothes. All our limbs were simply aching because of the long ride up and down the mountain roads. But on taking a refreshing bath we found all the aches gone and new energy instilled within us.

We prepared our meal for the night and for the next day. One should cook only once a day while journeying in these regions. This enables one to save time and to reach the next destination around sunset.

We started at eight in the morning from Simse-Kharbu for Kargil. To reach that place we were to cover fifteen miles.

CHAPTER—9

Soon we reached the bank of river Suri flowing through the valley of Shingonala Deosai. We had come across river Shingo in the village of Kharbu. And now we were at the confluence of the two rivers. The valley of Deosai is full of bears and deer. People come here on hunting expeditions. We met an European couple in the valley who had come to hunt bears. Accompanied by servants, they had rigged up a tent where they intended to stay for a day or two.

Our route lay through ascents and descents along the bank of river Suri. We were proceeding towards east and so had to face the sun. Its rays proved to be scorching and a violent gale was blowing from behind. It seemed as if we were being pushed along by an invisible hand in the direction of Tibet. On our way we had to alight from our horses and cross a hanging bridge on foot. At this point we found that one of our porters was missing. A search had to be made for him. After a while we found him sitting astride a huge block of stone at a little distance ahead. How he could overtake on foot people riding on horses was a mystery. But the man explained with a broad grin that he had used a short-cut unknown to us. These hill people are very simple and guileless.

We took our lunch and a little rest at a place where potable water was available. We saw telegraph wires running along the deep valley spread before us and lying across rivers and mountain peaks. This spoke of great engineering skill.

A little onwards we found across river Suri a huge hanging bridge made of iron and wood. Built under the auspices of Maharaja of Kashmir, it is known as Skardu Bridge. A sentinel keeps guard over the same. He will not allow one to enter Skardu if one is not equipped with necessary permission to do so. The region of Skardu is also known as Little Tibet. To the west of Skardu lies Gilgit.

Skardu is situated on a very wide valley at a height of nearly 9000 ft. It is encircled by summits of soaring height. From here the Indus flows southwards. There is a fortress near the confluence of Suri and Indus. At a short distance from there stands a palace belonging to the former king of Baltistan. The spot chosen for building this palace clearly indicates that the person who got it erected for him was more bent on luxury and enjoyment than on self-defence against the enemy.

To reach Skardu from here we would have to trek for seven days during which no dak bungalow or serai would be available. Food was also not to be had anywhere along this route. Travellers were to fend for themselves with regard to food and accommodation. It is because of this that tents had to be carried from place to place all along the route.

We could see the ruins of what was once a bridge not far from the point we had reached now. It was built by Sepal-Inamgyal, a former king of Tibet. It came to be destroyed by Zarowar Singh in 1034. We found the following notification engraved on a huge block of stone by the bridge :

"Sepalnamgyal, king of Tibet, is having this bridge erected for the benefit of his subjects. Anyone who will dare to cast an evil eye on this bridge will be blinded by the king's order. Anyone who will dare to do harm to the bridge will have his hands cut off. Anyone who will dare to speak ill of this bridge will have his tongue cut into pieces."

The block of stone on which this terrible warning had been inscribed now stood split in two. But the king's signature and seal looked quite distinct.

There is a serai on the other side of river Suri where travellers on their way to Skardu can put up without having to make any payment for their stay. The town of Kargil is only four miles to the north-east from here. On our way we found pebbles of various sizes and hues along a stretch of at least one furlong. The Swami said, "This clearly indicates that this spot was under water in the distant past"

Most of the mountain routes here were built by charging dynamites into rocks almost impregnable. Landslides often cause road-blocks in these regions. To lift them also dynamites have to be used.

We arrived at the dak bungalow at Kargil around half-past

five in the evening. While going to see the Tahasildar, the Swami took Gania with him. Kargil, the capital of Baltistan, is a centre of trade and commerce. Surrounded by high hills on all sides, it is situated by the river also called Kargil. There is a huge hanging bridge on this river made of iron. Known as Edward Bridge, it was built in 1901 under the auspices of Maharaja of Kashmir. You have to cross this bridge to reach Ladakh and Central Tibet. Leh, the capital of Ladakh, is at a distance of nearly 200 miles to the north-east from Kargil. Those bound for Ladakh or Skardu should halt for at least a day at Kargil and take some rest. This would relieve their distress caused by their long and arduous journey.

This region is at so high an altitude and so cold that it takes long to boil rice, pulse or potato while preparing meals. Mutton fails to become edible unless boiled for at least eight or nine hours. Hills eternally clad in snow surround the place. As a result of this the average day temperature at Kargil is 50 degrees centigrade, while the average night temperature stands at zero degree. During winter all roads get blocked with snow.

Travellers with permission issued by the Joint Commissioner at Srinagar to visit Ladakh or Skardu are not allowed to proceed further from this point. All travellers are required to present themselves before the Tahasildar and get their names, address and purpose of coming here put on record. This rule is meant specially for Europeans. Tibetans do not like the idea of allowing Europeans to visit their country. Many a foreigner has lost his life or limbs while trying to enter Tibet without permission.

The night over, we left the horses we had brought from Drass and took fresh ones on hire. The local postmaster and others came to the dak bungalow to see the Swami. After talking to them for a few minutes the Swami took his meal and we all set out.

Our destination was now the village of Maulaba Chamba, twenty-three miles to the north-east from Kargil. Our route lay across Edward Bridge and after that a wide valley. There is an older route which people used before the bridge came to be constructed. Traces of this route are still to be seen. There is not a tree or spring in this valley. You have to carry water with you. Those unused to climbing mountains feel greatly exhausted and are plagued by nausea. This is called mountain-sickness to which one is prone at a height of 16000 ft or more. One feels breathless and is compelled to rest after taking every two or three steps. The air contains very little oxygen and one must carry oxygen-inhaler if one intends to climb 20000 ft and above. Beneath the valley flows river Suri and our route lay along its bank. Soon we came across a few springs whose waters are somewhat whitish in colour. We found a whitish substance scattered near these springs. Our guide asked us not to use this water for drinking purpose, since that would prove to be injurious to health.

At daytime during summer the scorching rays of the sun cause great distress to travellers and the hills radiate unbearable heat. It is therefore the usual practice to cover as much distance as possible very early in the morning and after sunset. Unless one sets out from Kargil at very early dawn one cannot hope to reach Maulaba by evening. With heavy luggages to carry, one cannot cover more than two miles an hour on this route. And it is impossible to set out at early dawn unless one can finish packing and cooking in the late hours of the night.

We reached a big village on our way. Most of the houses in the village are two-storeyed and made of stone and clay. There is a shed attached to every house for domestic animals. Haystacks and dry logs are there on each house-top to be burnt during winter. Surrounded by enclosures the houses have wide courtyards within them. Hardly any window is to be found in any of these houses. Those inside them can have a view of people moving about outside the house through very small openings on the wall. Each house is guarded by a stout and hairy dog or two. We were surprised to find boys playing hockey and lamas playing polo in this village. The Swami said, "Hockey and polo are games that have been played in India since ancient times It is from India that these games travelled to the West."

The villagers were watching us with eyes full of wonder. A girl of twelve or thirteen with a baby in her arms stood among them. We asked her in Hindi what relation the baby was to her. The girl could not follow Hindi and kept silent. A lama standing nearby said, "It is her husband." Surprised beyond measure on hearing this we asked Gania to explain the matter.

Gania told us that the baby was the youngest brother of her husband. So she was its wife, too. Among Tibetans the usual custom is that the elder brother's wife has to consider all his brothers as her husbands. It is the eldest son who has exclusive right to inherit paternal property. Men far outnumber women in Tibet. Hence the widespread practice of polyandry in that country. The Swami said, "The same was the practice in Gandhar (Kandahar) in the age of the *Mahabharata*." Women in Tibet do not observe 'Purdah'. They are very hard-working and labour unflinchingly side by side with their menfolk.

In a field in this village we saw a kind of crop red in colour and round in shape like turnips. We were greatly surprised when Gania said that it was nothing but radish. We asked Gania to purchase a few of these radishes which, on being tasted, were found to be smelling exactly like radishes we were familiar with in our part of the country but their taste was rather hot.

After covering eighteen miles from Kargil we came across for the first time a *gumpha* (lamasery) and a *chhorten* (Buddhist stupa). From a distance the gateway to the *gumpha* looked like a wonderful picture carved on the hillside. The *chhorten* looked exactly like a temple of Siva. We did not have enough time for a visit to the *gumpha,* since the day was about to be over and we were far away from our destination. Gania assured us that we would soon come across *gumphas* much more spectacular.

We covered another five miles and reached the dak bungalow at Maulaba Chamba a little after dusk. The dak bungalow was situated on the bank of a mountain river far below the village proper. Moulaba Chamba has a small population of roughly fifty families. There is a serai and a small shop in the village where you can buy few necessary things. At the centre of the village stands the village deity,—a gigantic idol of Lord Vishnu with four hands. The idol is known as Chamba. In one hand it holds a rosary, in another a pot for carrying sacred water. The third hand holds a lotus while the fourth hand holds nothing. The idol wears a sacred thread hanging from its neck. There is a crown on its head while its legs are adorned with anklets. Since Buddha is considered to be an incarnation of Lord

Vishnu, the lamas worship the latter with great devotion. Flags white, blue and red, were fluttering around the idol. On the flags were written the incantation *Hulu Hulu Rulu Rulu Hulu Hum Phut*.

After spending the night at the dak bungalow we got ready in the morning to start again. We changed horses here and set out on our journey at half-past eight in the morning, our next destination being Bodh-Kharbu, sixteen miles away to the north-east. We had to traverse a region as dry and barren as a desert. The peaks around us were capped with snow and we shivered with cold. The huge rocks on both sides of our route were of various colours. Ten miles away from Moulaba Chamba we had to scale a steep ascent and proceed along a path that extended across a mountain top (Namikha-la, by name) 13000 ft high. The scenery around this place is extremely charming but it is terribly cold even at noon during summer because of its high altitude. The skin on the nose-tip, lips and the cheek get cracked at being exposed to the fierce gale constantly blowing. As a result the lips get awfully blackened and swollen. Even a little attempt at speech or a smile proves to be a painful exercise resulting in blood oozing out from the cracked lips. Application of vaseline brings some relief to this pain.

As we proceeded along we saw two or three villages at a distance in the valley in front of us. We came across people coming from Yarkand and also men belonging to the Dard community. Muslims belonging to the locality of Drass are known as Dards. From them we purchased apricots. These people shave off all the hair at the centre of the scalp on which they place a diminutive cap around which they wear long tresses.

On entering Kharbu we saw ruins of a fortress and ancient buildings on the hillside. They belong to the time of king Dildan who had his capital here long ago. Around the fortress he built a moat which we found to be not entirely dry as yet. Dildan reigned here from 1620 to 1640. Later he came to be defeated by the Muslims who completely destroyed his capital.

We saw a few *chhortens*, (Buddhist Stupas) big and small, at this place. In them are preserved ashes of the dead kept in urns. These urns are placed on stones bearing the inscription, *Om Manipadme Hum*. Near the *chhortens* stand walls made of tablets of stone, each bearing the same inscription. The incantation is written twice or thrice or many times over if the tablet is a big one. The Swami collected a nice-looking tablet of stone for himself to be taken home as a memento of this journey.

Kings of Ladakh in the past considered it to be a pious act to build *chhortens* and walls like this. These are regarded as holy objects to be sincerely revered. No lama will pass by these walls and *chhortens* keeping them to his right. He will always keep them to his left. This practice is sure to remind one of the rule, 'keep to the left'.

On certain days in the year villagers all assemble in the morning in front of the *chhortens*, worship them and make offerings of food to their dead ancestors. Then they all go round and round the *chhortens*, reciting in chorus the incantation, *Lamla Kep Shunchha, Ke Ke Lama Idam*.

Next day we reached around half past five the dak bungalow at Bodh-Kharbu. There is a *Triratna* or *Parameshra* here. *Parameshra* is a variant of the word *Parameshwar*. It means three small brick-built temples painted black, yellow and white symbolising Buddha, Dharma and Sangha respectively. If you add eyes to these temples at the top, the black one would come to represent Jagannath, the yellow one Subhadra and the white one Balaram. The Swami said, "Although Jagannath, Balaram and Subhadra in the temple at Puri symbolise Buddha, Dharma and Sangha, the whole thing has come to assume a different meaning in course of time".

Nearly forty Ladakhi families live in this village sprawling across a mile-long plateau. There is no shop or post office here and local contractors would supply you with horses, logs to make fire with, butter, milk etc.

Ladakhis enjoy tobacco from hookahs made of horns of yaks. These hookahs are not available in any shop and are made in every home by the people themselves. We saw women on the river bank filling their pitchers in a novel manner in this place. They were using ladles for the purpose.

A Muslim divine hailing from Chapra in Bihar came to see us at the dak bungalow. He was just back from Tibet and was putting up at the local serai. The Swami gave him some money since he was in financial distress. After he had left the Swami said. "I have some doubt regarding the true identity of that man. He may be some criminal in the disguise of a saint to evade arrest. Otherwise why should he be in this perilous region without a penny in his pocket?"

In the morning we set out again with the intention to reach the village of Lama-uru before the day was over. To do this we were to cover fifteen miles. We were caught in a snow-storm very shortly after we had left the dak bungalow. Soon the route that lay ahead, and the hills, our horses, and our clothes came to be covered with flakes of snow. It was white all around. We had never seen such a wonderful sight in our life before and we enjoyed the same to our hearts' content.

After crossing ten miles from Bodh-Kharbu we found ourselves at the foot of a mountain pass at a height of 13400 ft. There we took our lunch and got ready to scale the height.

A fierce gale was blowing through the pass and it sent shivers into our very bones. It was freezing cold. The sun looked dim behind layers of cloud. We felt the cold less pinching whenever the speed of the gale slackened to some extent. But the gale also took away much of our exertion in climbing ascents and in descending steep slopes. So long we thought that the nearer one was to the sun, the warmer one would feel. But we now realised that this was not the case.

The village of Lama-uru seen from a distance proved to be an unforgettable sight. It looked like a fairyland and it seemed that we had reached a point in course of our journey beyond which there was nowhere else to go. Houses that did not seem to belong to the everyday world familiar to us lay scattered at the foot of the hill, on the hill top, and also along the hillside. An unbelievably wonderful looking *gumpha* (lamasery) stood with its proud pinnacle challenging the glory of the snow-clad mountain-top.

At about five in the evening we reached the village dak bungalow. As we finished taking tea a lama came to invite us to pay a visit to the village monastery. After giving necessary instructions to Gania, we accompanied him to the *gumpha* which was situated at a height of 12000 ft. It was built with stones, clay, glass and bricks. We found tridents planted on the roof along with five or six flags wound with dark clothes. Yaktails and sheep-horns were hanging from the tridents. There were also two gigantic wind-driven prayer-wheels. There is hardly any window in the temple which is therefore very dark inside. You have to light a lamp there even at daytime. On wooden racks stood arranged side by side nearly four hundred manuscripts in Tibetan bound with silk. On another side we found images of great preceptors like Atish Dipankar, Padmasambhava, Kushak etc. Along with them there were images of Tara, Shakathuba, Thug-Je-Chhin-po, Sakyamuni, Chenreji etc. In a room within the *gumpha* we found gigantic images of Avalokiteshvara, Vajratara and Buddhadev. Some of these images are entirely made of brass while others are of wood with layers of gold and silver on it. In front of each idol were placed thirteen small bowls of brass full of drinking water. We found numerous paintings in the temple depicting heaven and hell, Yama, the God of Death, and various stages and aspects of Buddha's life. We found valances and frills of silk both behind and in front of the idols. The wooden pillars inside the temple were painted red and blue and the rafters on the ceiling were highly decorated. Above the idols were hung wonderful looking canopies. A few cots lay on the floor with rugs spread on them. The lamas sit on these cots while reading scriptures and performing their daily worship. The lamas place their manuscripts on a kind of prayer-desk while studying them. After evening prayers the lamas assemble to hear their chief reading out from religious texts. Their scriptures are of two types,—*Kanjur* and *Tanjur*. *Kanjur* means *Tripitaka* translated into Tibetan, while *Tanjur* seeks to annotate the same. *Kanjur* consists of one hundred and eight chapters and *Tanjur* of two hundred twenty-five. Each chapter is a separate manuscript with a wooden covering on which are to be found engravings of various kinds.

Worships are held at early dawn, at nine in the morning, at twelve noon, at three in the afternoon and in the evening. A horn is sounded asking lamas to come to prayer. They all assemble in the temple, sit down in silence with their eyes fixed on the idol in front of them and then chant the incantation,

Om Arghom, Chargham Bimanase, Utsumma Mahakrodha Hum Phut. While doing so they think of the sinful thoughts in their minds. After this the horn is sounded once again and all start chanting another incantation. With this a dinning sound is made by them by clashing cymbals, beating on drums, blowing on a special kind of horn which they call 'Dor-je' and by ringing bells. They light lamps in honour of gods and goddesses not with oil but with butter. We found a huge quantity of butter kept in a big brass pot in a corner of the room for this purpose. The pot had various decorations on it and was placed on a wooden tripod.

Srong-tsen-Gampo (613-650 A.D.), king of Tibet, sent Thon-mi Sam-bho-ta, one of his ministers, to India with sixteen followers to receive training in Buddhism. He did this at the behest of his two queens, — Bhrukuti Devi who was of Nepalese parentage and Weng Cheng who was of Chinese. The minister and his companions translated many a Sanskrit religious texts into Tibetan. They took these translations with them to Tibet. Before this there was no separate alphabet for the Tibetans. So the minister devised an alphabet on the model of Sanskrit letters. In doing this he took his cue from Lipidatta and also from Pandit Singha Ghose of North India. On return to Tibet he taught the people this newly devised alphabet. In course of time this came to be known as Lama Alphabet or Buchan Alphabet.

Later in 747 A.D. Padma Sambhava went to Tibet on being invited by king Trisong Detsan to preach Buddhism. He was accompanied by Mandarba, his wife, and Shantirakshita, his father-in-law. He had studied all the Buddhist scriptures in Nalanda. The lamas refer to him as Guru Rinpoche. He lived in Tibet for long and died there after winning much fame and universal respect. He had a band of twenty-five disciples all of whom were well-known for their spiritual attainments.

After this during the reign of king Ralpachen (845-860 A.D.) Ratna Rakshita, Dharma Rakshita, Jay Rakshita, Jin Sen, Ratendra Seal, Manjusree Varma, Surendra Bodhi, Bodhi Mitra, Dan Seal and many other scholars from Kashmir and North India went to Tibet to preach Buddhism. They all preached the *Mahayana* tenets.

The *Tantras* began to spread to Tibet from 1041 A.D. onwards. Atish Dipankara Srijnan was the man behind this development. He was born in 980 A.D. at Vajrayogini, Vikrampur in East Bengal. His father's name was Kalyan Sree while his mother was called Prabhabati. Dipankara learnt Buddhist tenets and mastered the Tantrik lores in various places of India and Ceylon. He gave up the exalted post of the chief of the monastery at Vikramshila and left for Tibet to preach Buddhism among the people there. Tibetans hold him in high reverence. He died in Lhasa at the age of seventy-three in 1053 A.D. His images in various monasteries show him adorned with a scarlet headgear.

Kublai Khan who ruled in Central Asia conquered Tibet and reigned over it from 1259 to 1294. Converted along with his entire family to the religion of the lamas, he invited many a Buddhist scholar from India for its propagation. A large number of Buddhist preachers and people engaged in propagating the Tantric cult left India during the period between the twelfth century and the thirteenth and settled in Tibet. They translated various Sanskrit religious texts into Tibetan. In this way the Buddhist religion and the Tantric cult entered Tibet from India and through transformation in course of time became the religion of the lamas. Prior to this the Tibetans worshipped stars and planets and believed in ghosts and spirits.

It is the custom among the Tibetans that every family should send a male child to join some monastery. He has to observe celibacy and get initiated into various religious practices. After this he is allowed to join the chief monastery of the country if he can fulfil the necessary conditions. He then has to spend quite a few years in studying scriptures and receiving instructions in religious matters at another monastery selected for him by the chief lama. Then he returns to the monastery he had joined earlier. There in a solitary cell he has to spend twelve years and twelve days in the worship of God and in the practice of Yoga. No one is permitted to see him or to speak to him during this period. Through a small opening in the wall his daily food and drink are supplied to him. On completion of this period of meditation and worship he is given the title of 'Kushak' which means 'preceptor of the world' and is appointed the chief of a monastery with many disciples under him. As a mark of respect to him he is given very costly dresses to wear along with a golden cap to adorn his head.

Tibetans believe 'Kushaks' to be highly advanced in matters spiritual. After they die, their images are installed in temples for daily worship. They are believed to be gifted with immortality. And if they at all choose to die they announce to their disciples the date and time of their demise at least one year before the same. They also predict at the time of their death where and when they would be born again.

Near the temple about a hundred lamas reside in a two-storeyed house. On them are given the responsibility to conduct various rituals. Some of them visit their disciples in the village and perform on behalf of them the daily worship and prayer. Some of them look after property attached to the monastery. Some of them cook while others revolve the prayer-wheel or make idols of wood or paint wonderful pictures. Some of them take care of the trees around the monastery.

The lamas get up from bed long before sun-rise and make the following prayer :

"Oh my highly compassionate preceptor! Pray listen to me! Oh my kind preceptor, give me the strength to follow in letter and spirit all the two hundred and fifty-three rules enjoined upon me ! Let me never be addicted to ugly music or dance ! Let no impure thoughts or worldly riches ever succeed in tempting me !

"Listen to my humble prayer, Oh Buddha in your different incarnations and Buddhists spread all over the world ! I am a mendicant with a heart free from all pollution. It is my earnest desire to employ all my energy for the welfare of all living beings. I have made it my aim to work for the good of all creatures in the world by using all my wealth and physical strength."

After saying this he turns the prayer-wheel in his hand over and over again and repeats the following incantation seven times :

Om Sambhaba Sammaha Yab Hum.

This incantation is followed by repeating three times :

Om Khrakar Jnanaya Hreen Preen Swaha.

As these words are uttered the lama has to spit on his feet. This is done because the lamas believe that this practice helps the microscopic beings crushed under their feet to reach heaven.

After this a horn is sounded asking all to come out of their cells and join the morning prayer. On return from prayer at the monastery the lamas salute the rising sun and address it with the following incantation :

Om Marichinam Swaha

This is followed by the prayer given below :

"Oh save us always from our enemies, from fear of mighty robbers, wild beasts and snakes !"

The lamas take food nine times throughout the day and night. While eating they pray to Buddha, the gods and their dead ancestors with the following incantation :

Om Guru Vajra Naivedya Ah Hum.
Om Sarba Buddhabodhisattva Vajra Naivedya Ah Hum.
Om Deva Dakini Sri Dhammapala Saparibara
Vajra Naivedya Ah Hum.

CHAPTER—10

A custom we came across in the monasteries struck us as somewhat unusual. We moved about within the precincts of the temple with our shoes on and took snaps to our hearts' content and nobody objected. We paid a small donation which the lama-in-charge accepted and gave us some grapes along with his blessings.

We came down to the dak bungalow soon afterwards accompanied by the lama who had escorted us to the temple. His name was Lama Ten-Zing. He requested us to send him copies of the photographs we had taken.

When at night we had finished our supper, done our packing and were about to retire to bed, this Lama Ten-Zing approached us with blood-shot eyes and tottering steps as a result of having taken an enormous quantity of *chhang*. We made him sit on a chair and asked him the reason behind this strange visit at such a late hour of the night. He then took out a picture rolled like a map from the recesses of his clothings around his belly and requested us to buy the same from him on a payment of rupees twenty only. It was a picture of the Buddha sitting in meditation with an expression on his face that struck us with its wonderful naturalness. It was quite an ancient portrait but it retained its glaze to a great extent. We felt like taking this picture as a memento of our visit to Tibet but finally decided not to accept this stolen property. The lama insisted on our purchasing the picture from him and said that he was prepared to reduce the price. But still we refused to oblige him. Finally he left us in great sorrow when all his persuasion had gone unheeded. Before taking leave of us he urged us not to speak of this incident to anyone. We later came to know that Europeans often bribed the lamas with big sums of money into making them give away pictures, manuscripts, musical instruments, etc.

Next morning we set out from Lama-uru. Our destination that day was Nurula, a place situated eighteen miles to the north-east of Lama-uru. We had to mount very steep ascents on the way. A mountain river had to be crossed in course of our journey and our route lay across a narrow valley flanked by lofty mountains. We found the banks of the Indus stretching before us at the end of this valley. The Indus flows here at a height of 9500 ft above the sea level. We found here huge rock-cuttings done by British engineers in search of gold at the behest of the government of Kashmir. It seemed to us that their laborious efforts had not led to anything worthwhile. The spot we had reached then was on the upper Indus valley along which the British engineers had conducted their investigations with a view to striking gold mines. In ancient times the waters of this place used to be found containing gold-dust. Greek historians have mentioned this in their writings. The Indus is quite narrow here but very deep. Its current is very swift and the waters have a bluish tinge. We came to understand now the meaning of the expression *Neel Sindhujal* (the blue waters of the Indus). These waters have to struggle hard against the barrier of huge boulders in their onward progress ahead. We went on and crossed a hanging bridge of iron built by king Nagloog in 1150 A.D. The bridge is fifty feet in length and four feet in width. Since we found the bridge shaking under the weight of several horses or men on the move, we decided to cross it one by one. The bridge is surrounded by high mountains covered with snow. They are all barren with no trees on them. On a mountainside men could be seen driving flocks of sheep in their vain search for grass. They all looked like tiny ants from below. On the other side of the bridge stood a fortress called Bragnas built with stones and clay. There is a granary within this fortress where corns were stored in the past to meet the shortage of food during war-time.

From here onwards we found our route to be full of gravel, sand and stones. On covering a short distance we reached a big village called Khalatsa. The place is almost equidistant from Lama-uru and Nurula. On entering the village we came across a stationery shop and a tailoring shop combined into one. From there we purchased apricot and apples. They do not grow locally but are brought from Kashmir. A priest belonging to the Moravian Christian Mission engaged in preaching Christianity lives in the village. He runs a small school in his bungalow. Although people here have great regard for him, his efforts as a preacher are hardly being rewarded with success. Lured by the prospect of getting food and clothing, lamas or Muslims in very small numbers agree sometimes to be converted but they return to their own fold as soon as such prospect fails.

At the centre of the village the ruins of a huge mansion can be seen on the top of a lofty hill. This mansion was the palace of Nagloog, king of this region. In 1150 he was defeated and dethroned by Mughals. The hill on which he had built his palace is known as Bragnag.

We left this village behind and once again found ourselves on our way at the foot of the hills and along the bank of the Indus. On crossing roughly two miles we found a small cabin made of pebbles erected by the road-side. Such cabins known as 'dak' were to be found after every four miles. They are meant to serve as resting place for the postman. We found two yaks with parcel bags fastened to their backs proceeding along from Saspul to Khalatsa under the guidance of postmen who are all lamas. On the walls of the cabins for their rest we found the words *Om Manipadme Hum,* written in bold letters. As a matter of fact we found this holy incantation written and inscribed all along our route. We saw lamas working hard with chisels and hammers engraving the sacred words on hilltops, by the river banks and on huge blocks of stone by the road-side. They look upon this work as service to God.

Near the village of Nurula we found a small temple all scarlet in colour. Planted on the pebbles, stones and clay we found horns of at least twenty yaks. The presiding deity of the temple is Tara Devi. Temples dedicated to her are almost always painted all over in scarlet. People throw coins into the horns as donations. Near the temple there is a small *chhorten* on which are planted flags red, blue, white and of other colours. On the flags we found the following incantation written in bold letters :

Hulu Hulu Rulu Rulu Hum Phut.

Lamas believe that these words are a very effective antidote against evil spirits. On each of the four sides of the *chhorten* we found three blocks of stone placed one above another. We were told that they represented the Buddha, the Dharma and the Sangha.

We reached the dak bungalow in the village of Nurula

nearly at four in the afternoon. Very near the dak bungalow there was the house of a local lama. We felt like entering the same because we wanted to examine its interiors. It took the owner of the house a very long time to answer our call. But at long last he came out, prostrated himself at our feet and welcomed us with the words, "Zule, Zule,". On being told of our intention he took us inside his house. The ground floor of the house was made of stone-chips and the first floor of bricks and clay. The courtyard and the verandah had a coating of clay. The rooms had insufficient light because the windows were extremely small. The floors were also coated with clay inlaid with white gravel. Inside one of these rooms we found two movable earthen ovens and a few low wooden seats to be used during meals. We also found dry hedges and horse-dungs placed in a corner of the room to be used as fuel. There were various implements for cooking and for preparing tea arranged neatly. It should be mentioned that tea is prepared in this part of the world in a novel manner. Tea and butter are mixed in hot water put in a bamboo cylinder and the mixture is churned for a few minutes. Then salt, crushed pulse and a bit of sodium bicarbonate are added to it. This concoction the lamas take with pleasure. To add milk and sugar to tea is something unknown to them. We found two Ladakhi women in an adjoining room spinning yarn on a distaff out of wool sheared from mountain goats. Wrappers and blankets are made with these yarns. We found a heap of horse-hair in a corner of the room. Horses in this part of the country and yaks have long hair with which ropes are made.

We then mounted the extremely narrow staircase made of wood leading to the first floor where in a room images of Shakathuba, Thug-Je-Chhin-po and of some goddesses were there for daily worship.Facing the altar was a bench on which there were seven lamps burning and twenty-one small brass-bowls containing water and pulse-powder as offerings to gods and goddesses. In the room next to it lay a patient. We were told that this room was reserved for patients only. They received treatment in the form of exorcism conducted by lamas specially trained in occult lores. There is also a village apothecary who administers occasional drugs.

We took leave of the lama and returned to the dak bungalow. The local contractor came to us with the information that a lamb had been slaughtered by the villagers living nearby. So if we desired to buy some meat he would make necessary arrangement. But we did not feel like sending him to bring meat for us because from our previous experience we had come to learn that mutton takes a long time to be boiled in this region. We however felt curious to know how animals are slaughtered by the Buddhist lamas. We asked a monk to tell us the procedure people adopted here for the purpose. In reply he told us that according to *Mahayana* doctrine it is no sin to kill an animal if before doing that one repeats the following incantation seven times :

Oh Abora Ne Ir Re Hum.

Then we asked him to give us his opinion on taking *chhang* (the wine brewed by the lamas). He said that it is no sin to take wine if before taking it one offers the same to God with the following incantation repeated thrice :

"Oh *Triratna* (Buddha, Dharma and Sangha) ! May I and all my kindred be never separated from you either during this life-time or ever afterwards. Let your blessings be showered on this wine."

We spent the night in the dak bungalow and set on our journey next morning, our destination being a village named Saspul. To reach this place from Nurula one has to cross fourteen miles and a half. We went ahead through a field of rye. All the corns had been reaped and fresh digging was taking place for sowing the seeds for the next harvest. They do not use ploughshares in this region and do all digging with the help of small spade-like implements. The sowing operations take place in early winter. The fields get covered with snow as soon as saplings start sprouting. The latter remain hidden between layers of snow till April or May. In springtime the snow begins to melt and soon the saplings grow to full shape. Fields are irrigated with water from the springs. Use of fertilisers is almost unheard of in this region. Horse-dung and the stool of yaks are the only fuel used by the people here. We scanned the faces of the villagers at work in the fields. Some of them were Mongolian in appearance while the others looked like genuine Indians. It was our surmise that the ancestors of these men had come from India in some dim past. But who can penetrate the darkness that surrounds the history of the past and ascertain the real truth?

We found women separating rye from dirt with the help of winnowing platters and singing in a strange and enchanting voice. They were all gay and smart. Cows looking like yaks were grazing nearby. We had to cross a field and go down along a slope. There was now a dilapidated bridge ahead. It is always the case everywhere that roads not used by the head of the state usually remain in a state of disrepair and officials are inclined to neglect them. The king of Kashmir never visits the region we were traversing now. So the roads we were negotiating at present were not in a very good shape. On crossing the bridge we wended our way across a plateau with wonderful scenery all around. We found multicoloured thorns and grasses on the hillside rendering the entire place extremely beautiful. Our route lay along the bank of the Indus. Just as in a crowded city a pedestrian sees to his delight on both sides of and along the thoroughfare he is using innumerable mansions, carriages and horses on the move, in the same way we now feasted our eyes on endless rows of hills, glaciers, springs and fountains. We had to cross mountains big and small along our route which proved to be very dangerous at times and troublesome in many respects. We had been advised beforehand by our guide not to take sturdy and spirited horses along this perilous route. So we had selected horses for our journey at Nurula that were rather meek and gentle although fairly strong.

We entered the village of Saspul at about half-past four in the afternoon. It is a village fairly big in size. A large number of respectable gentlemen mostly Buddhists with a very small number of Muslims live here. We found the two-storeyed dak bungalow quite neat and clean and very well-furnished. There is a 'dharamshala' close by. Although there is no shop anywhere in the village, all necessary things can easily be obtained through the local contractor. After a short rest we went to see the ruins of an ancient monastery called Nazia Doog. It is situated on the top of a hill, 11180 ft high. The monastery was established nearly four hundred years ago. There was a time when more than a hundred priests lived here. Images of gods and goddesses made of gold were worshipped in all the ten rooms of the monastery. We found all the walls decorated with pictures. The monastery was spread over quite a large area. A fierce battle was fought between Delegs Namgyal, the king of this region, (1640-1680), and the Muslims of Baltistan. During this battle the monastery came to be destroyed by the Muslims.

Even now a mock fight depicting this battle is enacted here at a fair annually held in December. Some men play the role of the Muslims of Baltistan while others represent the soldiers of king Delegs. They all take their stand on a huge block of stone and make a show of fighting. It is said that this block of stone was hurtled down the hill by the soldiers of Baltistan during this battle.

At present an old mendicant and some priests live in a monastery built here much later. At the foot of the hill in a two-storeyed house lives Lama Shan-Kushak, a mendicant who is a married man. Members of his family live with him.

An ancient *gumpha* called Alchi is another place worth visiting in this village. To reach this *gumpha* one has to cross the bridge over the Indus and proceed for two miles. This *gumpha* and the bridge came to be built during the reign of king Sengi Namgyal (1590-1620). Many a fine work of Kashmiri art is to be seen in this *gumpha*. Rare and valuable varieties of shawls with excellent embroidery and beautiful wooden furniture with exquisite engravings that we saw here bear testimony to the ancient glory of Kashmir. These wonderful pieces of art are nearly a thousand years old. The reading room and the various images of gods and goddesses are also fit to be treasured in memory.

At break of dawn we left Saspul and started for Nimu. On covering four miles we came to a path leading to the famous *gumpha* at Likir. The distance to be crossed that day was eleven miles and a half. So we thought that we had plenty of time for a visit to the *gumpha* at Likir. On the way we felt that the ground we were traversing had minerals of various kinds underneath. At one spot we found the soil to be pitch black suggesting the presence of anthracite. At another spot we found the soil to be dazzlingly white and we deduced that it contained mica. At yet another spot we got the pungent smell of kerosene. At first we thought that our lantern had been upturned by the porter. But on enquiry we found that the lantern had been left undisturbed. Be that as it may, it matters little to India whether there are minerals under the soil here or not. For, after all these areas lie on the other side of the Himalayas. Gradually we came to the vicinity of the village of Likir. On crossing a dried-up streamlet we entered the village. When snow begins to melt in spring, streamlets are formed all over the place. They all flow into the river. In summer these streamlets get completely dried up.

A very small number of people live in this village situated on plainland surrounded by a number of hills. Fields of rye, three or four *chhortens,* big and small, and a small *gumpha* on the top of a hill constitute the main features of the place. The *gumpha* owes its name to the village. We crossed the village and went ahead along the side of a spring. The spring is a large one and, its bed is strewn with pebbles. Its waters are bluish and ice-cold, and its current is very swift. The place is surrounded by barren hills on all sides.

Gradually the Likir *gumpha* heaved into view. The scene was simply breathtaking. The mountain before us proudly stood with its crown of gold placed on its majestic pinnacle. At its rear lay a panoramic glacier at a height of 26000 ft. Did it not resemble the matted locks of Lord Siva? We got down from our horses just at the foot of the Likir *gumpha.* A difficult ascent had to be climbed now. Before that we took a little rest on the river-bank where we sought to refresh ourselves with warm tea stored in our thermosflasks. We were all feeling very much thirsty after our long trek and felt like drinking to our hearts' content water from the spring flowing swiftly before us. But our guide prevented us from doing this and warned us never to drink water from springs born of melted snow. To do this is to invite hill diarrhoea or pneumonia. Many have lost their lives because they could not resist the temptation of taking such water to quench their thirst. It is always advisable to carry warm water while travelling in these regions.

A lama acting as sentinel was watching us from the top of the mountain at Likir. We told him at the top of our voice that we were innocent travellers from Kashmir on our way to the Likir *gumpha.* We left our luggages with our porters and the guide and proceeded along the acclivity towards the mountain top. The Swami was on horse-back. The ascent was almost perpendicular. As a result the saddle constantly slid back towards the horse-tail again and again. So the saddle had to be properly fastened from time to time. Still it was somehow possible to climb up the hill on horse-back; but while coming down one ran the risk of sliding along with the saddle in front over the neck of the horse. The Swami decided therefore to make his descent on foot.

The mountain at Likir is 14000 ft high. A plateau extends above the same for about half a mile with beautiful trees on all sides. We found springwater frozen into snow at various places. If this be the condition during summer, what happens in winter is best left to imagination. Not a drop of water is to be come across then. While in need of water one has to take a lump of ice, put it in a vessel and melt it on an oven.

Apart from the gumpha there are a few houses on the mountain top belonging to the local inhabitants. We found their goats moving around. They had shaggy hair all over their body and looked like lambs. Dogs looking like bears began to bark furiously at us. It was lucky for us that they were all chained to posts. We crossed three gates one after another and then had to climb steps leading to the gumpha. These steps are nearly a hundred and fifty in number. At the top of them stood the main entrance to the door of the gumpha. All this while lamas from different sides watched our movements with keen interest. An old lama was working in a field of rye not far from where we were. He asked us to wait for a while and went to inform the head of the monastery of our arrival. By this time we were utterly exhausted after having climbed steep ascents for a long time at a stretch. So we got down from our horses, sat down on a block of stone and took a little rest. Shortly afterwards more than a score of lamas approached the Swami and received him with the words, "Zule, Zule" (We salute you). They escorted us into a big hall richly furnished and crowded with images of various gods and goddesses. On the floor of the hall were spread rugs of different types. There were racks holding sacred books and musical instruments. On two small benches were arranged vessels containing pulse powder and salt. In front of the benches lay a thick mattress meant to be used by the chief lama. The walls were covered with curtains of silk, red and blue and also of other different colours. We found the pillars wound from top to bottom with rich clothings. The beams and rafters on the ceiling were full of varied decorations. There were paintings on the wall and also on the pillars, depicting religious themes. The hall also contained images of Gedun Groove[1] and other Dalai Lamas. These images are so wonderful that one cannot but entertain great admiration for the men who shaped them. Serenity is stamped on their faces radiating kindness and peace.

In the centre of the hall is preserved a 'mendong' i.e., a mound serving as a memorial of great lamas of the past. In mendongs are preserved their hair, nails, hones and other bodily remains. These mounds are made of silver and gold and decorated with precious stones. The images of gods and goddesses have different types of visages. Some of them have a Mongolian stamp while others show Aryan features.

On a bench in front of the images were arranged tiny bowls with water in them. On another side were displayed small icons of brass and old shoes, turbans and articles of clothing belonging to great preceptors who lived and died long ago. Among the images of gods and goddesses the most important are those of Vajrapani, Lokeswari, Vajratara, Avalokitesvara etc.

In the adjoining room we found gigantic images of Shakathuba, Manjusree and others along with various items of worship. The room had no window and was steeped in darkness. A lama carried in his hand a lamp in the light of which we saw the images one after another. The faces of these images were full of compassion. We saw at least two hundred and fifty manuscripts wrapped in cloth on a shelf. Hundreds of small icons of brass stood in another room on the outer wall of which were painted scenes of the town of Lhasa, the *Potala* (the palace of Dalai Lama) and portraits of the Buddha. These paintings speak of great skill and artistic sense. We found many an adept in the art of painting among the lamas in the monastery.

---

[1]Gedun Groove (1389-1473) assumed the title of Gal-Ba-Rin-Poche and became the first Dalai Lama. Lamas hold the belief that when Bodhisattva Avalokitesvara decides to incarnate himself in this world, he emits a wonderful ray into the body of the person he enters. This person comes to possess divine qualities as a result.

The door leading to the next room was so small that we had to bend ourselves very low in order to enter it. What we saw on entering the room was quite astonishing. Nearly a hundred and fifty swords in their scabbards, more than a score of shields, a number of country-made guns and daggers and a golden Buddha on a throne greeted our eyes as we stood at the centre of the room. The throne was placed on a chariot also made of gold. Two pitchers made of black stone stood in two different corners of the room, possibly containing a secret treasure.

We came out of this room and began to stroll about on the roof-top. A panoramic view lay before us stretching up to the horizon. Far in the distance stood the Karakoram ranges all covered with snow. A lama pointed out to us Te-see (Mount Kailas), Po-Chhung (Little Tibet) and Senge Kharbu (the Indus). It was rather difficult to communicate with the lama because of his extremely scanty knowledge of Hindi. Of course he was the only man in the monastery who could at all follow the language even to a very small extent. The treasures in this monastery are only second to those in the Himis *gumpha* in richness and glory. That a monastery inhabited by priests and mendicants could contain so much of arms and riches was simply unbelievable.

Before we took leave of all the people in the monastery, the Swami gave some money to the chief priest and requested him to arrange *Puja* to the gods and goddesses in the temple.

———

After taking rest at the foot of Likir *gumpha* we set out for Nimu. A short distance ahead was a water cascade. Leaving this behind we reached a table-land where we took a path bestrewn with sand and gravel. A little distance more and we had to climb a hill. No sooner had we reached its top than the ruins of the town of Basgo came into view. The wonderful natural scenery of the town captures the fancy of tourists in a trice. We feasted our eyes on the abundance of fascinating views all around the place. One desires to keep them engraved permanently on one's heart. This famous town of Basgo has found a niche in the minds of historians. A study of its history enables one easily to have a full grasp of the political and social conditions of the entire region for all times, — its rise to eminence and its fall therefrom. In no time we reached the interior of the town.

In the middle of the town stand two many-peaked mountains consisting of stones somewhat greyish in colour. On them are to be found the ruins of the old palace together with two or three springs of sweet water flowing since times immemorial. At the foot of the hill is the garden house of the British Joint Commissioner of Leh. In the garden there are fine spots for camping where anybody can come for a stay. But the bungalow is not open to all.

The new town of Basgo sprawls across an area nearly two and a half miles long and one mile wide on an extensive valley. It is inhabited by nearly a hundred people most of whom are peasants. They are rather well-off since the soil here is quite fertile. All people are Buddhists and there are no Muslims here.

From 1590 to 1620 the place was used as the capital of the kings of the Senghe Namgyal dynasty. It was then considered the biggest town of the entire province. During the period from 1380 to 1400 the lamas of Baltistan, out of fear of losing their life, had to embrace Islam under the torture of Sikandar Khan, the king of Kashmir who was an iconoclast. Nor could the lamas of Bodh Kharbu escape his inhuman persecution and ruthless plunder. During the period from 1620 to 1640

Dildan Namgyal, the king of Basgo defeated twice in battle the Muslim ruler of the province,—once at Kharbu and again at Drass,—and thus recovered the area from Muslim domination. Even now there stands a slab of stone at Bodh Kharbu with the entire episode written on it.

One of the famous deeds of king Dildan was the construction of the largest holy wall in the mountain pass called Tewar at Leh. It is 850 cubits long. Its first *chhorten* is of the Namgyal-type having a circular staircase, while the second one is of the Yangchub-type having a straight one. This wall he raised with a view to invoking divine blessings on his mother.

In olden times a widely practised custom among kings of this province was to erect walls with holy incantations engraved on them for the welfare of their near and dear ones. King Dildan built a *gumpha* like the one called Pituk at Se, the ancient capital of Western Tibet. In addition, he raised there a five-storeyed *chhorten* and set up an image of Maitreya Buddha as high as a two-storeyed structure. He also built a large palace in the modern capital, Leh, where he placed an idol of Avalokitesvara as high as a two-storeyed building and also founded a *chhorten* made of silver in the council chamber.

Sometime between 1640 and 1680—the period during which Delegs Namgyal, the son of king Dildan, remained in power— the Mongols attacked Basgo and beseiged the capital. King Delegs fled the fortress of Basgo and took refuge in a fort called Ting Mo-gang at a distance of thirty miles to the west. He sent a messenger to Emperor Shah Jahan of Delhi asking for military aid. The latter complied with his request and sent to Basgo General Fateh Khan at the head of a large army. A pitched battle took place at a meadow called Jargal situated between Basgo and Nimu. The Mongols suffered a defeat and retreated to the shore of the lake Ponggong. They built a fortress at Trasigang where they settled for the time being. Having won his victory through the help of the Mughal General King Delegs went from Ting Mo-gang to the tent of Nawab Fateh Khan to offer him thanks for his timely intervention. But the Nawab, at the behest of Emperor Shah Jahan, served the king with a letter in which the following conditions were laid down :

1)　King Delegs must embrace Islam and agree to be named Akbal Mahmud Khan after his conversion.

2)　The king's wife, his son Jigpal and his daughter must all be converted to Islamic faith and then take their abode at Kashmir.

3)　To proclaim to all that king Delegs had embraced Islam a new coin called Zou with his newly acquired name Akbal Mahmud Khan engraved on it must be put into circulation.

4)　All help must be rendered by the king for the propagation of Islam in Ladakh and a mosque would have to be built at the town of Leh.

5)　The best quality wool of Tibet must not be sold anywhere except at Kashmir and its price must be fixed at Rs.2 per seven bowls of wool.

6)　Every year eighteen ponies, eighteen pieces of musk and eighteen fans made of white yaks' tail must be sent by the king as a tribute to the Nawab of Kashmir. In return the Nawab would send five hundred bags of rice to Ladakh.

King Delegs accepted all these conditions and Fateh Khan with his large army left Ladakh. No sooner had the king had some respite from his recent troubles than the Tibetan and Mongol soldiers came in swarms from the shore of the Ponggong Lake and encircled the fort of Ting Mo-gang. They forced Delegs to enter into a treaty with Dalai Lama. To do this they had brought with them a lama named Mipan Wangpo who acted as his representative.

The kingdom of Delegs came to be much reduced in size as a result of this treaty. The treaty also required that the king of Ladakh would send every three years to Dalai Lama a tribute consisting of thirty grams of gold, ten pieces of musk, six entire sheets of calico and one sheet of cloth made of soft thread. In return Ladakh would receive every year from Lhasa two hundred bags of tea. No one in Ladakh would be permitted to consume any tea other than what had been sent from Lhasa.

Even though king Delegs had been forced to accept Islamic faith he had not given up the Buddhist religion inherited from his father. He made every effort to keep Buddhism firmly entrenched in Ladakh and helped the lamas in various ways.

Every tourist should visit the *gumpha* at Basgo which contains the image of eighty-year old Maitreya Buddha, three storeys high and made of wood, brass and gold-leaves. This *gumpha* was constructed by Dildan's father, king Senghe Namgyal. His mother, though a Muslim convert, used to dress herself in scarlet like the lamas and remained ever devoted to Buddhist and Tantric religion. She earned imperishable fame by having a large number of temples and monasteries built at various spots near Basgo. She had also brought to Ladakh by invitation the famous lama named Stag-Sangh-Room-Chen. It was he who built the holy wall at Linga-Sed near Basgo. He also established *gumphas* at Himis Chemre, Asisgang and Hanley in Central Tibet and visited Kashmir and many other places of India including Uddyan, the birth place of Padmasambhava. He is often referred to as Tiger Lama.

We did not succeed in seeing the ruins of the old palace and monasteries on the top of the Basgo hill, since the lama entrusted with the keys to these places had then gone on a visit to Leh. So after a little while we got upon our horses and started for Nimu at a distance of four miles from this place. While passing through the middle of the village we saw on both sides of our road corn-fields in which lamaist men and women, boys and girls were at work.

The village slopes downward from one side to the other so that the corn-fields look like so many steps in succession. A sudden spring flowing over the road had made it quite muddy. Of course the spring would soon dry up,—a common feature in this part of the country. We saw ruins of the ancient town and houses of the village near them as we proceeded onwards. On finally reaching the end of the village we found four mill-wheels being operated with the help of the current of a large spring, turning out wheat from rye.

We came out of the village and reached an open table-land nearly five miles wide. The sight thrilled us immensely. On seeing plain land before him, the Swami gave free rein to his horse. Gania followed us with the horse carrying our luggages. The entire land was bestrewn with dust, sand and gravel. This made it difficult for one to proceed with quick steps. Under the scorching rays of the sun the whole area looked like a desert without a trace of water anywhere. In the distance could be seen the village of Nimu just like an oasis in a desert. This is the place called Jargal where once a fierce battle was fought between Nawab Fateh Khan and the Mongols. The guide pointed out to us all the spots associated with this historic battle. In the middle of the field stands a wall half a furlong in length made of nearly a million stone slabs on each of which the holy incantation *Om Manipadme Hum* is inscribed. This is the holy wall of Linga-Sed. By and by we arrived at Nimu.

On seeing our arrival the chowkidar of the dak bungalow came swiftly out and offered salutations to the Swami. The latter decided to take a little rest in the cool shade offered by the garden surrounding the dak bungalow. It was then three in the afternoon. After we had rested for a while it was decided not to halt here for the day but to forge ahead for another fourteen miles to the dak bungalow at the village of Pituk and spend the night there. From Pituk to Leh it is only six miles. So it would be quite possible on our part to visit the famous *gumpha* at Pituk and reach Leh before the sun became unbearable. But the horse-dealers at Saspul did not approve of this plan. It was not their practice to accept any alteration in the itinerary already fixed. From Saspul to Nimu and then from Nimu to Leh,—this was the plan laid out earlier. So they wanted us now to hire fresh horses if we wanted to change plans. We asked the local contractor to bring four horses for us. Within half an hour he brought them. When we asked the horse-dealers if they were prepared to come along with us up to Himis they said that they would go only upto Leh. For our journey to Himis we would have to hire horses again at Leh. We were rather surprised at these unalterable arrangements which reminded us of the trade-union spirit prevalent in the U.S.A. After a thorough check-up of the horses brought to us we fastened our luggages on their backs in the proper manner and then started again. It was then about four in the afternoon. We were eager to reach Pituk before nightfall. With this aim we rode with great speed and soon left Nimu far behind. We crossed a river, passed quite a number of holy walls and cornfields and then started climbing a huge mountain. The ascent was very steep and we had a tough time while negotiating the same. After quite a hard exertion for about half an hour we finally reached the top, its altitude being 14000 ft. A fierce gale was blowing then and the wide valley before us offered a fascinating view. The land was entirely plain for a stretch of no less than twenty miles beyond which stood the Karakoram ranges eternally clad in snow.

After this our route lay along a slope for a long distance. The horses proceeded at a canter along the slope and we crossed ten miles and a half within less than three hours and reached a fertile valley called Nala. A spring greeted our eyes here. Its water was cool and soothing and it ' moved   along with a sweet murmur as if inviting the weary traveller to come and quench his thirst. A beautiful garden lay spread on one side of the path and we took a little rest there in its cool shade. There were quite a number of fine spots where one could rig up a tent for rest. The spring could be seen flowing through the valley across a long distance flanked by innumerable trees. It was like a veritable oasis in the midst of this desert-like region without a single tree or creeper.

At a short distance from here stands the famous Fiang *gumpha* on the top of a hill. It offers a sight very much soothing to the view. The *gumpha* is quite old, its history extending over more than four centuries. Many an event of the past in the region is associated with this *gumpha*. We had no time now for a visit to it and decided to halt there on our way back.

On crossing another three miles we reached the bank of a large river and were soon at the dak bungalow of Pituk situated on a lovely spot. The evening was then far advanced. We saw small hills, gardens and a tiny spring before us.

The chowkidar had to be summoned from his house nearby and all necessaries were obtained through the contractor. We had gone through plenty of hardship throughout the day. So we quickly finished our supper and went to bed. It was essential to keep logs burning in the fireplace all the night because of the terrible cold.

Next morning we finished our breakfast and got ready to start again. Our grooms however had not turned up as yet.

They had gone to a village nearby to spend the night in the house of a relative. We had asked them to be back to the dak bungalow at early morning. But we waited for them in vain for more than an hour. In an adjacent room there was an Englishman waiting just like us for his groom. This man was simmering with anger and we saw him sitting with a whip in his hand to give his groom a hot reception as soon as the latter would come to wait his master's pleasure.

The grooms presented themselves at the dak bungalow after a long time. Like a ferocious tiger the Englishman hurled himself on them and rained kicks and blows to his heart's content. Our horse-dealers trembled in fear at the sight. The Swami was surprised to see this kind of high-handedness but remained silent. He only said that our grooms who had proved themselves to be lazy and irresponsible could not expect tips from us. After this we arranged our luggages and set out on our journey again. Lamas of this region are used to receiving this kind of harsh treatment from Englishmen. We saw similar thrashing in the dak bungalow at Bodh Kharbu.

We went ahead for about an hour along the bank of a river branching out from the Indus and reached the Pituk gumpha situated in the valley of Leh. From a distance it offered a picturesque view. This gumpha was built five hundred years ago by Gampo-Boomalde. The village of Pituk lies spread out to the east of the hill on whose top the gumpha is situated. The houses of the villagers and the corn-fields all looked spick and span without a speck of dirt anywhere. The steps leading to the gumpha were hewn out of rocks on the hill-side. After climbing one thousand feet of easy ascent we arrived at the gumpha's gate, a beautiful structure made of black stone. By its side there is a chhorten. We alighted from our horses and sat down to rest on a block of stone. A mendicant came out to receive us. He escorted us inside, made us sit and offered us in wooden bowls black tea, butter and salt. He gave us fried powder of rye in a wooden bowl with a tiny spoon made of animal bone. We mixed this powder with tea and got immense pleasure in taking the mixture. The place where we were thus entertained was the dining room of the monastery. There were a number of wooden seats and small stools on which plates and bowls were placed. On one side there was a mattress to be used by the chief lama. We found on a stool in front of it a pot

'Leh'-market with Lamas standing in front

Fiang *Gumpha* beyond the desert

Tomb of Jesus Christ at Khana-Yari

containing rye-powder and a wooden bowl serving as a tea-cup. The room had two doors, one leading to the kitchen and the other to the bed-room of the chief lama. We first entered the kitchen. Nobody objected to our having shoes on. The floor of the room was spick and span but the walls and the ceiling were dirty with soot and smoke. We found tea being brewed on an oven. Logs were being used as fuel instead of coal. There was a pot containing salt at a corner and some butter wrapped in lamb-skin.

The floor in the bed-room of the chief lama was almost entirely covered with a huge mattress on which were arranged three cushions to be used as back-rest. There were numerous photographs in a niche. Some of them were of the chief lama, some of the Dalai Lama, while some were of the Tashi Lama. On the mattress were spread white sheets of paper, a few letters and some writing material. The letters had an appearance quite novel. One cubit in length and only two inches in breadth they have to be rolled and placed within a bamboo cylinder. On the wall were hanging a few paintings. In another niche there were a few manuscripts. We found nearly ten pairs of very excellent shoes in a corner of the room. Some of them were of a very small size. The lama explained to us that they were meant for very young trainees for lamahood.

In yet another niche we found a number of icons made of brass and copper. The most important among them were the images of Surasundari and of Karna-Pisach Sundari, deities mentioned in the *Tantra*.

We climbed on the roof of the monastery and spent some time there enjoying the incomparable beauty of the valley of Leh. The Swami took a few snaps. At a distance could be seen the Fiang *gumpha*, the town of Leh, the village of Stog, the Indus with its branches numbering five or six and the wide valley on all sides spread over a distance of no less than fifty miles. The panoramic view got imprinted into our hearts for ever. To the south of this spot extend the Himalayan ranges all white with snow. And in the north stand the colossal Karakoram ranges as sentinels guarding our frontier. In the south-east the proud summit of the Kailash looked like an ancient and venerable sage with his matted locks all snow-white. Huge prayer-wheels covered in black cloth, flags and tridents adorned the roof.

On the first floor of the monastery we found cells all ill-lighted in a row serving as bed-rooms for the lamas. They were bare except for a very humble bed, a prayer-wheel, a lamp and a few manuscripts. On the verandah there was a huge prayer-wheel. While we stood before the same, a very rude incident took place all on a sudden. A lama came out of his cell, revolved the prayer-wheel as a gesture of seeking divine grace for his own welfare, made salutation to it and then left. No sooner had he done this than another lama emerged from his cell and stopped the motion of the wheel. Then he gave a push to it to invoke divine blessings for himself. As the second man was going to make his salutations the other lama rushed to the scene almost mad with rage and stopped the wheel's motion. After this he set the wheel moving in his favour and dealt a big blow to the second lama with the words, "How dare you stop the wheel revolving in my favour?" In blind fury the two fought with each other and were seen rolling on the verandah locked together in a firm and desperate grip. Attracted by the hue and cry raised an old lama came out of his cell and separated the two. On being told what all this hullabaloo was about he set the prayer-wheel revolving in the name of both. This helped in restoring peace and the two lamas stopped fighting.

On the ground floor of the monastery there was a big hall almost steeped in darkness containing the colossal image of Shakathuba. The hall was very nicely furnished and we found incense burning in it emitting a sacred aroma. We prostrated at the feet of the image and after donating some money took leave of the lama. Soon we found ourselves at the foot of the hill.

At a small distance from this *gumpha* could be seen the ruins of Kaochi *gumpha*. It was destroyed by the Muslims. From here the town of Leh is situated at a distance of four miles and a half. To cover this distance one has to climb a very mild ascent all the way across a field. Since there is nothing to hinder the vision of the climber, the town is visible to him all along. The entire route is a stretch of sand. On coming very close to Leh we saw small hills on both sides. It was here that a horse suddenly threw off a lama from its back and darted ahead. Some men rushed behind the horse to catch hold of it. Had this accident taken place on a mountain-path, it would have been fatal for the rider. But since we were proceeding along ground almost plain, the man escaped sure death. We found a sacred wall and *chhorten*, the largest in this region, by the side of our route.

We arrived at Leh nearly at ten in the morning. The 'tahashildar' was shown the two letters of introduction we were carrying and he arranged our stay in the house of the Wazier. We, however, had our lunch in the house of the 'tahashildar'. After resting for an hour the Swami started writing letters to the Belur Math and other establishments of the Ramakrishna Mission at Srinagar, Lahore etc informing the people there of our safe arrival at Leh.

It was freezing cold at night and we did not have a good sleep in spite of the logs burning at the fireplace. In the morning we saw heavy snowfall all around. Within half an hour everything became covered with snow and it seemed as if somebody had spread a white bed-sheet over the entire landscape before us. It was an unforgettable sight and the Swami took a few snaps.

After having breakfast we came out for a stroll around the town with a guide to help us. He was a local man but could speak Hindi quite well. In the marketplace we saw merchants hailing from Yarkand, Dard, and the Punjab with their merchandise of shawls, wrappers etc. All other necessaries were also available in the market. Members of the fair sex predominated among the sellers. Some of them were selling *chhang* in earthen pitchers. At another place we saw quite a number of women standing with loads of grass on their back patiently awaiting prospective buyers. At the centre of the market we saw a post and telegraph office. Beyond Leh there is no postal service.

This market closes down in winter when all the roads around the place lie under a thick layer of snow. The snow starts melting in April and the merchants also start arriving then. The houses are mostly made of bricks and clay, stones and wood. Their roofs are slanting and so the snow cannot accumulate on them. The entrance to the market lies through a huge portal by the side of which we found a charitable dispensary.

At the extreme end of the marketplace stands an ancient palace, a monastery and a few other structures on the top of a small hill. It has been mentioned before that they all belong to the time of Senghe Namgyal. The palace is ten-storeyed and from its top one can get a panoramic view of the town all around. To the north of the town stand the sky-scraping peaks of the Kailash ranges eternally clad in snow. They simply took our breath away as we gazed at them in wonder. To the south can be seen the Lohit ranges. Their rocks and stones are all red and fascinating to look at.

Inside the palace we came across big halls with their walls adorned with excellent paintings and decorations. The council chamber and the assembly hall are extremely beautiful and impressive. They appear to have been built very recently. The monastery standing adjacent to the palace was plundered by bandits and foreign invaders many times. As a result of this we found it in a derelict condition. In the seventeenth century Sarder Sher Ali, the Muslim ruler of Skardu, set fire to the chief idol of the monastery and a large number of ancient manuscripts and they all got destroyed. Zarowar Singh, an army chief of Kashmir, also destroyed many idols and manuscripts. We found heaps of torn papers at the centre of the hall and were told that these were remnants of the ancient manuscripts referred to above. We begged of the lama to be allowed to take at least one page from them but he refused to accede to our request. He explained to us that it was a kind of sacrilege to give away parts of religious books to strangers.

The huge idol of Maitreya Buddha in this monastery is worth seeing. The people here think that the bigger the idol, the more beautiful it is bound to be. This idol of Maitreya Buddha simply compels admiration. It exudes rare charm. The compassion which its eyes radiate is bound to win the heart of the onlooker.

After this we went to visit the garden near the dak bungalow, the burial ground of the Muslims, the crematorium for the lamas, the court and the polo ground where the lamas come every afternoon to play. They put anklets round the feet of their horses which produce a sweet jingling sound that fills the air and reverberates throughout the polo-ground with the play going on.

The distance between Leh and Simla is four hundred and thirty miles. Tradesmen come to Leh across this distance to buy leather jerkins, yaks' tail etc. From Leh to Yarkand it is four hundred and seventy-seven miles. Along the route between the two there lies a mountain pass at a height of 18000 ft on the Karakoram ranges. Throughout this long distance nothing of daily use is available and you will find only snow-clad hilly tracts all around. Before making this journey one has to take all necessaries from Leh including tents to serve as shelter at night and logs to be used as fuel. There is a school run by Moravian missionaries at Leh. It is a charitable institution in which about fifty Ladakhi boys are taught Tibetan and English. At a short distance from the market stands the bungalow serving as quarters occupied by the British Joint Commissioner. Near this is a small spring on one side and a wide expanse on the other.

The Ladakhis are sturdy and short in stature. They seldom take any bath or wash their clothes. Both men and women have massive and rounded faces. They are not fair in complexion. The men wear a woolen garment covering their bodies from the neck to the knees. Around the waist-line of this garment is wound a woolen scarf in which are tacked various articles like distaff, tobacco-box, hookah made of yak's horn, needle and thread, comb, etc. They also carry within the fold of this scarf small globules of pulse-powder and flints. Inside the recesses of the woolen garment near their chest they keep a wooden cup to drink water from. Their legs are protected from cold by puttees fastened around them. They also wear boots made of the same stuff as used in making blankets. Their caps are made of lamb-skin. Often they put on an overcoat of leather on top of the woolen garment extending from the neck to the knees. And this is their dress all the year round.

All wear long pig-tails. The women use the same dress as men do, the only difference being that on their backs hang a full-length lamb-skin. They tie their hair in a bun and adorn their earlobes with small leather pieces. There is a big leather piece at the centre of the head on which valuable stones are set. The women wear boots like men but do not use caps like the latter.

Agriculture is their chief occupation. Rye, radish, potatoes, apricots etc grow here in abundance. The cultivation is done with the help of bullocks known as 'Jho', a mixed breed. Every family here owns yaks, goats and sheep. The region is full of various kinds of wild animals.

The people are mostly illiterate. Their daily fare consists of pastes of rye, pulse-powder, meat and its juice, skimmed milk, tea with salt and butter, *chhang* (a kind of wine) and bread. They are a very hard-working people quite satisfied with their lot. Social ties for both men and women are not very exacting. Polyandry is largely practised and it is usual for all brothers in a family to marry one and the same girl.

Tibetans call their own country 'Po'. The name 'Tibet' derives from 'Tibba' which means 'hillocks'.

Next day we visited a very old monastery on the top of a mountain called Namgyal Seemo. This was built in 1520 by Trashi Namgyal.

After spending four days at Leh we set out on our journey once more, our destination being the convent at Himis at a distance of twenty-four miles eastward. The road to it runs all along the valley of the Indus. You will find no hills while journeying along this route. Nearby is the village of Stog where now lives the last descendant of the Ladakhi royal dynasty, Sednam Namgyal, the grandson of Jigsmed Namgyal. He has been living in this village since his defeat in battle in the hands of the king of Kashmir.

There is now hardly anything to suggest that he had once been the monarch of this region. Lavish in his expenditure, he spends recklessly the entire amount he receives every year as an allowance from the king of Kashmir. At present he is burdened with a heavy debt. To repay this he has mortgaged his entire property to the chief priest of the Himis monastery. The latter will continue enjoying his hold on this property till all his dues with interest are cleared. Even such a humiliating state of affairs has not cured him of his incorrigible habit of incurring debts. Of late on being unable to pay off a very small debt he had to ask for help from the king of Kashmir. Nothing gives him more satisfaction than holding in his house sessions of dance and music attended by comely Ladakhi women. Whenever any dancer or singer from a far-off region comes to this place he invites the 'Tahashildar' to join him in attending her performance.

The palace he lives in is situated on a hill not very high. Its small windows from a distance look like so many pigeon-holes. This old stone-made palace was built in 1820 by Sepal Dandrub Namgyal.

The village is quite small in size with a population just above one hundred. Beneath its level rushes the Indus with a mighty roar. All around is a wide and open area dotted with cornfields on the bank of the Indus or with gardens here and there. The road is sandy. At the centre of the vast expanse can be seen a cluster of small hills having on their tops so many lamaseries. On the opposite bank of the Indus there is yet another road along the hillside which runs from Leh to Himis. We decided to take that road while on our return journey. The road we were now traversing was plain. This enabled us to hasten our speed. At nearly three in the afternoon we found ourselves very near the village of Himis situated at the foot of a mountain on the other side of the Indus. It is not visible from the road. Nor can its existence be easily detected by one who is not acquainted with the topography of the place. Many a monastery being thus concealed could escape the ravages inflicted by the Dogra general Zarowar Singh. We left the bank of the Indus behind and entered a narrow valley and while proceeding onwards came across quite a large number of cornfields and houses. We had covered a distance of about two miles when at the end of the valley we found several houses looking like big pigeon-holes from a distance,—some grooved into the mountain-side and some lying at the foot of the mountain. This is the famous Himis monastery nearly 11000 ft high with a vast landed property at its command. We found some fourteen or fifteen lamas in a nearby field engaged in reaping rye while singing in chorus. We learnt from them the rules and regulations to be followed while on the way to the monastery. A lama went into the monastery to inform the chief priest of our arrival. To the left of the road is a ravine beyond which could be seen a number of cornfields. To the right were the houses of the Ladakhis with small temples of various deities interspersed among them. At one spot several temples stand huddled together. In them are to be found the images of Vishnu, Buddha, Yama etc engraved on blocks of stone and painted in various colours. The houses of most of the villagers are grouped around the monastery. Quite a number of boys and girls, men and women, and lamas were watching us with curiosity from roof-tops or through small openings on the wall. Some of them came out on the open road to have a more satisfying view of us. Huge dogs guarding the households furiously barked at us to our great annoyance. On crossing the big portal to the monastery we had to get down from our horses since these animals are not allowed to go inside. There is a big prayer-wheel on the way. We went a little distance along the covered metalled road, reached a fairly big courtyard, and finally arrived at the guest-house of the monastery. The lamas came and unlocked the door leading to it for us. One side of this guest-house was completely exposed to the elements. The lamas at once covered the same with valances and carpets. We put our beddings at the right place and then began unpacking our luggages. The lamas sent to us milk, eggs, kerosene, wood, butter etc and made all necessary arrangements for our cooking. They were all attentive to our needs and did their best in seeing that we were not put to any inconvenience. At night it was terribly cold. We kept our primus burning and in the mild heat thus provided we somehow managed to pass the hours before dawn.

Accompanied by the lamas the Swami went to visit the monastery in the morning. He was invited to sit in the office room of the chief lama. A huge visitors' book was produced before us in which we were required to write down our names and addresses. The Swami gave his name, identity and address in this book as follows : 'Swami Abhedananda, Vice-President of the Ramakrishna Mission, Belur Math, near Calcutta.'

The Swami glanced through the pages of the Visitors' Book but could find not a single Bengalee name. The room in which we were sitting was fairly large in size. A bed was spread over the floor in the Marwari-style. Several clerks were doing correspondence work and writing accounts. Some repair work was going on in the sanctum sanctorum and the prayer hall. Quite a number of masons and labourers were engaged in the work. Many boys and girls and some women were serving as helpers to them. The chief mason pleaded with the Swami to give some tips to the labourers. The Swami acceded to the request and gave them some money. Upon this the labourers started singing gleefully in Tibetan which we could not follow. The melody of their song was typical of the hilly region now quite familiar to us.

We came to know that Maharaja Pratap Singh, the former ruler of Kashmir, had sanctioned Rs.30000 for this repair work. When Pratap Singh of the Punjab had attacked this region, the chief priest of the monastery rendered help to the King of Kashmir and promised to provide his army with food for six months and quarters for their stay. Since then his monastery is tied in bonds of friendship with the royal house of Kashmir.

We saw prayer-wheels of different varieties in different corners of the monastery. At one place we found a huge prayer-wheel revolving automatically under pressure of the waters of a spring and a bell attached to it ringing continuously as a result. At another place we found rows of small prayer-wheels arranged in a line. We also saw images of various gods and goddesses in different rooms. In a dark room could be seen the image of Stag-shun-rom-chen, a lama preceptor and founder of this monastery. He has a divine bearing, a superb body and broad forehead,—all indicating his courage and valour. It has already been mentioned that he is referred to by many as 'Tiger Lama'. Most of the images here are made of gold and silver. Images made of other metals in this monastery are very few in number. The 'stupas' are entirely made of silver inlaid with precious stones and gold. The ornaments decorating the images are also made of gold and valuable stones. We came across a goddess whom we were meeting for the first time in our life. Her name is Mandara or Kumari Devi. She is the spouse of Padmasambhava (Guru Rinpoche) and sister of Shantirakshita whose famous *Tattva Samgraha* was published some time ago in the state of Baroda. Mandara accompanied her husband when the latter came to Tibet to preach Buddhism. The two came from Uddyan, a place in North India, and reached Tibet in 749 AD. Their images are worshipped in the monasteries of Shung-je, Ching-fug etc. The lamas regard Padmasambhava as an incarnation of Manjusree.

We came across in the Himis monastery mendicants numbering nearly a hundred and fifty and belonging to the *Dugpa* sect. They all wore scarlet caps. Each had a separate cell allotted to him. In a room on the roof-top lived the Khang-po or the head of the monastery. He knew a little bit of English and Hindi. Excepting the lama looking after us all other inmates of the monastery knew no language other than Tibetan. We would have been put to much inconvenience, had there been no interpreter with us.

The monastery is spread over quite a large area. On all its sides save the east there are rows and rows of high mountains. Some portions of the monastery seem to be merged in the hills adjoining them. Under its jurisdiction there are other monasteries, big and small, and villages with cornfields. Its chief priest is known as 'Kushak'. He has numerous followers and disciples whom he visits once a year. They make big offerings of money to him as a token of respect. He also visits them when they are ill or when some evil spirit has entered them. He drives these evil spirits away and extracts huge fees for his pains. All expenditure of the monastery is met with the money thus earned by him.

Several years ago a Russian traveller, Nicolas Notovitch by name, came on a visit to Tibet. He fell from a hill near Himis

Lama-uru *Gumpha* (p.85)

Swamiji and Gania on way to Drass from
Mechohi amidst snowfall all around. (p.73 - 74)

Swamiji and the Lamas on the roof of 'Pituk'
Gumpha, Ladakh. Snowfall all around. (p.109)

Swamiji and Gania in front of Himis Monastery, (p.115)

Swamiji and the treasurer Lama at the gate
of the Himis temple, (p. 123)

Gandharaball-Ghat (p.124)

JESUS CHRIST
This picture is the oldest known,
found on a Tomb in the Catacombs.

The Himis Monastery in Ladakh

Madona With Christ

monastery and broke one of his legs. Local people brought him to the rest house of the monastery. The lamas nursed him for a month and a half and restored him to normalcy. He came to learn from one of the lamas that Jesus Christ had been to India according to records in a manuscript preserved in the library of the monastery. He had the manuscript brought to him and got it translated into Russian. On his return to his native land he wrote a book entitled *The Unknown Life Of Jesus Christ.* In this book he discussed thoroughly the matter of Christ's sojourn in India. While in America the Swami had gone through the book and felt deeply interested in its subject. As a matter of fact he had taken so much trouble in coming all the way to the monastery of Himis to check up the truth of what he had read. He now made enquiries with the lamas and came to know that it was true. Then he requested to be allowed to see the book containing this information.

The lama who was acting as our guide took a manuscript from the shelf and showed it to the Swami. He said that it was an exact translation of the original manuscript which was lying in the monastery of Marbour near Lhasa. The original manuscript is in Pali, while the manuscript preserved in Himis is in Tibetan. It consists of fourteen chapters and two hundred twenty-four couplets (slokas). The Swami got some portion of the manuscript translated with the help of the lama attending on him.

Below are given the activities of Jesus Christ in India according to this manuscript :

* * * * * *

10. "Issa stepped into his thirteenth year by and by. According to the national custom of the Israelites, this is the right age for matrimony. His parents lived the life of humble folks."

11. "Their humble cottage came to be crowded with people proud of wealth and pedigree. Each of them was eager to accept Issa as his son-in-law."

12. "Issa was unwilling to marry. He had already earned fame through his expounding the true nature of God. At the proposal of marriage he resolved to leave the house of his father in secret."

13. "At this time his great desire was to achieve full realisation of god-head and learn religion at the feet of those who have attained perfection through meditation."

14. "He left Jerusalem and started on a journey to Sind in the company of a band of merchants. These merchants procured various commodities from Sind and exported the same to different lands."

* * * * * *

(5)

1. "At the age of fourteen he (Jesus) crossed Sind and entered the holy land of the Aryans."

2. "As he was passing all along through the land of the five rivers, his benign appearance, face radiating peace and comely forehead attracted Jain devotees who knew him to be one who had received blessings from God Himself."

3. "And they requested him to stay with them in their monastery. But he turned down their request. / this time he did not like to accept anyone's service."

4. "In course of time he arrived at Jagannath Dham (Puri), the abode of Vyasa Krishna, and became the disciple of the Brahmins. He endeared himself to all and learnt how to read, understand and expound the Vedas."

* * * * * *

"___After this he went on pilgrimage to Rajagriha, Benares, etc. This took six years and then he started for Kapilavastu, the place where Buddha had been born."

"___Then he spent six years in the company of Buddhist mendicants, mastered Pali to perfection and studied all the Buddhist scriptures."**

"___From here he went to Nepal and travelled in the Himalayan region."** Then he went westwards."**

"___By and by he came to Persia, the abode of Zoroastrians."[1]

"___**His fame soon spread in all directions."**

"Thus he returned to his native land once again at the age of twenty-nine. After this he started preaching his message of peace among his brethren suffering under oppression."

The lama said that after resurrection Jesus Christ came secretly to Kashmir and lived in a monastery surrounded by many disciples.[2] He was looked upon as a saint of a high order and devotees from many lands came to see him and joined him as disciples. The original manuscript in Pali was prepared three or four years after Christ's demise on the basis of reports given by Tibetans who actually saw him at this time of his life and the accounts received from wandering merchants who had witnessed his crucifixion. If someone collates in a single book all the observations made by scholars on the subject of Christ's sojourn in India, it will no doubt prove to be a valuable addition to literature on Jesus.

In an autobiographical essay published in *Prabasi* (Magh, 1333) Bipin Chandra Pal, the great savant and political leader, gave a very interesting account of the connection between the Nath Yogis and Jesus Christ. We are quoting him in full below :

"Once I heard from the venerable Vijaya Krishna Goswami that he had been in the Aravalli ranges along with a band of Nath Yogis. These monks referred to Ishainath, a holy man, as one of the great preceptors of their order. The story of the life of Ishainath was read out to Vijaya Krishna Goswami by one of the Nath Yogis from their holy book. It bears close resemblance to the story of Christ as narrated in the *Bible*."

---

[1] During this journey Jesus performed ablutions at a pond and took rest for a while on its bank. The pond is still in existence and is called Isha-Talao. A fair is held every year at this spot to commemorate the incident. This matter has been described in *Tarikh-i-Azham,* a book in Arabic.

[2] The tomb of Christ at Khana-Yari is still in existence. The late Ramatirtha, the famous monk and preacher, has left a description of his experience regarding this matter.

Bipin Chandra Pal comments on this as follows : "According to the life-story of Jesus as recorded in the *Bible,* what he did and where he was during the eighteen years of his life between the age of twelve and thirty are shrouded in mystery. Some people guess that he was in India during these eighteen years. It is also their conjecture that Jesus Christ and this Ishainath are one and the same person."

In Palestine there used to be a community called Essenees[1] in the time of Christ and before. Jesus belonged to this community. Regarding this Arthur Lillie, the great savant and archaeologist, writes in his book, *India in Primitive Christianity* (p. 200) : "Jesus was an Essenee and he meditated for long in the manner of Indian Yogis for union between his self and the Brahma and for achieving heavenly bliss."

To us it seems that the name Essenee' derives from 'Ishan' which is another name for Siva, the great deity and also a great Yogi. It will not be wrong to conjecture that the name 'Essenee' is another form of 'Ishani' which means a devotee of Lord Siva. 'Ish' is also another name of Siva and 'Ishainath' in all probability means of worshipper of Siva. The word 'Nath' is also associated with the same deity. It is possible that Jesus Christ received initation into the order of monks known as 'Nath Yogis' and came to be called 'Ishainath'. The word 'Isha'[2] means 'Lord'. The meaning of the word 'Nath' is also the same. Jesus often spoke of God as 'Lord'. He himself was also addressed as 'Lord' by his followers.

In July every year a big fair is held in the monastery of Himis. Lamas with great mystic attainments come to this fair from various places and demonstrate supernatural and magical feats. Along with this there is plenty of dance, songs and fun of many kinds. A large number of people assemble in this monastery at this time. To come from Kashmir at this time of the year is very difficult on account of heavy snow-fall. A few

---

[1]Swami Abhedananda has given an authentic account of the Essenees in his book *India and Her People.*

[2]Jesus is referred to as Issa in the holy book of the Muslims. It seems clear that this name derives from 'Ishai'. 'Masih' is a perverted form of 'Messiah' and among Muslims Jesus is often referred to as 'Issa-Masih.

years ago Sir Francis Younghusband,[1] formerly Commissioner of Kashmir, came here to witness this fair. Hundreds of people can be easily accommodated in the big hall of the monastery and its courtyard. The small cells in the monastery are, however, not well-lighted. Although the walls and the ceilings are made of bricks, the floors are made of clay. They are, therefore, rather damp. We saw cooking going on in the huge kitchen. Four big ovens were ablaze and the inside of the kitchen was dark with smoke and soot. The windows were very few in number and there was not much light within. There were of course sky-lights and chimneys to let out the smoke from inside. The Joint Commissioner of Leh had come and stayed in this guest-house some time ago.

We were very much exposed to cold and a gale that was furiously blowing at the time. So the chief priest shifted us to another room on the first floor.

During our stay here the lamas looked after us with great care. The wonderful scenery all around filled our heart with joy. The lamas frequently came to our room and we talked with them on different subjects. The Swami spoke to them about the Great War (1914-18), Sri Ramakrishna, Vivekananda, Mahatma Gandhi and topics related to India. And he enquired of them about their methods of prayer and the incantations they recited. He also discussed in their presence various creeds and opinions regarding them.

The chief priest presented the Swami with an excellent head-gear usually worn by a 'Kushak'. On coming to know that the Swami had some difficulty in riding on wooden saddle, he gave him a saddle of leather. We took a number of snaps in the monastery of Himis and finally took leave of its inmates before returning to Leh.

We were to take the road to Leh along the hills on the other side of the Indus. For this a route different from the previous one had to be taken. There is an excellent hanging bridge across the Indus on the other side of which lies the village of

---

[1]Sir Francis Younghusband wrote a voluminous book on his travels in Tibet. This book is full of valuable information. He participated and spoke in the centenary celebration held in honour of Sri Ramakrishna in 1937.

Himis. On crossing the bridge we wended our way through the
village. We had to climb hills and proceed along the bank of
the river and that of the canal at their foot and gradually
arrived at a place called Golap Bagh. It is a place equidistant
between Leh and the monastery of Himis (twelve miles from
each). A soothing breeze was blowing when we reached the
place. The dak bungalow of the Commissioner is very near this
spot around which many people pitch their tents for their stay.
Near it stand a few houses belonging to the lamas. Our route
after this lay along gardens, cornfields, and hamlets. On our
way near a village considerably large in size we had the
wonderful view of the *gumpha* at Seh. Seh is also a village
quite big in size. This was formerly the cap tal of Western
Tibet. Later it was shifted to Leh. Dense forests lie around the
village where the houses of the lamas are all made of stone
and clay.

We found yaks tethered to posts near which lama women
were engaged in winnowing corn. As we entered the village we
found people watching us. The *gumpha* at the village of Seh
was built by Dildan Namgyal. There is another *gumpha* on the
top of a very lofty hill in a village nearby. At both these
gumphas one finds images of holy personages. In particular
are to be seen images of Buddha of the height of a two-storied
building. On the hill near this is engraved a colossal image of
Shakathuba (Shakya Sthavir). On huge chunks of stone we
could see the incantation *Om Manipadme Hum* engraved in
bold letters. From this spot our route lay along the bank of the
Indus. We arrived at the town of Leh by and by. It was terribly
cold at the time and a heavy snowfall was on. So we took rest
at Leh for four days only and then left for Kashmir. On the
twenty-third of October we were once again back to our
houseboat lying at anchor near Gandharball Ghat. On the way
nothing happened worth recall except that there was incessant
snowfall everyday. We gave appropriate rewards and tips to
the guide, the horse-dealers, the porters and the chowkidar at
Gandharball who acted as watchman during nights and saw
that our boat came to no harm. Then we parted from them
and started in our houseboat for Srinagar.

With a mind to relieving the exhaustion resulting from our
long and arduous journey we took rest at Lalmundi Ghat,
Srinagar, for a week. On coming to hear of the enchanting

view of the fields of saffron at Pampur the Swami went on a visit to the place in a tonga. We found these fields stretched along a distance of five or six miles in the midst of hilly surroundings. Innumerable flowers of saffron, dark violet in colour, unfolded before us an unparalleled view. From a distance the fields covered from end to end with these enchanting flowers looked like richly embroidered Kashmiri shawls of panoramic proportions. The flowers, however, did not have much fragrance. Here and there we found female labourers plucking those flowers and collecting them in baskets. At another place we found heaps of these flowers being dried on huge mats spread on the ground. At yet another place we saw pollen-tubes and flowers being separated with the help of sieves. The pollen-tubes are of two varieties, — one of them being dark red in colour and the other yellow. The yellow pollen-tubes are regarded as inferior to the red.

This place is situated at a distance of eight miles to the south east from Srinagar. While on the way to it one can have a view of the ruins of Pandarthan.

The village of Pampur is on the southern bank of the Vitasta. A few wooden mosques in the Kashmiri style, gardens of *chenar* and a bungalow belonging to the Maharaja are among the objects worth mentioning in this village. A nice-looking wooden bridge spans the river. A king called Padma reigned here in the past. A number of structures in ruins bear testimony to this. The vilage next to Pampur is known as Bhil. A few sulphureous hot springs are there in this village. A bath in these hot springs has cured many of skin diseases.

On returning to Srinagar from this place we rested for a few days. On eighteenth November we left Kashmir in a lorry belonging to the Punjab Motor Company and headed for Rawalpindi. We arrived there in safety and the Swami became the guest of Lala Nandaram, the secretary of Sanatan Dharma Sabha, and stayed at his *dharamshala*. Dr Sri Ram took upon himself the responsibility of looking after the Swami. He had recently given up his job at Srinagar and come to Rawalpindi. Lectures by the Swami were arranged at the Sanatan Dharma Sabha. He spoke on two consecutive days on 'Sanatan Dharma' and 'Soul's Immortality'. On both the days four or five hundred people had assembled to hear him. Bengalee families at

Rawalpindi number nearly a score and a half. The locality where the Bengalees reside is known as Babu Mahalla. The Swami was invited one day by the residents of this locality. N. N. Datta, M. B., the well-known physician of the place, arranged devotional music and reading of scriptures at a holy gathering and escorted the Swami there. After the function was over the Swami spoke a few words of advice before the gathering. At night the Swami had been invited by the physician to his place. He obliged him by accepting the invitation and returned to the *dharamshala* in his car.

Next day, the Swami went by Lalaji's car on a visit to the ruins of Taxila situated at a distance of thirty-three miles to the west of Rawalpindi. Taxila was a city of great renown during the Buddhist period. Its ruins are now being unearthed by the famous archaeologist, Sir John Marshall. Mr. Manindra Nath Gupta, his assistant, showed the Swami around the place with great respect and care. Taxila was a part of Gandharva Desh (Gandhara) in the past. From the *Ramayana* we come to know that Bharat conquered Gandharva Desh at the order of Sri Rama Chandra and put prince Taksha on its throne. Since then the place has come to be known as Takshashila (Taxila). King Janmejoy, son of Parikshit, held a big snake-Yajna (Sacrifice)[1] in order to avenge his father's death caused by snake-bite. Many have advanced the conjecture that the place is called Takshashila, because it was once ruled by kings belonging to the Takka dynasty. The Buddhists call this place Takkshasir. According to them, the Lord Buddha in one of his past incarnations made a gift of his own head at this place to a Brahmin.

A branch of the Scythians known as the Abaras used to rule here around 126 B.C. The place was later conquered by Kanishka. Some coins and inscriptions of his time are to be found in the local museum. In the first century B.C. Taxila was a part of the empire ruled by Euphratedas. When in 327 B.C. the great Alexander beseiged this city, Ambhi, the king of this region, entered into a treaty of alliance with him and joined him with an army of five thousand soldiers in the battle against Porus.

---

[1] We asked the Swami to explain to us the meaning of this. He explained that tribes with the totem of snakes were converted to Hinduism through this Yajna.

In the fourth century Fa Hsien, the mendicant traveller from China, came to Taxila. He was followed in 630 A.D. by Hiuen Tsang who also visited this place. At this time the ancient royal dynasty ruling over the region was extinct and Taxila was under the sway of Kashmir.

Excavation work is going on over an area of six square miles. Among the ruins of the ancient city now being unearthed are a large number of Buddhist temples, monasteries and stupas. Images of Lord Buddha of different models are to be seen among them. Although full of ruins the ancient city offers fascinating views all around. At the north-west corner of the place there is a tank full of various kinds of lotus blooms. The tank, named after Nagraj Elapatra, is a magnificent sight. To the south of this tank there is a cave reported to have been built by Emperor Asoka.

The town of Taxila can be divided into six localities. Wide roads leading to them have been preserved as far as possible. The names of these localities are as follows: (1) Vir, (2) Hatial, (3) Barkhana, (4) Shir Kapka Kote, (5) Shir Sukka Kote and (6) Kachh Kote. On the plinth of a dilapidated house could be seen the image of an eagle with two beaks. The Swami pointed it out to us as a specimen of Greek art. He also pointed out to us the remains of underground drainage here and there among the ruins and remarked, "Do you see how these people of ancient times had mastered engineering knowledge and skill?" After making this comment, he moved around the premises of another dilapidated building, paying special attention to its bathroom, drawing room, cistern and walls surrounding them. Near the museum stands the railway station of Taxila with a fine orchard near it.

Manindrababu began to show the Swami with due respect and care all the things preserved in the museum. Ornaments made of gold and silver inlaid with precious stones have been dug out of the ruins. They have all been sent to England while their models have been kept in the museum. Two objects attracted the Swami's notice here and he was surprised to find them. They were a set of razors and garlands of glass beads. He said, "Existence of razor in our country in very ancient past can be surmised from the words in the *Upanishad*, 'Kshurasya

dhara nishita duratyaya'.[1] To day I find from what I see before
me that razors and things made of glass were in use in our
country during ancient times.". The floor around the 'stupa'
was paved during the Buddhist era with bricks of glass three or
four inches thick. The Chinese came to learn from India
during this period how to manufacture glass. It is a matter of
regret that Indians later forgot the art. After happily spending
the whole day here the Swami returned to Rawalpindi in the
evening.

From Rawalpindi the Swami left for Peshawar and reached
there at nine in the evening. The place is full of ruffians and so
the police do not allow anybody to go out of the precincts of
the railway station after dark. Hence we had to spend the night
in the railway waiting room. Next day we went to the local
'Kalibari' to arrange our stay there. In every city and town in
Western India there is a 'Kalibari' where local Bengalees assemble
to listen to religious discourses and music. There is good
arrangement for the daily worship of the goddess here. For
Bengalees coming from their homeland shelter at a 'Kalibari'
like this is really covetable. The Swami accepted hospitality at
the house of Byomkesh Chakravarti at noon. And in the afternoon
he went to the house of Charu Chandra Ghose, the most well-
known physician at Peshawar. He is highly popular among the
Afghans in the same manner as Sir Kailash Chandra Basu is
popular among the Marwari community residing at Calcutta.

After spending two days at Peshawar the Swami left for
Jamrud on the way to Afghanistan across the Khyber Pass. A
railway track was being laid at this time from Jamrud to
Khyber. Innumerable labourers were at work and workshops
had sprung up in many places. The Swami left for Afghanistan
in a lorry carrying mail. The vehicle rattled along the uneven
road up hill and down dale. Almost everywhere on the way
could be seen work on the railway track in progress which
included hewing a tunnel from one end of a hill to the other.

The natural scenery of Peshawar is simply incomparable.

---

[1]The reference is to the verse 1/3/14 of the *Katha Upanishad* where it is
given : *'Kshurasya dhara nishita duratyaya durgam pathastat kabayo
badanti'* (Like the sharp edge of a razor is that path,-so the wise say,-hard to
tread and difficult to cross.)

Tier after tier of hills surround the city on all sides. Gandhara is the name given to this region in the *Mahabharata*. Kings belonging to the Chandra dynasty used to reign here with their capital at Purushpur,—the name gradually changing to Peshawar. More than a thousand Buddhist monasteries and 'stupas' were once to be seen here in the past. The chief among them was the one built upon the begging-bowl of Lord Buddha. These monasteries and 'stupas' came to be destroyed during foreign invasions launched at different periods of history. Great authors of Buddhist scriptures like Narayana Dev, Ananga Bodhisattva, Basubandhu Bodhisattva, Dharmatrata, Monohita, Arya Paschik etc were born in Gandhara. The place was visited by Fa Hsien in 400, by Sunga-Phul in 520 and by Hiuen Tsang in 630 A.D.

The Swami arrived near the famous military contonment at Landikhana three miles away from Peshawar. We did not see so many soldiers anywhere in course of our travels in the region. Full regiments, four or five in number, were stationed here to guard the frontier between Afghanistan and India. We saw innumerable cavalrymen and infantry soldiers on parade. The lorry came to halt here for half an hour. During the recess the Swami went to visit the tents of local Bengalee officers. A Mr. Kar entertained the Swami with tea and snacks. One is not allowed to proceed further from here unless one has a passport. But Mr. Kar gave his pass to the Swami and requested him to use it. Equipped with this pass the Swami once again boarded the lorry and left for Afghanistan.

At long last we were on Afghan soil and found men both young and old and also women and children,—many of them with guns in their hands moving about. The place was dotted with cottages surrounded by earthen walls and roofs thatched with hay. Almost every house has a lofty minaret fifty or sixty cubits in height. When fighting breaks out villagers fire from their guns from the top of these minarets. The people here are very fond of guns. When they succeed in killing an enemy and capturing his gun, they declare with great joy *'Mujhe ek bhai mil gaya'* (I have found a brother).

Extremely ferocious by temperament these people are all crack-shots. Entrusted with the task of guarding the frontiers they receive regular salary from the king of Kabul. Gradually we reached Landikotal, a town with a military cantonment. The

British rule extends up to this place. We found a very large number of soldiers here and a fortress equipped with all kinds of arms and fighting material. The soldiers have to be always on the alert and constantly on their toes. They shoot at the merest sound seeming to be unusual. A police officer belonging to the intelligence department escorted us to a high official. This gentleman was an Afghan Muslim. He spoke to us with politeness. He made the Swami sit on a chair and asked him the reason behind our visit to this region. After examining the pass we were carrying he allowed us to take leave of him. Trucks carrying mail do not proceed any further from here. They go back to Jamrud once again. So after enjoying the mountain scenery of Afghanistan for a while we returned to Jamrud via the Khyber pass. A railway train bound for Peshawar was about to start from Jamrud. At this time we found another man of the intelligence department on our trail. He now approached us and pestered the Swami with question after question. The Swami replied to some of them. But finally he got irritated and gave him a piece of his mind and at once the man beat a hasty retreat. We boarded the train and duly arrived at Peshawar once again. There we visited the zoo and the military cantonment. Then the Swami went to see the town of Atak[1] and the Kabul river. After five days we resumed our journey, to Lahore.

Kalowant Singh whom we have mentioned before, Teja Singh and others were there at the railway station in Lahore, waiting to receive us. Two carriages were hired for carrying us with our luggages and we were all taken to their house. It had been decided that the Swami would be in Lahore this time for a fortnight. Before our journey to Tibet the Swami had stayed for two or three days in the house of Sushil Kumar Chattopadhyaya, an advocate at Lahore. People whom we had come to know during our previous visit now came to see the Swami everyday. A lecture by the Swami was arranged in the Arya Samaj College with Lala Hansarajji, the leader of the Arya Samajists, in the chair. So many people attended the lecture that the Chairman had a very trying time in maintaining order during the meeting. The

---

[1]Atak is situated on the eastern bank of the Indus. The battle between Alexander and Porus was fought here in 325 B.C. The fortress of Atak was built during the reign of Akbar in 1581. The railway bridge at Atak built in 1883 starts at the point from which Alexander crossed the Indus. At present Atak is well-known for manufacture of cement and its trade.

topic the Swami chose for his scholarly and highly interesting speech was 'My Experiences in America'. Hansarajji said, "In 1897 I had asked Swami Vivekananda to join the Arya Samaj. In reply he said, 'It is better that you come and join us'." (Laughter). The speeches took nearly two hours to be over and after that the meeting came to a close.

For the next few days the Arya Samajists came to the Swami again and again and put abstruse questions to him with the intention to win him over to their point of view. But they were worsted by the Swami in debate. One day they invited the Swami to the house of Sri Nanak Chand Pandit. They served him with delicious food and drink and then the big shots among the Arya Samajists challenged the Swami to a debate.

First question: Are the *Vedas* complete in themselves according to you ?

The Swami : The question of their being complete does not arise, since none of them is available to-day in full. Apart from this, the *Vedas* themselves declare that to one who has come to realise the true nature of Supreme Reality 'the Vedas are no more the Vedas'.[1]

Second question: You often say that this world is an illusion and that Brahma alone constitutes reality. But where exactly do the *Vedas* say this ?

The Swami: The *Vedas* proclaim, *'Ekamebadvitiyam'* (It is one and without any peer). Brahma alone is the Supreme Reality,—nothing exists apart from Him. Truth is one and indivisible. If you count the world as true and real, Brahma comes to be meaningless and non-existent. On the other hand if you look upon Brahma as true, the world comes to be without meaning and substance. Both the world and the Brahma can be true at the same time if they are one and the same thing. When we say that the world is

---

[1]The reference is to the verse 4/3/22 in the *Brihadaranyaka Upanishad* where we find a discussion on the form of the Self which is directly perceived in the state of dreamless sleep and which is beyond all relations and all social and scriptural obligations. "In this state a father is no more a father, a mother is no more a mother, the worlds are no more the worlds, the gods are no more the gods, the Vedas are no more the Vedas."

an illusion and Brahma alone constitutes the truth, we mean that what appears to be the world around us is actually a manifestation of the Brahma. It is wrong to look upon a piece of rope as a live snake. It may look like a snake but is actually nothing but a piece of rope. In the same way is this world an illusion.

The Arya Samajists were put out by the cut and dried answers to their questions and soon they beat a hasty retreat. A few Sanatanis (a sect opposed to the Arya Samajists) were present. They were very happy at the Swami's victory and requested him to stay on at Lahore. They further requested him to set up an 'Ashram' and assured that they would provide him with all assistance in the matter. The Swami told them that he would discuss these matters later. He was rather tired and so after supper retired to bed quite early.

Next day the Swami spoke at the Foreman Christian College,—his subject being 'The Doctrine of Karma'. Professor Lucas, the principal of the college, was in the chair. Students crowded in great numbers to hear the Swami. The Swami spoke for nearly an hour and a half. The Chairman said at the close of the meeting, "I have been a Christian missionary all my life. But I have heard nothing equal to to-day's scholarly discourse of the Swami. I have heard lectures of all the great seers of India. But it seems that the Swami's eloquence surpasses anything I have heard before. I heard of him while at New York but did not have the good fortune to hear him then. To-day on listening to him I am more than fulfilled."

Next day the Swami went to see Sir Gangaram who was at that time engrossed in the social movement of the re-marriage of widows. He had spent a lot of money in fostering this movement. He told the Swami, "Sometime ago a monk called Sevananda from the Belur Math came here. He set up here an 'Ashram' which he could not run for long. If you agree to build one, I shall provide you with all the money needed for the purpose." The Swami told him that he would let him know his decision later.

A little after this the Swami accompanied by Raghubir Singh went to visit the Anglo-Vedic School and Hostel founded by Dayananda Saraswati. Then he went to the Lahore museum. It was not possible to see the exhibits in it in all their details. So the Swami just sent a sort of cursory glance at them while hurrying through all the rooms in the museum. An image of Buddha made of touchstone drew our attention. Buddha was represented in this image as a very lean and emaciated person. The perfection with which his bones, arteries and veins were set indicated great knowledge of anatomy on the part of the sculptor. This image has been found at a place called Taktibhai.

On our way back from the museum we saw the statue of Lawrence wielding a sword in one hand and a pen in the other. A number of attempts have been made to mutilate this statue. So a policeman always stands guard near it. During our stay at Lahore the Swami accompained by Kalowant Singh went on a visit to Amritsar. Teja Singh and others saw them off at the railway station.

What Benares is to the Hindus and Mecca to the Muslims, Amritsar is to the Sikhs,—the holiest of all their holy places. Nearly four hundred years ago there was a small hamlet named Chak at the spot where Amritsar is situated now. There being no tank or pond here, travellers had a very hard time when passing through this place. While touring this region with a few disciples Guru Nanak created a tank full of clean and transparent water with the help of his miraculous power.

About sixty years after this in 1574 during the reign of Emperor Akbar the fourth guru of the Sikhs, Ramdas, enlarged this tank by further excavation. He erected many small temples on all its four sides and called this place Ramdaspur after his own name. His disciple Guru Arjun Singh later made this place the capital of the Sikhs and gave the name Amritsar to it. Its present population is about 143000. Walled on all sides the town has thirteen gates for entrance and exit. In earlier times there was a moat all around it which is now almost completely filled up with earth. To protect the town from the attack of enemies the Sikhs had also built a fortress which exists no more. In 1800 Maharaja Ranjit Singh raised here another fortress called Govindagarh surrounded with a trench. It exists even now.

In 1762 Timur, the son of Ahmed Shah, destroyed the chief temples of this place, apart from profaning them by slaughtering cows, and raised some mosques on their sites. Later the Sikhs recaptured the area and began slaughtering pigs in the mosques. The present big temple called the Darbar Saheb was built at that time. It is situated just in the midst of the tank, Amrit Sarovar. The temple and its precincts resound constantly with recitation from the holy book, the *Granth Saheb*. One is charmed with the strikingly beautiful reflection of the temple on the still waters of the pond. Just at its centre stands a big tree with branches outspread; from these branches huge bats, quite large in number can be seen hanging. The floor of the temple and the paths leading to it are all paved with white marble stones. The dome is plated with copper leaves gilded with gold. This was done under the orders of Maharaja Ranjit Singh at the cost of a fabulous sum. The Sikhs plucked precious stones from the tomb of Jahangir and that of other emperors and set them inside this temple.

As you enter through the main gate into the temple's courtyard you find yourself in front of the Bhung Palace of the Akalis. There is a collection of arms used by the Sikh Gurus inside this place. We found people singing devotional songs and playing on musical instruments at different corners of the courtyard. Pilgrims were having a holy dip in the tank and monks were sitting here and there in meditation. We found some people engaged in copying the *Granth Saheb*. Tradesmen were busy selling clothes, combs, ornaments and different iron wares. On the eastern side of the tank there is a huge tower from the top of which the scenery all around looks very charming. Very near this stands the famous Baba Atal. By the side of this is to be seen the Kaulsar hallowed by the memory of the wife of Guru Govind Singh. Beneath a tree on a copper plate is given the details of how Guru Govind Singh brought Kaul, his wife, to Lahore.

The Swami took off his shoes and entered the temple inside which recitation of the *Granth Saheb* was in progress. The Swami prostrated himself before it and the Sikh priest handed him a flower as a token of God's grace. The Swami took the same, placed it on his head and came out of the temple. Then after a visit to the Santsar we all left the precincts of the temple through the main gate. After this we went to the Jallianwala Bagh. It was there that General Dyer opend indiscriminate fire on hundreds of men, women and children on a fatal evening under the orders of Governor Michael O'Dyer resulting in a cruel massacre.

Then we went to the local railway station, boarded a train and proceeded towards Nankana Sahib, the birthplace of Guru Nanak. Not far from Amritsar it is the chief pilgrimage spot for the Sikhs.

On getting down from the train a tonga was hired for the Swami. What struck us as out of the ordinary as we entered the town was that everybody both young and old, carried a dagger fastened at the waist. Even housewives could be seen with daggers likewise as well as girls on their way to school. It appeared that we were in the midst of martial people always ready for a fight. There was no knowing as to whether more such strange sights still awaited us. With this thought in mind we arrived at Nanak's birthplace where now stands a huge Gurdwara. As the Swami approached it, members of the Gurdwara Prabandhak Committee sitting in front of its main gate and transacting official work gave him a rousing reception and offered him a chair. They told us that a few days ago a violent clash had taken place at this very spot between the Sikhs following Sadhu Narayan Das and the Akalis. The Akalis have taken the responsibility of running this temple from the government by force. These members had now sat together to review the situation and to decide on all issues related to it under the leadership of Sardar Gurudit Singh. This gentleman had a talk with the Swami on various topics. After this the Swami entered the courtyard of the temple in his company. The rioters had killed many people and then set fire on them. Marks of this fire were still there for all to see. The doors and windows also bore marks of heavy and indiscriminate exchange of fire. Bullets had hit the walls inside the temple resulting in plasters falling off. Even the *Granth Saheb* had not been spared and it lay on the floor riddled with bullets. People were not being allowed to be within the temple for long because of this recent outbreak of violence. So after taking a few snaps the Swami soon left the temple and made for the railway station. He boarded the train there and was back to Lahore within a short time.

At Lahore the Swami addressed the students of the National College in the pandal set up for the annual session of the Indian National Congress. It was a cogent speech rich in content that he delivered to them. Accompanied by Bhai Paramanand the Swami went to visit the National College after the speech was over. Next day the Swami spoke on the philosophical thoughts permeating the *Vedas* at the Sanatan Dharma College with Lala Haridas in the chair. Many respectable persons and the students in general were all highly impressed on hearing the Swami speak. They were overwhelmed by his extraordinary scholarship. The Swami was invited to supper at the house of Lala Haridas. He was plied with questions on various subjects by all the important people of the town who had gathered there to meet him. The Swami was asked to describe and explain his own religious convictions. Next day the Swami went to see Yajna being performed under the aegis of the Arya Samaj and to listen to the recitation of the *Vedas*. At this time the annual gathering of the Arya Samajists was taking place on an extensive ground fenced with huge tarpaulins. Arya Samajists from all corners of the country had set up tents on this ground and Brahmin scholars had arrived in large numbers to conduct Yajnas and other holy rites. This was the first time that we were witnessing Yajnas being performed on such a large scale. This filled our hearts with great joy.

From this site the Swami went to the house of Mr. B. K. Lahiri at Sabji Bagh where he had been invited to lunch. His next programme was a visit to Babu Mahal where some Bengalees messed together. Upendranath De, one of these Bengalees, welcomed the Swami and offered him tea. In all cities and towns in Bihar, U.P. and the Punjab are to be found localities populated by Bengalees. These localities are usually designated as Bangalitola or Babu Mahalla. Such localities grew because in earlier times quite a large number of Bengalees migrated to these places in search of jobs. They held important posts and were highly respected. But things have changed with the spread of education among the local people and the number of Bengalees in different offices and establishments is now on the decrease.

In this way passed a fortnight and the Swami started for Kurukshetra from Lahore. Thieves operate freely in this part of the country. So we kept awake all through the night during the journey to prevent our luggages from being stolen.

We arrived at Kurukshetra in the morning. Arrangements were made for the Swami and his party to stay at the local *dharamshala*. We took our meals in the house of Nilkantha Panda. Then we went out sight-seeing in course of which we covered Lake Dwaipa-yana where Duryodhana had hid himself at the end of the great battle fought between the Kauravas and the Pandavas. The Swami visited the spot where Bhima and Duryodhana had their duel, mace in hand, and where the latter was killed. Then we went to the spot called Jatismar where Sri Krishna had recited the *Gita* to Arjuna. A banyan tree now stands at this spot. Our next place of visit was Bhadrakali Peeth. We spent the night in the *dharamshala* and took the train for Hardwar on the next day. On our arrival there a large number of monks and ascetics from the Ramakrishna Mission received the Swami amidst shouts of joy and cheer. The Swami stayed at the Ramakrishna Mission Sevashram for a week in course of which he paid a visit to Rishikesh. During this visit he was accompanied by Swami Kalyananandaji, founder of the Sevashram and a direct disciple of Vivekananda. Memories of the past revived in the mind of the Swami while at Rishikesh. Long ago he had been a begging mendicant here during the years between 1888 and 1890. At that time he used to live in a cottage made of grass and studied *Vedanta* at the feet of Dhanaraj Giri, founder of the Kailash Math. Dhanaraj Giri used to hold the Swami in great affection. He highly admired his intellect and described it as something extra-ordinary. The Swami went to visit Kailas Math during his stay at Rishikesh. Govindananda, the chief priest of the Kailash Math, had long ago been a friend and classmate of the Swami. He, too, had been a disciple of Dhanaraj Giri. Though old and blind now, he still cherished the memory of the Swami. He now gave the latter a warm reception and entreated him to stay at the Kailash Math for a few days. The Swami assured him that he would do this on some later occasion. Then he took leave of him.

The Swami took his lunch at a charitable eating house run by the Punjabis. Then he came back to Kankhal. The programme there consisted of visits to Daksha-Yajna Ghat, Sati-Sarovar, Rishikul Ashram etc. The Swami laid the foundation of a new ward which was to serve as an annexe to the Savashram meant for patients attacked with cholera. Then he gave initiation to a few inmates of the Ashram into celibacy and monasticism.

From Hardwar the Swami came to Benares and stayed at Ramakrishna Sevashram for three days. After paying visits to important places at Benares the Swami started by the down Punjab mail on the night of the tenth of December on the last lap of his journey to Belur Math from where he had been away for six months. He was back on the eleventh of December, the hallowed birth-day of Sarada Devi. He returned amidst happy celebrations on this occasion. The monks and devotees were all very happy to see him in their midst once more after his long sojourn at Amarnath, Tibet and various other places.

CHAPTER—13

Buddhism in Western Tibet or Ladakh

History tells us that during the reign of Asoka (273—236 B.C.) the third Great Buddhist Conference was held in Pataliputra (Patna). After this conference Asoka sent Buddhist monks as preachers to Nepal, Kashmir, Tibet, Western Tibet (Ladakh), Bactria, Yarkand, China, Mongolia, Egypt and various other places.[1] They spread Buddhism among people of these countries and along with it a civilization based on ethics and morality. They founded colonies in sparsely populated regions of Tibet. At this time two branches of the Aryan race called Mens and Dard used to reside in Western Tibet. They were the first to be converted to Buddhism, —a fact borne out by the ancient Buddhist art and sculpture as enshrined in the ruins at Janskar. A stone tablet belonging to the second century B.C. and bearing inscriptions in Brahmi script tells us that monks from India had spread the message of Buddha in Ladakh (Western Tibet).

Buddhism in China

It was at this time that monks from Nepal went to China for

---

[1]From ancient Buddhist literature we come to know that the Third Great Buddhist Conference was held under the chairmanship of Bhikshu Mangali-putta Tish (Upagupta). The following chief monks were sent to different countries for the propagation of Buddha's message :

Preacher's Name	The country to which he was sent
1. Majjhantik	Kashmir and Gandhara
2. Maha Rakshit	Ionia or Greece
3. Majijham	Himalayan regions
4. Dharmarakshit	Aparantaka (Upper Burma)
5. Mahadhammarakshit	Maharashtra
6. Mahadev	Mahishmondal (Mysore)
7. Rakshita	Vanavasita
8. Sona and Uttara	Suvarnabhumi
9. Mahendra and others	Lanka (Ceylon)

Apart from these preachers Asoka sent Buddhist monks to Egypt, Greece, Macedonia and other countries of the West and the Far East. As a result of this Indian civilization and culture spread all over the world.

the spread of Buddhism in that country. During the reign of Emperor Shi Hwang-Ti the first batch of missionaries consisting of eighteen Buddhist monks went to China. This was in 217 B.C. But the religion got firmly entrenched in China when in 61 B.C. Emperor Ming-Ti embraced Buddhism. History tells us that in 65 A.D. the Chinese Emperor sent officials to India to bring to China Buddhist scriptures and sacred bones of the Buddha or any article used by him. They returned two years later in 67 A.D. With them came two Buddhist monks from Magadh named Kasyapa Matanga and Gobharan or Dharmarakshak, carrying scriptures and various samples of Buddhist art and craft collected from Gandhara. During this period of history Sanskrit was the spoken language of the people throughout the region from Gandhara to Khotan and also in parts of China and Turkestan. Within a few years after the arrival of these monks the first Buddhist temple in China came to be built in the town of Loyang in the district of Chhopan. Matanga died at this town, but Dharmarakshak survived him for long. He was a great scholar and translated *Buddha Charita Suttra* from Sanskrit into Chinese.

The emperor who ascended the throne after Ming-Ti invited many an Indian scholar to China in 76 A.D. Among these scholars mention must be made of Aryakala, Sthavir Chilukaksha and Sraban Subinoy. In 222 A.D. a Buddhist monk called Dharmakala went from India to China. He was followed by Mahabal and Bighna in 224, by Kalyanaruna in 225, by Kalyan and Dharmaphala in 281, by Dharmaraksha in 381, and by Gautam and Sanghadeva in 388 A.D. Bhikshu Kumarjiva stayed in China during the years between 383 and 412. He translated *Sad Dharma Pundarika*, a Buddhist scripture, into Chinese. The famous Chinese traveller, Fa Hsien, was one of the disciples of this Kumarjiva who, in turn, had sat at the feet of Bimalaksha, a great Buddhist preceptor residing in Kashmir. At this time another Buddhist monk called Buddhabhadra boarded a ship bound for South China and on reaching there set up a school of followers engaged in constant meditation. He stayed there for thirty-one years and breathed his last in 429 A.D.

In 400 AD. Gunavarman, Prince of Kashmir, set out on a travel across Ceylon and Java and then in 428 A.D. sailed aboard a ship bound for Canton. He set up two Buddhist monasteries, —one in Canton and the other in Nanking. Associations of

Buddhist monks and nuns came to be formed in China around this time. Along with this Buddhist painters like Dharmadut and Gunavarman propagated Indian arts in that country. From Kabul a scholar named Sanghabhatta had gone to China sometime before Buddhabhadra went there. In 380 A.D. there went to that country Shraman Dharmapriya. The others to go there included Punyatrata (414 A.D.), a colleague of Kumarjiva, Buddhajiva (423 A.D.) and Dharmamitra (424 A.D.)

In 520 Bodhidharma, a Buddhist monk from India, went to Malaya and from there to China on foot. While in Nanking he took a vow of silence and did not utter a single word for nine years during which he remained absorbed in meditation. On hearing this the Chinese Emperor came to see him. This earnest meditation won his admiration and he built a temple in his honour.

In 500 Pandit Paramartha, the biographer of Basubandhu, went to Nanking and spent eight years there, practising Yoga. He created a sect in China called Yogachar.

In 399 A.D. the famous Chinese traveller, Fa Hsien, came to Pataliputra (Patna). There he studied Buddhist scriptures for fourteen years at the feet of Guru Revati, the famous teacher of Buddhaghose. He returned to China in 414 carrying a number of Buddhist scriptures with him.

Buddhism in Korea

In 374 A.D. two Chinese Buddhist monks, Ah Tao and San Tao by name, were invited by the king of Korea to go there and spread the message of Buddha. These two monks were received by the king with great honour on their arrival at Korea. They preached Buddhism in that country and finally succeeded in converting both the king and the queen to the new religion. The royal couple gave up all their earthly possessions and took to monastic life. Since then Buddhism became firmly entrenched in Korea. As a result of this many a Chinese monk went to Korea and set up Buddhist temples and monasteries there. An Indian Buddhist monk, Matananda by name, also went to that country and was accorded great honour by the king.

Buddhism in Japan

In 522 A.D. the king of Hiaksai in Korea sent to the king of

Japan an image of Buddha made of gold and Buddhist scriptures as gifts. A year later the Mikado (King of Japan) found on the seashore near his capital a colossal image of Buddha made from the trunk of a camphor tree. Fascinated by the beauty of this image he brought it to his palace and installed it there. At that time the king of Hiaksai sent seven Buddhist monks from Korea to the Mikado of Japan. These monks belonged to the Jo-jit-su and Sun-ron sects.

In 544 the king of Korea sent another batch of Buddhist monks, nine in number, to Japan. During the reign of Mikado Bidatsu-Tenno there came from Korea to Japan monks and nuns belonging to Ritsu and Zen sects carrying with them a large number of Buddhist scriptures. Along with them came teachers, sorcerers, masons and idol-makers.

In 584 two men from Japan brought from Korea images of Sakyamuni and Maitreya Bodhisattva as well as holy bones of the Buddha. The first pagoda in Japan was built by a man named Sogo-No-Iname.

During the reign of the next Mikado a large number of Buddhist monks came from Korea to Japan on invitation and preached the message of the Buddha. It was at this time that the famous Tennoji Buddhist temple at Osaka, Udjumasa Buddhist temple near Kyoto, Asukdera-darumaji temple in the town of Yamado as well as the temples called Tayema-dera, Kume-dera and Tachi-ban-dera came to be built.

* * * * *

The Chinese Buddhist monks first came to Japan in 623 A.D. They set up temples and monasteries and in course of two years Buddhism spread among the people of Japan.

In 645 Mikado Kodoku-Tenno of Japan came to be converted to Buddhism. He sent a Japanese monk, Do-so by name to the famous Chinese traveller, Hiuen Tsang, to learn from him the inner truth of the gospel of the Buddha. Do-so received initiation into the mysteries of various processes of meditation from a Buddhist monk belonging to the Zen community.

* * * * *

During the years between 673 and 686 Mikado Temmu-Tenno of Japan gave to Buddhist monasteries plenty of landed property and made them autonomous and free from the control of the government to a great extent. He set up the famous Buddhist temple called Jukushji near the town of Nara and proclaimed an edict, making it compulsory for all his subjects to worship Lord Buddha and to have Buddhist scriptures in every house. In 700 the custom of burning the dead came to be introduced in Japan for the first time. In 710 a huge Buddhist monastery, Kobuku-ji came to be set up in the town of Nara. Mikado Shomu Tenno ordered in 737 that Buddhist monasteries must be there in every district. He also had a seven-storied Buddhist shrine built. At his orders came to be erected the famous Buddhist temple of Nara and an image of Buddha made of eight metals (gold, silver, copper, bronze, bell metal, zink, lead and iron) twenty-five cubits high. The temple and the image are to be seen even today. It was during the reign of the same Mikado Shomu Tenno that a Brahmin monk from India, Baraman So-jo by name, arrived at Osaka aboard a ship. In all probability he was a Bengalee and he carried with him to Japan manuscripts written in the Bengali script of the time. This manuscript continues to be worshipped in the Buddhist temple at Nara. Mikado Shomu Tenno finally gave up his kingdom and became a monk. Since then Buddhism has remained firmly entrenched in Japan.

CHAPTER—14

Buddhism in Tibet

History tells us that it was in the fourth century A.D. that Buddhism came to be established in China as state religion with royal sanction. It spread to Central Tibet but found no general acceptance there. The king of Tibet, Srong-tsen-Gampo (613—650) invaded China in 641. The then Chinese Emperor, Tai-tsung of the Tang Dynasty (618—906), had to enter a treaty with the Tibetan king according to which he had to yield his daughter Weng-Cheng in marriage to the conqueror. Two years later Sron-tsen-Gampo married another princess, Bhrukuti, the daughter of king Amsuvarman of Nepal.

Both the queens had been brought up in an environment permeated with the Buddha's teachings. They succeeded in converting the king to the new religion. He became an ardent admirer of the high ideals and tenets of Buddhism and sent his ambassador, Thon-mi Sam-bho-ta, to India. The said Sam-bho-ta stayed at different parts of India and learnt Sanskrit and philosophy from Brahmins and Buddhist scholars. He returned to Tibet in 650 A.D. and introduced an elaborate system of written characters based on the Nagri alphabet as current in Bengal and Magadh during the seventh century and the eighth. Even to-day the same alphabet is current in Tibet, though in Bengal and Magadh its form has undergone a sea change. Sam-bho-ta not only introduced the new alphabet in Tibet but also wrote a grammar in Tibetan. Thus Srong-tsen-Gampo, the first important king of Tibet, brought to his country the language it still uses in writing. He also introduced under the inspiration of his two wives Buddhism in the form then most popular in India. He made Lhasa ('the place of the gods') his capital and erected a large temple in honour of Lord Buddha. This temple exists even today.

Primitive Races in Tibet

In the pre-Buddhistic period the original inhabitants of Tibet were a race of cannibals steeped in barbarism. They had no religion to boast of. They went in constant dread of ghosts, spirits, monsters, gnomes, goblins, demons, witches etc and in order to propitiate them practised various shamanistic rituals, involving sacrifice of both men and beasts. They looked upon rocks and trees as endowed with a kind of human personality and saw in lightning, storm and thunder dreadful spirits ready to do ill to man unless propitiated with offerings and worship. They used to pay homage to trees which they considered to be the abode of devils and also to rocks, snakes, etc. They wore frightful masks and executed horrible dances as a form of worship offered to these devils.

'Bon' Religion in Tibet

Such worship of ghosts and spirits went by the name of 'Bon' or 'Pon' among Tibetans. A holy man of Western Tibet, Shen-Rab-Mi-Bo by name, introduced this blood-curdling ritual. According to tradition, he had learnt various languages and had acquired proficiency in arts and medicinal sciences. He had three hundred thirty-six wives who bore him innumerable children. At last at the age of thirty-one he began practising religious austerities and in a short time obtained divine grace. He acquired miraculous powers through the worship of the god named Shen-Hao-Kar (which means 'full of white splendour') and spent twenty-five years of his life in popularising this god in China. Finally he succeeded in converting Kong-gong-see, the Chinese king, to his religion. Shen-Rab-Mi-Bo taught the people of Tibet this religion. He instructed them how to invoke gods and how to propitiate goddesses who grant fortune to men. Along with this he initiated them into the mysteries of ghosts and spirits and their terrific dance, the procedure of offering drinks to goblins, rituals to be followed while cremating the dead, making of talismen to ward off evil influences coming from supernatural sources and various other magic cults and mumbo-jumbo. This religion spread to Tibet, China, Mongolia, Turkestan and other places of Central Asia and was in vogue for a long time among people in these countries. The priests who upheld this religion were known as Bonpos.

The Bonpos invoked spirits, demons, ghosts, and other supernatural beings through recitation of various incantations and made use of them in curing diseases and warding off evils. These incantations were supposed to be safeguards against dangers and losses brought about by conjunction of stars and planets and also by mischievous spirits. They were also regarded as having the power to release man from the bondage of all earthly sorrows and miseries and to help in his salvation. The name of the chief god of Bon religion is La-Chhen-po-Mig. Supposed to be equipped with nine eyes but only two legs he is regarded as the glorious monarch of the world and the universe. The other gods are of two kinds, — givers of sorrow and givers of peace. The goddesses in this religion are greater and more powerful than the gods.

The chief goddess is Ji-Briji-dangtha-Yasma. She is supposed to be the source of all powers. Her face is of snow-white complexion. In each of her two hands she carries a mirror on the top of which stand four lions supporting a throne on their backs and a torch in their claws. On the throne there is a seat lotus-like in structure. On it sits a goddess, La-Chhen-po by name. She is the spouse of Lord Mahadev who sits on the back of a white bull, carrying a book in hand gilded with silver. There are other goddesses too, their names being Bagdevi, Lakshmi, Dayamayee, Buddhidatri etc. Each sits on a throne and each has a god for her partner. Bag-devata is one of these gods. There are other male deities as well all of whom are seen riding on bulls. Thus in the Bon religion there are five gods and five goddesses. The ultimate purpose of the saints of this religion is to win salvation and to do good to all living beings. Another purpose which they cherish is to overcome all those who put obstacles in the path of doing good to every soul and to attain heavenly bliss. They also aim to cross all the thirteen stages to be gone through before one can hope to achieve the ultimate goal of complete deliverance from all earthly bondage. In this religion there is no place for the cult of Nirvana as in the doctrines of the Buddha.

In the seventh century A.D. King Srong-tsen-Gampo of Tibet founded Buddhism in his country. The lamas look upon him as the incarnation of Bodhisattva Avalokitesvar and honour him as such. The two queens of this monarch started being worshipped as incarnations of Taradevi (the Divine Mother). One of them was the Chinese Princess, Weng-Cheng while the other was the Nepalese Princess, Bhrukuti. Weng-Cheng came to be defied as Shubhra Tara (the White Tara) while Bhrukuti was apotheosised as Shyamal Tara (the Green Tara). Their images are still worshipped in temples in Tibet. Since they bore the king no children they are looked upon as goddesses by the lamas.

What was the nature of Buddhism planted in Tibet in the seventh century? A thousand years had gone by at this time after the demise of the Buddha and his teachings had undergone many a change. As it took within its fold various unenlightened tribes it had to accommodate various totems, images, ghosts and spirits which they cherished. Their rituals based on superstitions found a place in Buddhism in the form it spread in Tibet. To preserve the original purity of Buddhism religious councils were summoned a number of times. One of these was held in the first century A.D. at the behest of the Scythian King Kanishka at Jullundhar. Deliberations in this council resulted in a split among Buddhists. Some chose to adhere to the religion in its ancient purity. Buddhism as practised by them was accepted by Ceylon, Burma and Thailand and came to acquire the name of 'Southern Buddhism'. The others preferred having a mixture of Buddhism and worship of gods and goddesses of various kinds. They also insisted on preserving ideas and superstitions of old. This mixture between the new religion and the old spread to Tibet, China, Japan, Korea, Mongolia, Central Asia, Russia etc and came to be labelled as 'Northern Buddhism'. 'Southern Buddhism' is called *Hinayana* (low vehicle or inferior means of salvation) by Buddhists, while *Mahayana* (great vehicle or superior means of salvation) is the name given to 'Northern Buddhism'. At the outset there was not much difference between the religious practices of these two sects and their final goal was more or less the same, i.e. Nirvana. But during the first century A.D. Nagarjun preached with vigour in the North-western parts of India the tenets of *Mahayana* school and offered new interpretations to the message of Lord Buddha.

The *Mahayana* camp placed Lord Buddha in the position of God in heaven. His great qualities and attributes came to be personified in their eyes and they looked upon them also as gods. The divine Bodhisattava Avalokitesvar came to be regarded as the very embodiment of kindness to all living beings. He was the constant dispenser of their well-being. On the other hand, the *Hinayana* camp was all the time anxious that each individual belonging to it should attain Nirvana. It observed rites prescribed in *Vinaya Pitak* and other Buddhist scriptures. The *Mahayana* camp, by contrast, believed that every effort should be made to enable every living being to attain salvation. It is their firm belief that all beasts and animals were once our ancestors. So we should strive hard to redeem them from the earthly existence full of sorrows and difficulties.

In the famous Buddhist scripture called *Ashta-Sahasrika-Prajna-Paramita* the *Hinayanists* have been taken to task for their selfish efforts at attaining Nirvana only for themselves and at doing good to only their own souls. The *Mahayanists,* on the other hand, have been highly praised for their universal approach and their prayer for salvation for every living being.

In the doctrines of the Buddha in their original purity there is no place for God as creator or preserver or destroyer. But soon after his holy demise his followers put him on the lofty pedestal of a god and started worshipping him under the title of Amitabha Buddha. He came to be regarded as a divinity without any origin or end, with his abode in heaven known as Sukhavati and having the attributes of Knowledge covering everything. His deeds and the incidents that took place during his life on earth came to be described as the manifestations of his everlasting self without any beginning or end. The idea of divine Bodhisattva came to germinate from this. The chief among the various incarnations of Bodhisattva is Avalokitesvar (Son of Amitabha). Such in brief are the ideas upheld by the *Mahayanists.*

During the fifth century A.D. there was a Buddhist monk named Asanga in Gandhara (Peshawar). He had reached salvation through the practice of Raja Yoga as propounded by Patanjali and included the same in the curriculum to be followed by the *Mahayanists.* In the centuries that followed worship of gods and goddesses like Siva, Sakti, Durga etc with incantations familiar to the Hindus came to be incorporated within the *Mahayana* doctrine. In this way Buddhism as preached in early times came to undergo transformation while spreading far and wide. The *Mahayana* doctrine was preached by Buddhist monks in Tibet during the seventh century A.D. At this time the influence of the ancient Bon religion was very strong there. Instead of coming into a head-on clash with it the *Mahayanists* chose a path of slow reconciliation and compromise.

Followers of the Bon religion used to wear black head-gears

and chogas (a long and loose robe). The *Mahayanists* sought to differentiate themselves from them by wearing scarlet head-gears and chogas. Even after persistent efforts of nearly a century the Buddhist monks failed to wipe out the superstitions and ghostly practices encouraged by the Bon religion. To lend strength to such efforts the next king of Tibet, Trisong Detsan, invited during the middle of the eighth century Shantirakshita, eminent Buddhist scholar and teacher at the University of Nalanda, to teach his people the doctrines of the Buddha in their purest form.

Shantirakshita (also called *Shantarakshita*)

Shantirakshita was the son of the king of Jashohar in Bengal. Given initiation by Jnanagarbha, the great Buddhist monk, he studied various scriptures with diligence, meditated long to reach inner realisation and finally attained monkhood. The Tibetans were much impressed by his saintly character and noble qualities of both head and heart. He came to be known among them as Acharya Bodhisattva, a name held in great esteem by the Tibetans even today. He was a Yogi belonging to the Madhyamik Yogachar sect. On his arrival at Tibet Shantirakshita spoke thus to king Trisong Detsan, "There lives in Udyananagar (Kabul) a prophet named Padma Sambhava who mastered Buddhistic *Tantra*. He has the power to drive out from Tibet all ghosts, goblins and spirits with his magic incantations. You are to invite him to come to your aid". The king of Tibet invited Padma Sambhava in obedience to this order of Shantirakshita. Padma Sambhava arrived at Tibet in 749 and was received by the king with great honour. On being appointed the chief Buddhist priest of the country, he started converting both men and women to the new religion. He taught them that it is posible for all to achieve Nirvana without giving up earthly possessions and taking to the life of monks. This applies to ordinary people and also to kings.

Padma Sambhava used to wear a double-crested scarlet cap. The chief lamas belonging to the sect established by him continue to wear caps of this variety.

Padma Sambhava (the 'Lotus Born')

Padma Sambhava is referred to as Guru Rinpoche by Tibetans.

This means the 'Precious Teacher'. The creed preached by him came to be known as Lamaism. He is given the same honour by the lamas which they accord to Lord Buddha. Many a story is current among the Tibetans as to how he subdued ghosts, demons and goblins etc by his magic incantations and saved the country from their evil influences. He gave assurance to these ghosts and demons that the lamas would daily worship them with due offerings. This practice of propitiating the malign forces has become an indispensable part of the daily worship of the lamas.

Padma Sambhava founded in 749 the first Buddhist monastery and convent for the Bhikkhus in Tibet under the patronage of king Trisong Detsan in the town of Sam-yas (Samya). He got Shantirakshita appointed as the first priest of this monastery and convent. This post the latter held for thirteen years. Padma Sambhava was later given by the lamas the title of Acharya Bodhisattva Mahaguru and they came to regard him as the incarnation of Lord Buddha in heaven. Many a book in Tibet contains descriptions of his supernatural feats. It is said that he could fly in the air, change his visage into that of a horse, bring back the dead to life, become invisible like the wind, turn ebb-tide into flow-tide and catch with his hands birds on their wings in the sky.

Within nearly a hundred years after the time of Shantirakshita and Padma Sambhava there went to Tibet from Bengal, Nepal and Kashmir no less than seventy-five Buddhist monks endowed with profound scholarship to preach the new religion there. They also translated various Buddhistic scriptures into Tibetan. The names of some of these translators are as follows : Dharmakirti, Vimalmitra, Buddhaguhya, Shantigarbha, Vishudda Sinha, Kamalsheel, Kushar, Shankar Brahman, Shilamanju (of Nepal), Ananta Varma, Kalyanmitra, Jinmitra, Dharmapala, Prajnapala, Gunapala, Siddhapala, Subhuti, Sri Shanti etc.

In the ninth century A.D. Ralpachen, grandson of king Trisong Detsan, ascended the throne of Tibet. He appointed competent Buddhist scholars to translate various Buddhistic scriptures into Tibetan. He made gifts of property to Buddhist monasteries and introduced the Chinese method of measuring time in Tibet, which, since then, the country has followed while recording historical events.

Buddhists under Repression

Lang Darma, the younger brother of Ralpachen, was dead against the new religion. The king's profound admiration of Buddhism irked him greatly. In 899 he had king Ralpachen murdered and captured the throne. On assuming power he let loose a spate of torture on the lamas and started defiling their temples and monasteries in various ways. He burnt their scriptures and ordered inhuman repression on them. The lamas were forced at his behest to do the work of butchers. For three years he continued to play the role of a hateful tyrant and his murky career came to an end with his being shot to death by an arrow thrown by a lama named Palgyi Dorje. It is said that the king while dying observed with great sorrow, "Had I but died three years earlier than this, I would not have been guilty of all the sins I have committed. And had I been killed three years later I would have succeeded in uprooting Buddhism altogether from the soil of Tibet". This murder raised Palgyi Dorje to the status of a great religious leader in the estimation of the lama priests. The hateful tyranny of the late king failed to do much harm to Buddhism. It rather strengthened the resolve of the lamas to spread the influence of the new religion on a permanent basis.

The word 'Lama' in Tibetan means 'a man with a great soul, or alternatively, the Superior One.' This title is bestowed on priests in monasteries and Bhikkhus who have attained full enlightenment. During the reign of Trisong Detsan and that of the two kings who succeeded him Buddhism spread and flourished in Tibet under their patronage.

Atisha Dipankar Sree Jnana

In the eleventh century many a Buddhist Bhikkhu went from Bengal, Nepal and Kashmir to Tibet. Among them there was a scholar without peer named Atisha Dipankar Sree Jnana. A Bengalee by birth and belonging to the royal family of Gour, he was born in 980 A.D. at a village called Vajrajogini, Vikrampur Parganas, East Bengal. His parents were Kalyan Sree and Prabhavati (also called Padmaprabha) who christened him Chandragarbha. In his youth he studied at the feet of Avadhut Jetari the holy scriptures of the *Hinayanists* as well as of the *Mahayanists,* the *Vaishesik* philosophy of Kanad, the *tantras* etc and mastered them all to perfection. He earned great fame by defeating eminent Brahmin scholars in debate. Finally, he took his initiation from Rahul Gupta, the chief preceptor in the Krishnagiri Buddhist monastery. At the age of nineteen he took further initiation from Acharya Shilabhadra (Shilarakshita), the chief monk of the Vihara of Odantapuri in Magadh. The latter conferred on him the title of 'Dipankar Sree Jnana'. At thirty-one Atisha gave up family life and became a Buddhist monk in a monastery. He studied logic with great diligence under eminent scholars of Magadh.

This was followed by his profound study of all Buddhistic scriptures for twelve long years at the feet of Dharmakirti in Suvarnadvip (Java) which was one of the chief centres of Buddhistic studies at the time. There he came into contact with highly talented and famous scholars in different branches of knowledge and benefited much from their teachings. After a voyage to and stay at Ceylon for sometime he returned to India.

On coming back to Magadh he continued with his religious studies in the company of eminent scholars among whom Shanti, Naropanta, Avadhuti and Tambhi deserve special mention. These scholars all respected Dipankar for his matchless erudition. During his stay at Mahabodhi he had debated with the atheists there and persuaded them to recognise the greatness of Buddhistic philosophy. They received conversion to Buddhism at his hands.

At the request of King Nayapala, son of King Mahipala, the Buddhist monarch of Magadh, Dipankar accepted the post of the Principal of Vikramsila Mahavihara. Reports of his extraordinary scholarship spread far and wide and eventually reached Tibet. The lamas extended an invitation to him to come to Tibet. The Tibetan chronicles tell us that Lha Lama Ye-shes-od, king of Tibet, had sent a letter to Dipankar inviting him to his country.

Thus invited, Dipankar started on his journey to Tibet in the year 1039 at the age of sixty. Accompanied by a lama named Nag-tsho he took the hilly track of Nari-kor-sum, crossed the Himalayas and on his arrival at Tibet preached the *Mahayanist* brand of Buddhism. It is said that while riding on his way to Tibet he kept himself all along at a height of one cubit above the saddle on his horse with the help of his miraculous power attained through Yoga. He had other miraculous powers besides this and could clearly recollect events in his previous incarnations.

The king of Tibet accorded Dipankar a very warm reception. He was charmed with his extraordinary scholarship and the miraculous powers he had attained through the practice of Yoga. He revered him deeply and gave him the title of Jo-bho-je (Lord and Master).

Atisha Dipankar Sree Jnana propagated in Tibet the *Mahayanist* doctrine in its purest form. Under his influence the lamas who had previously taken to the path of *Tantra* veered to the *Mahayanist* fold. He rid Buddhism of the manifold defects that had crept into it and founded a sect called *Kadampa* which name later changed to *Gelukpa*. This is now the dominant religious sect in Tibet. From this time onwards different sects among the lamas came to be classified according to rank and social order.

Atisha Dipankar spent thirteen years in Tibet during which he kept himself engaged wholeheartedly in the reform of Buddhism. He died in 1053 at the age of seventy-three in the monastery of Ne-tang near Lhasa where his memorial stands even today. The lamas of Tibet hold him in high reverence and consider him second only to Lord Buddha. His image is worshipped everywhere in Tibet.

Atisha Dipankar wrote more than a hundred volumes in Sanskrit and Tibetan. The most important among them include the following :

1. *Bodhipatha pradipa;* 2. *Carya Sangraha pradipa;* 3. *Madhyamopadesa;* 4. *Satya dvyavatara;* 5. *Sangraha garbha;* 6. *Hridaya nischita;* 7. *Bodhisattva manyavali;* 8. *Boddhisattva Karmadimargavatara;* 9. *Saranagatadesa;* 10. *Mahayanapatha sadhana varna sangraha;* 11. *Mahayanapatha sadhana sangraha;* 12. *Sutrartha samuchhayopadesa;* 13. *Desakusala Karmopadesa;* 14. *Karma Vibhanga;* 15. *Samadhi sambhara parivarta;* 16. *Lokottarasaptaka vidhi;* 17. *Guru Kriyakrama;* 18. *Chittotpada samvara vidhikrama;*

19. *Siksha samucchaya abhisamaya;* 20. *Vimala ratna lekhana.*

The chief disciple of Atisha Dipankar was Domton (Jinakar). He was a monk belonging to the *Kadampa sect.* The monastery called Ra-Deng situated in the north east of Lhasa was founded by him in 1058. This came to be the chief lamasery of the new sect.

The reforms introduced by Atisha Dipankar were accepted, though not in their entirety, by sects known as *Kargyupa, Sakyapa, Dugpa* etc. There were, however, people who entirely rejected these reforms and continued to practise the traditional rites and demonolatry as prescribed by the Bon religion. These people formed the community that came to be known as *Ninmapa* or 'the old ones', since they adhered to old practices. This community branched into seven different sects. Lamas belonging to them wear scarlet caps and chogas (a kind of loose robe). These sects have their monasteries in different places of Tibet:

After the murder of Lang Darma the lamas took charge of his minor son. They divided the kingdom into different parts that came to be ruled by different religious sects. This resulted in the country's fragmentation and the chief lamas belonging to the different sects started becoming owners of properties which they ruled from the strongholds within their monasteries and viharas. This state of affairs continued for nearly a century and a half. There was no mighty sovereign holding sway over the country. Bandits in Mongolia found this situation sufficiently alluring for them to launch an attack on Tibet in 1206 under the leadership of a Mongol Chief named Chingiz Khan. He was the man who later invaded India, plundered it to his heart's content and went back to his country with rich booty.

Chingiz Khan was succeeded by the great Chinese emperor, Kublai Khan, whose vast empire comprised Mongolia, Tibet and China. He was a man endowed with many a good quality. It was during his reign that Christian missionaries entered his empire. His conviction was that to civilise the various unenlightened tribes in his extensive empire it was necessary to encourage preaching of ethics and religion. With this end in view he convened an assembly where Christian missionaries and Buddhist lamas met face to face. The former had been sent to China by the Pope of Rome.

Emperor Kublai Khan notified both the Christian missionaries and the lamas that he would accord superiority to the religion of those who would show him some mighty miracle. The Christian missionaries failed to do this while a Buddhist lama raised the Emperor's wine-cup placed on a table not with his hand but with his Yoga-power and fixed its brim to the imperial lips. Struck with wonder and admiration the Emperor drank his fill from the cup. This strange miracle made him accept the superiority of Buddhism over Christianity and he agreed to be converted to the religion of the lamas. Just as in the ninth century Charlemagne had set up Christian Religious Order in Europe, Emperor Kublai Khan did the same in regard to Buddhism in Tibet. He gave away his Tibetan kingdom to the chief lama and created the post of Dharmadhyaksha whose word was law to all the Buddhists in Tibet. He was given the title of 'Pags-pa' which means the 'most powerful monarch'.

In 1270 Kublai Khan recognised the Sakya Pandita or the Sakya Grand Lama as the head of the lamaist church and made him the suzerain of Tibet. To express his gratitude for this generosity the Sakya Lama promised to consecrate or crown the Chinese emperors. Kublai Khan did much to foster Buddhism among the lamas of Tibet and founded monasteries and viharas in large numbers not only there but also in Mongolia. He even set up a very big monastery in Peking, capital of China.

The Sakya Pope, the monk suzerain, got the Buddhist scripture called *Ka-gyur* translated into Mongolian with the help of a staff of scholars. It is said that he was the man who devised the Mongolian alphabet. Since his time people in China, Mongolia, Manchuria and Russia started being converted to the religion of the lamas. The Sakya lamas became very powerful with the help of the Mongolian emperors and reigned in Tibet for nearly a century.

In 1368 the Ming dynasty came to power in China. Attempt was made by the first Chinese Emperor belonging to this dynasty to reduce the power of the Sakya lamas. He adopted an attitude of partiality to the *Kargyupa* and *Kadampa* sects and raised them to the status of Sakya lamas. This resulted in conflict among the people of Tibet. Lamas belonging to different groups came to be at loggerheads with one another with the intention to snatch absolute power.

In early fifteenth century there was a lama, Tsong Khapa by name, belonging to the *Kadampa* sect. Atisha Dipankar had joined this sect and had introduced reforms among its adherents. The meaning of *Kadampa* is 'those who obey rules with faith and devotion.' Tsong Khapa changed this name to *Gelukpa* ('those who follow the path of perfect virtue'). He abbreviated and simplified the rules regarding meditation as laid down by Atisha Dipankar and put greater emphasis on ritualistic practices. The *Gelukpa* sect became more powerful than other religious groups in course of time. The Dalai lama of Tibet belongs to this sect.

In 1409 Tsong Khapa founded a monastery in a place thirty-nine miles to the east of Lhasa and named it Ganden which means 'heaven' or 'place of joy'. Lamas belonging to the *Kadampa* sect were brought from different parts of the country to this monastery at his behest and they stayed there with his own disciples. Followers of Tsong Khapa wear patched robes of a yellow colour and move about with a begging-bowl and a prayer-carpet. It may be mentioned here that 'Sa-ser' in Tibetan means a 'yellow cap', and 'Sa-mar' is the Tibetan term for a 'scarlet or red cap'. Since the time of Atisha Dipankar the lamas belonging to the *Kadampa* sect had been wearing caps and robes of scarlet hue. Tsong Khapa instructed his followers to obey the two-hundred and thirty-five rules as laid down in the *Vinaya Pitaka* and asked them to wear yellow robes and caps after the fashion of the Indian monks.

Tsong Khapa had thoroughly mastered Buddhistic scriptures and was the author of a large number of books. Among them the chief is *Lam-rim* (the *Graded Path*). He also put down in writing rules to be followed by priests belonging to the *Gelukpa* sect.

On his death in 1417 the disciples of Tsong Khapa started worshipping him as Manjusree, an incarnation of Brahma. The lamas of the *Gelukpa* sect refer to him as Je-Rim-po-che. They consider him to be greater than Padma Sambhava and even

Atisha Dipankar. His image came to be placed by them on a high pedestal. They gave him the title 'Gyalwa' and started wearing small images of him as amulets.

Lamas of the *Gelukpa* sect believe that the message of Lord Buddha came to them from Asanga (the Buddhist monk who preached Yogachar doctrine in 500) via Dipankar, Dom-vakrisi and Je-Rim-po-che. These lamas regard Vajradhara as the Primal Buddha. In 1439 Gedendub (Ge-dun-grub), the nephew of Tsong Khapa, became the chief lama and head priest of the *Gelukpa* sect. He founded in 1445 the Tashi Lhumpo monastery (Mountain of Blessings). Je-She-rab-sen-age-Gyal-tsabje, one of his collegues, founded in 1414 the Depung monastery, the meaning of which is 'the pagoda of meditation'. This monastery was constructed on the model of Sridhanya Katak, the famous *Tantrik* monastery of *Kalinga*, India. Depung monastery is three miles to the west of Lhasa. Seven thousand lamas reside here at present. There is a small palace belonging to Dalai Lama within this monastery which he visits every year. Lamas from Mongolia in large numbers can be seen in this monastery receiving instructions in the intricacies of Buddhism.

Another colleague of Geden-dub named Khas-grub-je founded in 1417 the Sera monastery. Many other monasteries for the *Gelukpa* sect came up with the passage of years. Geden-dub died in 1473 in which year Jan-pob-Krasis came to be appointed as the abbot of the Tashi Lhumpo monastery A close rival to it was the Sera monastery situated at an extremely beautiful spot on the Tatipu mountain. The meaning of 'Sera' is 'compassionate hailstorm'. The significance of this name is that just as a hailstorm destroys paddy ripe for harvest, Sera would come to destroy Depung.

At present there live inside the Sera monastery five thousand and five hundred lamas. Inmates of this monastery came often into conflict with the lamas of Depung resulting in violent clashes and bloodshed. There are three big temples inside this monastery all as high as eight or ten-storied buildings. Each room in these temples is gold-plated. The Tibetan for gold is 'gesre'. According to some this monastery is called Sera because of these gold-plated rooms. Inside one of these temples there is a representation of thunderbolt (Dor-je) known as Tam-din-phur-bu held by the lamas in high respect. Every year it is carried at the head of a procession to Potala, the residence of Dalai Lama at Lhasa. All the lamas including the Dalai Lama himself touch it with their foreheads in deep reverence. It is said that the thunderbolt first belonged to a great Indian personage. Then it flew through the air and fell on a mountain adjacent to the Sera monastery and thus came into the possession of the lamas there. It is supposed to have miraculous powers with whose help dangers and malign influences can be warded off.

Towards the end of the sixteenth century during the reign of king Yonten Gyatso (Grand Lama), the fourth friar of the *Gelukpa* sect became very powerful with the help of Chong-kar, the Mongol minister of the Chinese government. He forced the lamas belonging to *Kargyu, Ninma* and other sects to enter his fold and to wear yellow caps.

In 1640 Lozang, the fifth Grand Lama of the *Gelukpa* sect, sought foreign aid and appealed to Gushri Khan, the son of the Mongolian Emperor, to attack Tibet. Gushri Khan promtly responded to the appeal and after making himself master of the whole country made a present of it to this Grand Lama. In this way Lozang came to be the ruler of Tibet. In 1650 the Chinese Emperor conferred on him the title of Dalai Lama. 'Dalai' is a Mongolian word which means 'vast as the ocean'. It is a word not in usage among Tibetans who refer to the Dalai Lama as Gyalwa-rin-po-che. This in its turn means 'a king endowed with great power and a jewel among men.'

Since then all the monasteries belonging to the different sects came under the control of the Dalai Lama. Gradually he came to be regarded as the incarnation of Bodhisattva Avalokites-var. According to Lamaism, Bodhisattva Avalokitesvar is the god of death in the manner of Yama belonging to the Hindu pantheon, the arbiter of human destiny and dispenser of life after death.

Potala, the colossal monastery-cum-palace in Lhasa, came to be built in 1645 and Lozang started ruling Tibet from within its precincts. His descendants (all known as Dalai Lama) have been using it as the royal palace. Potala is a nine-storied mansion situated on a red-coloured mountain named Marpo-ri. With its outer wall painted scarlet it presents an enchanting view.

There is an ancient Buddhist temple in Lhasa named Je-khang within which stands an image of Lord Buddha made of an alloy of five metals. The name of this image in Tibetan is Je-bho-rin-po-che. It is said that this image was built in Magadh during the life-time of Buddha by Visvakarma, the celestial artificer under the direction of Indra, the celestial king. During the Muslim invasion of India the Chinese Emperor rendered assistance to the king of Magadh who sent this image of Buddha to the former as a gift in gratitude. Tait-sung, the Chinese Emperor, gave his daughter Weng-cheng in marriage to Srong-tsen-Gampo, the king of Tibet. The Chinese princess took the image with her to Lhasa. Srong-tsen-Gampo founded this ancient temple in Lhasa and installed the image therein. The precious crown worn by this image was a gift from Tsong Khapa.

Various Diseases and Their Treatment in Tibet

The pharmacopoeia of the lamas is based on Charak and Susrut. The surgical instruments and tools for chemical analysis mentioned in *Susrut Samhita* are no longer used in India. But the apothecaries and medicine-men of China, Tibet and Mongolia are familiar with them.. It is said that Tibetans can cure dreadful diseases with the help of indigenous drugs and herbs. They are also well-known for their proficiency in surgery which they are reported to have acquired from China.

Smallpox often breaks out in Tibet. The Tibetan apothecaries do not know much about its treatment. Vaccination is unknown among them. They use the Chinese method of collecting germs of this disease from the body of a sturdy boy infected with it and then mixing the same with camphor. The mixture is next whiffed into the patient's nose through a tube. No remedy is prescribed so far as chicken pox is concerned and the patient is expected to come round in course of time.

Hydrophobia resulting from being bitten by rabid dogs is frequent in Tibet, China and Mongolia. Tibetans believe that symptoms of this disease would come out within a period ranging from seven days to eighteen depending on the dog's colour. The treatment prescribed for this disease in Tibet is highly effective. A bandage is tightly wound a little above the place where the dog has inserted its teeth and then the poison is sucked out with the help of a bowl-shaped implement. Blood is let out through the wound and then the infected place is branded with a red hot iron rod. The place is then treated with ointment in which are mixed clarified butter, turmeric, musk and roots of a kind of poisonous plant.

Goitre is another disease to be frequently encountered in South Tibet, Nepal, Bhutan and Sikkim. It results from taking water with heavy doses of lime (as is frequent in mountainous regions of Tibet) or quenching one's thirst from rivers that had frozen earlier. Goitre is of six varieties. Tibetan apothecaries recommend different treatments for them.

There are poisonous snakes in certain valleys of Tibet. Treatment for snake-bite is similar to the treatment for dog-bite. The only difference is that in the case of snake-bite the infected limb is washed with milk or curd. Sometimes the milk of a camel proves useful. It is said that if a snake bites a camel, the latter would come to no harm, but the former would die. There is a tribe in Tibet called Lalos who relish eating snakes. Before cooking the same they discard its head and its tail.

Apoplexy is very common in Tibet. The treatment and medicine prescribed for this is quite effective. Leprosy is rampant among Tibetans and its varieties are eighteen in number, each of them having different medicines and course of treatment. Dropsy is common in the southern and eastern Tibet. This also has varieties, twelve in number. Bone-ash and various indigenous herbs are of help in the cure of this disease. Dyspepsia and diarrhoea of nearly forty varieties are widespread among Tibetans. Due to climatic conditions Tibetans lose all their teeth by the time they are thirty.

Games and Sports in Tibet

Wrestling, archery, horse-race and polo are very popular with Tibetans. Among their favourite indoor games can be mentioned playing at cards, dice and chess. Even monks try to find out through lottery games whether they are destined for heaven or for hell.

Tibetans hold fairs to celebrate their new year's day, the birthday of Lord Buddha, the day on which he renounced family life and the day of his holy demise. On these occasions many people gather in temples and monasteries and dances, fun and frolic become the order of the day. Participants wear masks and dress themselves in garbs that make them look like skeletons. In their strange apparels they dance and sing to the delight of onlookers present. Even monks are given to music and dance.

Tibetans are also very fond of picnic. During the solar and lunar eclipse they observe religious rites in the manner of Hindus.

Funeral Rites in Tibet

When a patient in Tibet dies nobody save an ascetic lama is allowed to touch his body. The Tibetans do not believe that the patient has died or that his soul has left his body simply because his pulse is not beating any more or he has stopped breathing. They hold that the spirit called *She* resides in the corpse for at least three days. It is therefore considered a grievous sin to perform funeral rites immediately after death. But the souls of lama monks who have attained perfection through Yoga can rise to the heaven called *Tushita* or *Gadan* immediately after death.

When a common person dies, the Po-bo lama who knows the art of extracting the soul from the dead body is sent for. On his arrival he enters the death-chamber the doors and windows of which are then all closed. Alone he sits down near the corpse. While chanting incantations he forcibly plucks with the fore-finger and thumb a few hairs from its crown and occasionally makes a slight incision with a knife on the scalp. It is generally believed that the confined spirit of the deceased passes through the exit thus made and easily gets to the heaven above. If it goes out through some other aperture it is bound to go down to nether worlds. After this the lama by chanting incantation saves the spirit from the dangers which beset the road it has to pass and gives directions to it in finding its way to the paradise of the Amitabha Buddha. It takes nearly an hour to complete the ceremony. The grief-stricken relatives of the deceased are not allowed to approach the corpse until the said lama states with conviction through which exact route the spirit has passed.

Once this ceremony is over and done with the lama is paid his fees in terms of money, cows, yaks, sheep or goats. Next to come is the astrologer-lama who examines the horoscope of the deceased. On ascertaining the person's birthday and his age at the time of death he prescribes the mode of funeral rites suitable for him. No relative whose birth-date and other particulars coincide with those of the deceased is allowed to participate in these death-ceremonies, since it is believed that a breach of this rule will cause the spirit of the deceased to possess him. The fees to be paid to the astrologer-lama are similar to those given to the Po-bo lama.

Every family in Tibet and Mongolia, be it rich or poor, usually covers the dead with a white shroud and then with much care preserves it for three days in a corner of the death-chamber. The relatives and friends then come to see their dear one for the last time. They go round and round the dead body while praying for the welfare of the departed soul and revolving prayer-wheels. Near the head of the corpse five lamps are kept burning with a valance hanging in front. Behind this valance the spirit of the dead is offered food and drink at regular intervals. Even tobacco is offered to it. It goes without saying that the things thus offered are not later taken by anybody. These are simply thrown away since the general belief is that the dead man's spirit has consumed all their essence. The Tibetans also believe that the spirit of the deceased hovers near his relatives for as long as forty-nine days subsequent to his death and so his own bowl is kept filled everyday with food and drink and near it incense is kept burning.

On the fourth day the corpse is brought outside and carried to the nearest crematorium or burial ground. The lamas then blow their trumpets with vigour and the relatives follow the bier holding the end of a long white scarf tied to it. They prostrate themselves with deep reverence repeatedly on the way. The chief lama chants a liturgy while beating a drum with his right hand and ringing a bell with his left. Laying down the corpse anywhere on the road leading to the crematorium is considered to be an inauspicious act fraught with evil. If for some reason this becomes compelling, the funeral obsequies are to be performed at the very spot. There are two burial grounds, one at Phabonka and the other at Sherasha near Lhasa.

There is a huge block of stone in every crematorium or burial ground in Tibet. The dead body is stripped of all clothings and placed on it with its face downwards. An executioner among the lamas first makes lines with his sword across the body while chanting incantations. He then cuts it to pieces along those lines. Vultures and dogs feed upon them later on. The head is smashed and a paste is made of the brain matter and pieces of scalp. This grisly concoction is also offered as food to vultures and dogs. Then a fire is made of cowdung-cakes in a new earthen pot in which is burnt a mixture of clarified butter and barley. The earthen pot is then placed in a corner of the crematorium in the direction which the dead man's spirit is supposed to have taken. Then the pall-bearers wash their hands, take food and return home. The system of cutting the dead body into pieces as described above applies to most people. But in the case of eminent lamas a different course is followed. Their dead bodies are burnt in fire and after that ashes are collected and put in *chhortens*. Bodies of high-ranking lamas like Bodhisattva are preserved in the manner of Egyptian mummies and placed in *chhortens* made of gold, silver or copper. They are still to be seen in temples in the posture of Lord Buddha in meditation. Daily worship and rituals are held in their honour.

When Dalai Lamas or Tashi Lamas die all offices and market places close down for a week. For a whole month women do not wear new garments or ornaments. Other lamas observe mourning for ten days during which it is forbidden to shave or to use any headgear. When a rich Tibetan of high lineage loses either of his parents, he does not marry or join merriment of any kind and desists from travel outside his country for a year

The Buddhist lamas of Sikkim burn their dead and extinguish the funeral pyre with water in the manner of Hindus. The ashes are then collected to be thrown into some river. Only a small portion of them is placed in an urn which in its turn is kept buried in a *chhorten*. Bones of lamas who have attained perfection through meditation are smashed into powder and then mixed with clay. The mixture is then moulded into the shape of a tiny *chhorten* which is then kept preserved in a temple or monastery.

On the seventh day after death a ceremony of obsequies

known as *Ten-jung* is held. Relatives, neighbours, friends and admirers are treated to a feast on completion of the ceremony. Then as darkness descends a *Tantrik* lama wards off with his incantations ghosts, spirits and all harbingers of evil. Everybody present shouts at the top of his voice when this is being done.

CHAPTER—15

Jesus Christ—The Great Guide of Man

The following are extracts from the manuscript earlier referred to as found in the monastery at Himis.

I

1. The earth trembled and Gods shed tears in heaven at the dreadful sins committed by the sons of Israel.

2. This was because they had inflicted endless pain on the saint Issa who held within himself the soul of the Universe and did him to death.

3. In him was manifest the soul of the Universe to do good to all and to wash away all sinful thoughts.

4. He had come among men to remind sinners of the infinite compassion of God and bestow on them peace, happiness and divine grace.

5. Merchants of Israel came to this country and delivered this message.

II

1. The people of Israel lived on fertile lands tending herds of cattle and raising twin harvests every year. They incurred through their sins the wrath of God.

2. For this God took away all their possessions and decreed that they become slaves to the mighty Pharaoh of Egypt.

3. The Pharaoh inflicted inhuman tyranny on the sons of Israel. He caused them to be chained, maimed, deprived of food and clothing and put to hard labour.

4. He wanted that they should be in a state of continual terror and stand bereft of all human attributes.

5. The children of Israel thus fell into great hardship and agony. They implored the Lord of the Universe who had earlier saved their forefathers in their distress for mercy and aid.

6. At that time the Pharaoh was on the throne of Egypt. A famous conqueror, he was fabulously rich. All his palaces were built through the hard labour of his slaves.

7. The Pharaoh had two sons. The younger of the two was called Mossa. He was highly trained both in sciences and the arts.

8. He was dear to all for his nobility of character and for his kindness to those in distress.

9. It came to his notice that in spite of their endless misery and hardship the sons of Israel had not given up faith in the Lord of the Universe and had not taken to worshipping the petty gods of Egypt.

10. Mossa believed in God whom he considered to be one and indivisible.

11. Priests who acted as teachers to the Israelites prayed to Mossa that he should request his father, the great Pharaoh, to come to the aid of their co-religionists. This they thought would bring good to all.

12. Mossa made this request to his father. This, however, angered the Pharaoh who intensified his oppression on his subjects.

13. But within a short time a fierce epidemic spread all over Egypt. Men, women and children, both rich and poor, began to die in large numbers. The Pharaoh thought that God in His displeasure over his actions had decreed this punishment for him.

14. At this time Mossa told his father that the Lord of the Universe in His infinite mercy to His subjects in misery caused by the king's tyranny had ordained this punishment for the people of Egypt.

* * * *

Gradually by the mercy of the Lord of the Universe freedom and welfare came to be the lot of the sons of Israel.

IV

1. In His infinite compassion for the sinners the Lord and Father of the world willed to descend on earth in human form.

2. The eternal spirit without any beginning or end and in a state of complete inaction separated Himself from the all-pervading Supreme Soul and came to assume the form of a human being.

3. He descended on earth to show all living creatures the way to unite with God and to attain endless bliss.

4. He assumed human form with a view to setting an example with his own life of how to reach holiness of the mind and of how to attain immortality by separating spirit from the flesh and thus arrive at felicity without end in God's heaven.

5. A wonderful child was born in the land of Israel. God spoke of the impermanence of the body and of the soul's glory through the mouth of this child.

6. The parents of this child were poor but full of piety and born of families noted for their purity and innocence. They cared little for worldly possessions and sang the glory of the Lord. It was their conviction that sorrows and setbacks experienced by them had all been ordained by God in order to test their integrity.

7. To reward them for their patience and fortitude God blessed their first-born. He had sent him for the redemption of the sinners and the recovery of the diseased to health.

8. This divine child came to be named Issa. Even at a tender age he used to exhort people to revere God and ask sinners to desist from their evil activities.

9. People came from all directions to hear words of wisdom spoken by the child. Sons of Israel were unanimous that God the Eternal dwelt within him.

(The rest has been reproduced earlier in Chapter 12.)

*   *   *   *

Apart from this the Secretary of the Buddhist Society, Bombay, has made the following statement regarding Christ's sojourn in India :

"A recent New York despatch says that Prof. Roerich, a well-known archaeologist, who is conducting an American expedition to Central Asia announces that he has found manuscripts in a Buddhist monastery in Ladakh describing the visit of Jesus Christ to India to study Buddhism. Jesus Christ travelled through India preaching and returned to Jerusalem when he was 29 years of age.

There are not a few scholars who think that Christianity originated from Buddhism."

APPENDIX ONE

We have already referred to the similarity between the account which Swami Abhedananda collected from the Himis Gumpha with the help of a Tibetan interpreter of the sixteen years spent by Jesus Christ and the account given by Nicolas Notovitch. Notovitch also did his work of translation with the help of an interpreter. His book was published in French for the fist time in 1894. In all probability his translation was in the Russian language. It was retranslated in America into English.

We give below for the benefit of our readers some extracts from *The Unknown Life of Jesus Christ*[1] by Nicolas Notovitch (Fourth Edition, 1916). In the Introduction to his book he writes :

"After the close of the Turko-Russian War (1867-1878) I undertook a series of extended journeys through the orient. Having visited all points of interest in Balkan Peninsula, I crossed the Caucasus Mountains into India, the most admired country of the dreams of my childhood.

* * * *

In the course of one of my visits to a Buddhist convent, I learned from the chief Lama that there existed very ancient memoirs, treating of the life of Christ and of the nations of the Occident, in the archives of Lhassa, and that a few of the larger monasteries possessed copies and translations of these precious chronicles.

* * * *

During my sojourn in Leh, the capital of Ladakh, I visited Himis, a large convent in the outskirts of the city, where I was informed by the Lama that the monastic libraries contained a

---

[1] *The Unknown Life of Jesus Christ* by Nicolas Notovitch. Translated from the French by Alexina Loranger (Indo-American Book Company, Chicago, III U.S.A).

few copies of the manuscript in question. * * * * I took advantage of my short stay among these monks to obtain the privilege of seeing the manuscripts relating to Christ. With the aid of my interpreter, who translated from the Tibetan tongue, I carefully transcribed the verse as they were read by the Lama. Entertaining no doubt of the authenticity of this narrative, written with the utmost precision by Brahmin historians and Buddhists of India and Nepal, my intention was to publish the translation on my return to Europe'.

Besides this in the Chapter called 'A Feast in a Gompha' we find :

"While a young man kept]the prayer-wheel in motion by my bedside, the venerable director of the gompha entertained me with interesting accounts of their belief and the country in general, * * * *.Finally, yielding to my earnest solicitations, he brought forth two big volumes in cardboard covers, with leaves yellowed by the lapse of time, and read the biography of Issa, which I carefully copied from the translation of my interpreter This curious document is written in the form of isolated verses, which frequently bear no connection between each other."

I have long cherished the project of publishing the memoirs on the life of Jesus Christ, which I found at Himis, * * * * *.* * (pp.96—97)."

The writer discusses in the Epitome of his book : "In reading the life of Issa (Jesus Christ), we are at first struck by the similarity between some of its principal passages and the Biblical narrative: while, on the other hand, we also find equally remarkable contradictions which constitute the difference between the Buddhist version and that found in the Old and New Testaments" (p.147).

"The two manuscripts read to me by the Lama of the Himis Convent, were compiled from diverse copies written in the Tibetan tongue, translated from rolls belonging to the Lhassa library and brought from India, Nepal and Maghada two hundred years after Christ. These were placed in a convent standing on Mount Marbour, near Lhassa, where the Dalaı-Lama now resides.

"These rolls were written in the Pali tongue, which certain lamas study carefully that they may translate the sacred writings from that language into the Tibetan dialect.

"The chroniclers were Buddhists belonging to the sect of Buddha Gautama." (p. 151)

Notovitch, after considering various arguments for and against Christ's sojourn in India, is led to reach the following conclusion :

"It is to be supposed that Jesus Christ chose India, first because Egypt made part of the Roman possessions at that period, and then because an active trade with India had spread marvellous reports in regard to the majestic character and inconceivable riches of art and science in that wonderful country, where the aspirations of civilized nations still tend in our own age.

"Here the Evangelists again lose the thread of the terrestrial life of Jesus. St Luke says : 'He was in the desert till the day of his shewing unto Israel,' which conclusively proves that no one knew where the young man had gone, to so suddenly reappear sixteen years later" (pp. 161-162).

Swami Prajnanananda

APPENDIX TWO

FULL TEXT OF THE HIMIS MANUSCRIPT

On

LIFE OF SAINT ISSA

by

N. NOTOVITCH

Translated from the French
by
Violet Crispe
(1895)

APPENDIX TWO

THE LIFE OF SAINT ISSA
BEST OF THE SONS OF MEN

by
Nicolas Notovitch

CHAPTER—I

1. The earth has trembled and the heavens have wept because of a great crime which has been committed in the land of Israel.

2. For they have tortured and there put to death the great and just Issa, in whom dwelt the soul of the universe.

3. Which was incarnate in a simple mortal in order to do good to men and to exterminate their evil thoughts.

4. And in order to bring back man degraded by his sins to a life of peace, love, and happiness and to recall to him the one and indivisible Creator, whose mercy is infinite and without bounds.

5. Hear what the merchants from Israel relate to us on this subject.

CHAPTER—II

1. The people of Israel, who dwelt on a fertile soil giving forth two crops a year and who possessed large flocks, excited by their sins the anger of God,

2. Who inflicted upon them a terrible chastisement in taking from them their land, their cattle, and their possessions. Israel was reduced to slavery by the powerful and rich pharaohs who then reigned in Egypt.

3. These treated the Israelites worse than animals, burdening them with difficult tasks and loading them with chains. They covered their bodies with weals and wounds, without giving them food or permitting them to dwell beneath a roof,

4. To keep them in a state of continual terror and to deprive them of all human resemblance.

5. And in their great calamity, the people of Israel remembered their heavenly protector and, addressing themselves to him, implored his grace and mercy.

6. An illustrious pharaoh then reigned in Egypt who had rendered himself famous by his numerous victories, the riches he had heaped up, and the vast palaces which his slaves had erected for him with their own hands.

7. This pharaoh had two sons, of whom the younger was called Mossa. Learned Israelites taught him diverse sciences.

8. And they loved Mossa in Egypt for his goodness and the compassion which he showed to all those who suffered.

9. Seeing that the Israelites would not, in spite of the intolerable sufferings they were enduring, abandon their God to worship those made by the hand of man, which were gods of the Egyptian nation,

10. Mossa believed in their invisible God, who did not let their failing strength give way.

11. And the Israelitish preceptors excited the ardor of Mossa and had recourse to him, praying him to intercede with the pharaoh his father in favour of their coreligionists.

12. Wherefore the Prince Mossa went to his father, begging him to ameliorate the fate of these unfortunates. But the pharaoh became angered against him and only augmented the torments endured by his slaves.

13. It happened that a short time after, a great evil visited Egypt. The pestilence came to decimate there both the young and the old, the weak and the strong; and the pharaoh believed in the resentment of his own gods against him.

14. But the Prince Mossa told his father that it was the God of his slaves who was interceding in favor of these unfortunates in punishing the Egyptians.

15. The pharaoh then gave to Mossa his son an order to take all the slaves of the Jewish race, to conduct them outside the town, and to found at a great distance from the capital another city where he should dwell with them.

16. Mossa then made known to the Hebrew slaves that he had set them free in the name of their God, the God of Israel, and he went out with them from the city and from the land of Egypt.

17. He led them into the land they had lost by their many sins, he gave unto them laws, and enjoined them to pray always to the invisible Creator whose goodness is infinite.

18. On the death of Prince Mossa, the Israelites rigorously observed his laws, wherefore God recompensed them for the ills to which he had exposed them in Egypt.

19. Their kingdom became the most powerful of all the

earth, their kings made themselves famous for their treasures, and a long peace reigned among the people of Israel.

CHAPTER—III

1. The glory of the riches of Israel spread throughout the earth, and the neighboring nations bore them envy.

2. For the Most High himself led the victorious arms of the Hebrews, and the pagans dared not attack them.

3. Unhappily, as man is not always true to himself, the fidelity of the Israelites to their God did not last long.

4. They began by forgetting all the favors which he had heaped upon them, invoked but seldom his name, and sought the protection of magicians and sorcerers.

5. The kings and the captains substituted their own laws for those which Mossa had written down for them. The temple of God and the practice of worship were abandoned. The people gave themselves up to pleasure and lost their original purity.

6. Several centuries had elapsed since their departure from Egypt when God determined to exercise once more his chastisements upon them.

7. Strangers began to invade the land of Israel, devastating the country, ruining the villages, and carrying the inhabitants into captivity.

8. And there came at one time pagans from the country of Romeles, on the other side of the sea. They subdued the Hebrews and established among them military leaders who by delegation from Caesar ruled over them.

9. They destroyed the temples, they forced the inhabitants to cease worshipping the invisible God, and compelled them to sacrifice victims to the pagan deities.

10. They made warriors of those who had been nobles, the women were torn away from their husbands, and the lower classes, reduced to slavery, were sent by thousands beyond the seas.

11. As to the children, they were put to the sword. Soon in all the land of Israel naught was heard but groans and lamentations.

12. In this extreme distress, the people remembered their great God. They implored his grace and besought him to forgive them; and our Father, in his inexhaustible mercy, heard their prayer.

CHAPTER—IV

1. At this time came the moment when the all-merciful Judge elected to become incarnate in a human being.

2. And the Eternal Spirit, dwelling in a state of complete inaction and of supreme beatitude, awoke and detached itself for an indefinite period from the Eternal Being,

3. So as to show forth in the guise of humanity the means of self-identification with Divinity and of attaining to eternal felicity,

4. And to demonstrate by example how man may attain moral purity and, by separating his soul from its mortal coil, the degree of perfection necessary to enter into the kingdom of heaven, which is unchangeable and where happiness reigns eternal.

5. Soon after, a marvelous child was born in the land of Israel, God himself speaking by the mouth of this infant of the frailty of the body and the grandeur of the soul.

6. The parents of the newborn child were poor people, belonging by birth to a family of noted piety, who, forgetting their ancient grandeur on earth, praised the name of the Creator and thanked him for the ills with which he saw fit to prove them.

7. To reward them for not turning aside from the way of truth, God blessed the first born of this family. He chose him for his elect and sent him to help those who had fallen into evil and to cure those who suffered.

8. The divine child, to whom was given the name of Issa, began from his earliest years to speak of the one and indivisible God, exhorting the souls of those gone astray to repentance and the purification of the sins of which they were culpable.

9. People came from all parts to hear him, and they marveled at the discourses proceeding from his childish mouth. All the Israelites were of one accord in saying that the Eternal Spirit dwelt in this child.

10. When Issa had attained the age of thirteen years, the epoch when an Israelite should take a wife,

11. The house where his parents earned their living by carrying on a modest trade began to be a place of meeting for rich and noble people, desirous of having for a son-in-law the young Issa, already famous for his edifying discourses in the name of the Almighty.

12. Then it was that Issa left the parental house in secret, departed from Jerusalem, and with the merchants set out

towards Sind,

13. With the object of perfecting himself in the Divine Word and of studying the laws of the great Buddhas.

CHAPTER—V

1. In the course of his fourteenth year, the young Issa, blessed of God, came on this side of Sind and established himself among the Aryas in the land beloved of God.

2. Fame spread the reputation of this marvelous child throughout the length of northern Sind, and when he crossed the country of the five rivers and the Rajputana, the devotees of the. god Jaine prayed him to dwell among them.

3. But he left the erring worshippers of Jaine and went to Juggernaut in the country of Orissa, where repose the mortal remains of Vyasa-Krishna and where the white priests of Brahma made him a joyous welcome.

4. They taught him to read and understand the Vedas, to cure by aid of prayer, to teach, to explain the holy scriptures to the people, and to drive out evil spirits from the bodies of men, restoring unto them their sanity.

5. He passed six years at Juggernaut, at Rajagriha, at Benares, and in the other holy cities. Everyone loved him, for Issa lived in peace with the Vaisyas and the Sudras, whom he instructed in the holy scriptures.

6. But the Brahmans and the Kshatriyas told him that they were forbidden by the great Para-Brahma to come near to those whom he had created from his side and his feet;

7. That the Vaisyas were only authorized to hear the reading of the Vedas, and this on festival days only;

8. That the Sudras were forbidden not only to assist at the reading of the Vedas, but also from contemplating them; for their condition was to serve in perpetuity as slaves to the Brahmans, the Kshatriyas, and even the Vaisyas.

9. "Death only can set them free from their servitude' has said Para-Brahma. Leave them then and come and worship with us the gods, who will become incensed agianst thee if thou dost disobey them."

10. But Issa listened not to their discourses and betook him to the Sudras, preaching against the Brahmans and the Kshatriyas.

11. He inveighed against the act of a man arrogating to himself the power to deprive his fellow beings of their rights of humanity; "for," said he, "God the Father makes no difference

between his children; all to him are equally dear."

12. Issa denied the divine origin of the Vedas and the Puranas. "For," taught he to his followers, "a law has already been given to man to guide him in his actions;

13. "Fear thy God, bend the knee before him only, and bring to him alone the offerings which proceed from thy gains."

14. Issa denied the Trimurti and the incarnation of Para-Brahma in Vishnu, Siva, and other gods, for said he :

15. "The Judge Eternal, the Eternal Spirit, comprehends the one and indivisible soul of the universe, which alone creates, contains, and vivifies all.

16. "He alone has willed and created, he alone has existed since all eternity, and his existence will have no end. He has no equal either in the heavens or on earth.

17. "The Great Creator has not shared his power with any living being, still less with inanimate objects, as they have taught to you; for he alone possesses omnipotence.

18. "He willed it and the world appeared. In a divine thought, he gathered together the waters, separating from them the dry portion of the globe. He is the principle of the mysterious existence of man, in whom he has breathed a part of his Being.

19. "And he has subordinated to man the earth, the waters, the beasts, and all that he has created and that he himself preserves in immutable order, fixing for each thing the length of its duration.

20. "The anger of God will soon be let loose against man; for he has forgotten his Creator, he has filled his temples with abominations, and he worships a crowd of creatures which God has made subordinate to him.

21. "For to do honor to stones and metals, he sacrifices human beings, in whom dwells a part of the spirit of the Most High.

22. "For he humiliates those who work by the sweat of their brow to acquire the favor of an idler seated at his sumptuous board.

23. "Those who deprive their brethren of divine happiness shall be deprived of it themselves. The Brahmans and the Kshatriyas shall become the Sudras, and with the Sudras the Eternal shall dwell everlastingly.

24. "Because in the day of the last judgment the Sudras and the Vaisyas will be forgiven much because of their ignorance, while God, on the contrary, will punish with his wrath those

who have arrogated to themselves his rights."

25. The Vaisyas and the Sudras were filled with great admiration and asked Issa how they should pray so as not to lose their eternal felicity.

26. "Worship not the idols, for they hear you not. Listen not to the Vedas, for their truth is counterfeit. Never put yourself in the first place and never humiliate your neighbor.

27. "Help the poor, support the weak, do ill to no one, and covet not that which thou hast not and which thou seest belongeth to another."

CHAPTER — VI

1. The white priests and the warriors, becoming acquainted with the discourses of Issa addressed to the Sudras, resolved upon his death and sent with this intent their servants to seek out the young prophet.

2. But Issa, warned of his danger by the Sudras, left the neighborhood of Juggernaut by night, reached the mountains, and established himself in the country of Gautamides, the birthplace of the great Buddha Sakyamuni, in the midst of a people worshipping the one and sublime Brahma.

3. After having perfected himself in the Pali language, the just Issa applied himself to the study of the sacred writings of the Sutras.

4. Six years after, Issa, whom the Buddha had elected to spread his holy word, had become a perfect expositor of the sacred writings.

5. Then he left Nepal and the Himalayan mountains, descended into the valley of Rajputana, and went towards the west, preaching to diverse peoples the supreme perfection of man,

6. Which is — to do good to one's neighbor, being the sure means of merging oneself rapidly in the Eternal Spirit : "He who shall have regained his original purity," said Issa, "will die having obtained remission for his sins, and he will have the right to contemplate the majesty of God."

7. In crossing pagan territories, the divine Issa taught that the worship of visible gods was contrary to the law of nature.

8. "For man," said he, "has not been permitted to see the image of God, and yet he has made a host of deities in the likeness of the Eternal.

9. "Moreover, it is incompatible with the human consience to make less matter of the grandeur of divine purity than of animals and objects executed by the hand of man in stone or metal.

10. "The Eternal Lawgiver is one; there is no other God but he. He has not shared the world with anyone, neither has he informed anyone of his intentions.

11. "Even as a father would act towards his children, so will God judge men after their deaths accroding to the laws of his mercy. Never would he so humiliate his child as to transmigrate his soul, as in a purgatory, into the body of an animal."

12. "The heavenly law," said the Creator by the mouth of Issa, "is opposed to the immolation of human sacrifices to an image or to an animal; for I have consecrated to man all the animals and all that the earth contains.

13. "All things have been sacrificed to man, who is directly and intimately associated with me his Father; therefore he who shall have stolen from me my child will be. severely judged and chastised by the divine law.

14. "Man is naught before the Eternal Judge, as the animal is naught before man.

15. "Wherefore I say unto you, Leave your idols and perform not rites which separate you from your Father, associating you with the priests from whom the heavens have turned away.

16. "For it is they who have led you from the true God and whose superstitions and cruelties conduce to the perversion of your soul and the loss of all moral sense."

CHAPTER — VII

1. The words of Issa spread among the pagans in the midst of the countries he traversed, and the inhabitants forsook their idols.

2. Seeing which the priests exacted of him who glorified the name of the true God, reason in the presence of the people for the reproaches he made against them and a demonstration of the nothingness of their idols.

3. And Issa made answer to them : "If your idols and your animals are powerful and really possessed of supernatural strength, then let them srike me to the earth."

4. "Work then a miracle," replied the priests, "and let thy God confound our gods, if they inspire him with contempt."

5. But Issa then said : "The miracles of our God have been worked since the first day when the universe was created; they take place every day and at every moment. Whosoever seeth them not is deprived of one of the fairest gifts of life.

6. "And it is not against pieces of stone, metal, or wood, which are inanimate, that the anger of God will have full

course; but it will fall on men, who, if they desire their salvation, must destroy all the idols they have made.

7. "Even as a stone and a grain of sand, naught as they are in the sight of man, wait patiently the moment when he shall take and make use of them,

8. "So man must await the great favor that God shall accord him in his final judgment.

9. "But woe unto you, ye enemies of men, if it be not a favor that you await but rather the wrath of the Divinity—woe unto you if ye expect miracles to bear witness to his power.

10. "For it will not be the idols that he will annihilate in his anger but those who shall have erected them. Their hearts shall be consumed with eternal fire, and their lacerated bodies shall go to satiate the hunger of wild beasts.

11. "God will drive the impure from among his flocks, but he will take back to himself those who shall have gone astray through not having recognized the portion of spirituality within them."

12. Seeing the powerlessness of their priests, the pagans had still greater faith in the sayings of Issa and, fearing the anger of the Divinity, broke their idols to pieces. As for the priests, they fled to escape the vengeance of the populace.

13. And Issa further taught the pagans not to strive to see the Eternal Spirit with their eyes but to endeavor to feel him in their hearts and by purity of soul to render themselves worthy of his favors.

14. "Not only," said he unto them, "abstain from consuming human sacrifices, but immolate no creature to whom life has been given, for all things that exist have been created for the profit of man.

15. "Do not steal the goods of your neighbor, for that would be to deprive him of what he has acquired by the sweat of his brow.

16. "Deceive no one, so as not to be yourselves deceived. Endeavor to justify yourself before the last judgment, for then it will be too late.

17. "Do not give yourselves up to debauchery, for that would be to violate the laws of God.

18. "You shall attain to supreme happiness, not only in purifying yourselves, but also in guiding others in the way that shall permit them to gain original perfection."

CHAPTER — VII!

1. The neighboring countries resounded with the prophecies of Issa, and when he entered into Persia the priests became alarmed and forbade the inhabitants to listen to him.

2. And when they saw all the villages welcoming him with joy and listening devoutly to his sermons, they gave orders to arrest him and had him brought before the high priest, where he underwent the following interrogation :

3. "Of what new God dost thou speak? Art thou not aware, unhappy man, that Saint Zoroaster is the only just one admitted to the privilege of communion with the Supreme Being,

4. "Who ordered the angels to put down in writing the word of God for the use of his people, laws that were given to Zoroaster in paradise?

5. "Who then art thou to dare to blaspheme our God and to sow doubt in the hearts of believers?"

6. And Issa said unto them : "It is not of a new God that I speak but of our Heavenly Father, who has existed since all time and who will still be after the end of all things.

7. "It is of him that I have discoursed to the people, who, like unto innocent children, are not yet capable of comprehending God by the simple strength of their intelligence or of penetrating into his divine and spiritual sublimity.

8. "But even as a babe discovers in the darkness its mother's breast, so even your people, who have been led into error by your erroneous doctrine and your religious ceremonies, have recognized by instinct their Father in the Father of whom I am the prophet.

9. "The Eternal Being has said to your people through the medium of my mouth : 'You shall not worship the sun, for it is but a part of the world which I have created for man.

10. "'The sun rises in order to warm you during your work; it sets to allow you the repose which I myself have appointed.

11. "'It is to me, and to me alone, that you owe all that you possess, all that is to be found about you, above you, and below you!"

12. "But," said the priests, "how could a people live according to the rules of justice if it had no preceptors?"

13. Then Issa answered, "So long as the people had no priests, the natural law governed them, and they preserved the candor of their souls.

14. "Their souls were with God, and to commune with the Father they had recourse to the medium of no idol or animal,

nor to the fire, as is practiced here.

15. "You contend that one must worship the sun, the spirit of good and of evil. Well, I say unto you, your doctrine is a false one, the sun acting not spontaneously but according to the will of the invisible Creator who gave it birth,

16. "And who has willed it to be the star that should light the day, to warm the labor and the seedtime of man.

17. "The Eternal Spirit is the soul of all that is animate. You commit a great sin in dividing it into a spirit of evil and a spirit of good, for there is no God outside the good,

18. "Who, like unto the father of a family, does but good to his children, forgiving all their faults if they repent them.

19. "The spirit of evil dwells on the earth in the hearts of those men who turn aside the children of God from the strait path.

20. "Wherefore I say unto you, Beware of the day of judgment, for God will inflict a terrible chastisement upon all those who shall have led his children astray from the right path and have filled them with superstitions and prejudices;

21. "Those who have blinded them that see, conveyed contagion to the healthy, and taught the worship of the things that God has subordinated to man for his good and to aid him in his work.

22. "Your doctrine is therefore the fruit of your errors; for desiring to bring near to you the God of truth, you have created for yourselves false gods."

23. After having listened to him, the magi determined to do him no harm. But at night, when all the town lay sleeping, they conducted him outside of the walls and abandoned him on the high road, in the hope that he would soon become a prey to the wild beasts.

24. But, protected by the Lord our God, Saint Issa continued his way unmolested.

CHAPTER—IX

1. Issa, whom the Creator had elected to remind a depraved humanity of the true God, had reached his twenty-ninth year when he returned to the land of Israel.

2. Since his departure the pagans had inflicted still more atrocious sufferings on the Israelites, who were a prey to the deepest despondency.

3. Many among them had already begun to abandon the laws of their God and those of Mossa in the hope of appeasing

their savage conquerors.

4. In the face of this evil, Issa exhorted his compatriots not to despair because the day of the redemption of sins was at hand, and he confirmed them in the belief which they had in the God of their fathers.

5. "Children, do not give yourselves up to despair," said the Heavenly Father by the mouth of Issa, "for I have heard your voice, and your cries have reached me.

6. "Do not weep, O my beloved ones ! For your grief has touched the heart of your Father, and he has forgiven you, even as he forgave your forefathers.

7. "Do not abandon your families to plunge yourselves into debauchery, do not lose the nobility of your feelings, and do not worship idols who will remain deaf to your voices.

8. "Fill my temple with your hope and with your patience and abjure not the religion of your fathers; for I alone have guided them and have heaped them with benefits.

9. "You shall lift up those who have fallen, you shall give food to the hungry, and you shall come to the aid of the sick, so as to be all pure and just at the day of the last judgment which I prepare for you."

10. The Israelites came in crowds at the word of Issa, asking him where they should praise the Heavenly Father, seeing that the enemy had razed their temples to the ground and laid low their sacred vessels.

11. And Issa made answer to them that God had not in view temples erected by the hands of man, but he meant that the human heart was the true temple of God.

12. "Enter into your temple, into your heart. Illumine it with good thoughts and the patience and immovable confidence which you should have in your Father.

13. "And your sacred vessels, they are your hands and your eyes. See and do that which is agreeable to God, for in doing good to your neighbor you accomplish a rite which embellishes the temple wherein dwells he who gave you life.

14. "For God has created you in his own likeness—innocent, with pure souls and hearts filled with goodness, destined not for the conception of evil schemes but made to be sanctuaries of love and justice.

15. "Wherefore I say unto you, sully not your hearts, for the Supreme Being dwells therein eternally.

16. "If you wish to accomplish works marked with love or peity, do them with an open heart and let not your actions be

governed by calculations or the hope of gain.

17. "For such actions would not help to your salvation, and you would fall into that state of moral degradation where theft, lying and murder pass for generous deeds."

CHAPTER—X

1. Saint Issa went from one town to another, strengthening by the word of God the courage of the Israelites, who were ready to succumb to the weight of their despair; and thousands of men followed him to hear him preach.

2. But the chiefs of the towns became afraid of him, and they made known to the principal governor who dwelt at Jerusalem that a man named Issa had arrived in the country; that he was stirring up by his discourses the people against the authorities; that the crowd listened to him with assiduity, neglected the works of the state, and affirmed that before long it would be rid of its intrusive governors.

3. Then Pilate, governor of Jerusalem, ordered that they should seize the person of the preacher Issa, that they should bring him into the town and lead him before the judges. But in order not to excite the anger of the populace, Pilate charged the priests and the learned Hebrew elders to judge him in the temple.

4. Meanwhile Issa, continuing his preachings, arrived at Jerusalem; and, having learnt of his arrival, all the inhabitants, knowing him already by reputation, went out to meet him.

5. They greeted him respectfully and opened to him the gates of their temple in order to hear from his mouth what he had said in the other cities of Israel.

6. And Issa said unto them : "The human race perishes because of its lack of faith, for the darkness and the tempest have scattered the flocks of humanity and they have lost their shepherds.

7. "But the tempest will not last forever, and the darkness will not always obscure the light. The sky will become once more serene, the heavenly light will spread itself over the earth, and the flocks gone astray will gather around their shepherd.

8. "Do not strive to find straight paths in the darkness, lest ye fall into a pit; but gather together your remaining strength, support one another, place your confidence in your God, and wait till light appears.

9. "He who sustains his neighbor, sustains himself; and

XX APPENDIX TWO

whosoever protects his family, protects the people and the state.

10. "For be sure that the day is at hand when you shall be delivered from the darkness; you shall be gathered together as one family; and your enemy, who ignores what the favor of God is, shall tremble with fear."

11. The priests and the elders who were listening to him, filled with admiration at his discourse asked him if it were true that he had tried to stir up the people against the authorities of the country, as had been reported to the governor Pilate.

12. "Can one excite to insurrection men gone astray, from whom the obscurity has hidden their door and their path?" replied Issa. "I have only warned the unfortunate, as I do here in this temple, that they may not further advance along the darkened way, for an abyss is open under their feet.

13. "Earthly power is not of long duration, and it is subject to many changes. Of what use that man should revolt against it, seeing that one power always succeeds to another power? And thus it will come to pass until the extinction of humanity.

14. "Against which, see you not that the mighty and the rich sow among the sons of Israel a spirit of rebellion against the eternal power of heaven?"

15. The elders then asked : "Who art thou, and from what country dost thou come? We have not heard speak of thee before, and we know not even thy name."

16. "I am an Israelite," replied Issa. "From the day of my birth I saw the walls of Jerusalem, and I heard the weeping of my brothers reduced to slavery and the lamentations of my sisters who were carried away by the pagans.

17. "And my soul was filled with sadness when I saw that my brethren had forgotten the true God. As a child, I left my father's house and went to dwell among other peoples.

18. "But having heard that my brethren were suffering still greater tortures, I have come back to the country where my parents dwell to remind my brothers of the faith of their forefathers, which teaches us patience on earth to obtain perfect and sublime happiness in heaven."

19. And the learned elders put him this question : "It is said that thou deniest the laws of Mossa and that thou teachest the people to forsake the temple of God?"

20. And Issa replied : "One cannot demolish that which has been given by our Heavenly Father, neither that which has been destroyed by sinners; but I have enjoined the purification

of the heart from all blemish, for it is the true temple of God.

21. "As to the laws of Mossa, I have endeavored to establish them in the hearts of men. And I say unto you that you do not understand their real meaning, for it is not vengeance but mercy that they teach; only the sense of these laws has been perverted."

CHAPTER—XI

1. Having hearkened unto Issa, the priests and the wise elders decided among themselves not to judge him, for he did harm to no one. And presenting themselves before Pilate, appointed governor of Jerusalem by the pagan king of the country of Romeles, they addressed him thus :

2. "We have seen the man whom thou accusest of inciting our people to rebellion; we have heard his discourses, and we know him to be our compatriot.

3. "But the chiefs of the cities have made thee false reports, for this is a just man who teaches the people the word of God. After having interrogated him, we dismissed him, that he might go in peace."

4. The governor then became enraged and sent near to Issa his servants in disguise, so that they might watch all his actions and report to the authorities the least word that he should address to the people.

5. In the meantime, Saint Issa continued to visit the neighboring towns, preaching the true ways of the Creator, exhorting the Hebrews to patience, and promising them a speedy deliverance.

6. And during all this time, many people followed him wherever he went, several never leaving him but becoming his servitors.

7. And Issa said : "Do not believe in miracles wrought by the hand of man, for he who dominates over nature is alone capable of doing that which is supernatural, whilst man is powerless to stay the anger of the winds or to spread the rain.

8. "Nevertheless, there is one miracle which it is possible for man to accomplish. It is when, full of a sincere belief, he decides to root out from his heart all evil thoughts, and when to attain his end he forsakes the paths of iniquity.

9. "And all the things that are done without God are but errors, seductions, and enchantments, which only demonstrate to what an extent the soul of him who practices this art is full of shamelessness, falsehood, and impurity.

10. "Put not your faith in oracles; God alone knows the future; he who has recourse to diviners profanes the temple wnich is in his heart and gives a proof of distrust towards his Creator.

11. "Faith in diviners and in their oracles destroys the innate simplicity of man and his childlike purity. An infernal power takes possession of him, forcing him to commit all sorts of crimes and to worship idols;

12. "Whereas the Lord our God, who has no equal, is one, all-mighty, omniscient, and omnipresent. It is he who possesses all wisdom and all light.

13. "It is to him you must address yourselves to be consoled in your sorrows, helped in your works, and cured in your sickness. Whosoever shall have recourse to him shall not be denied.

14. "The secret of nature is in the hands of God. For the world, before it appeared, existed in the depth of the divine thought; it became material and visible by the will of the Most High.

15. "When you address yourselves to him, become again as children; for you know neither the past, the present, nor the future, and God is the Master of all time."

CHAPTER—XII

1. "Righteous man," said unto him the spies of the governor of Jerusalem, "tell us if we shall perform the will of our Caesar or await our speedy deliverance."

2. And Issa, having recognized them as people appointed to follow him, replied : "I have not said to you that you shall be delivered from Caesar. It is the soul plunged in error that shall have its deliverance.

3. "As there can be no family without a head, so there can be no order among a people without a Caesar; to him implicit obedience should be given, he alone being answerable for his acts before the supreme tribunal."

4. "Does Caesar possess a divine right?" further asked of him the spies. "And is he the best of mortals?"

5. "There should be no better among men, but there are also sufferers, whom those elected and charged with this mission should care for, making use of the means conferred on them by the sacred law of our Heavenly Father.

6. "Mercy and justice are the highest attributes of a Caesar; his name will be illustrious if he adhere to them.

7. "But he who acts otherwise, who exceeds the limit of power that he has over his subordinates, going so far as to put their lives in danger, offends the great Judge and loses his dignity in the sight of man."

8. At this juncture, an old woman who had approached the group, the better to hear Issa, was pushed aside by one of the spies, who placed himself before her.

9. Then Issa held forth : "It is not meet that a son should set aside his mother, taking her place. Whosoever respecteth not his mother, the most sacred being after his God, is unworthy of the name of son.

10. "Listen, then, to what I say unto you : Respect woman, for she is the mother of the universe, and all the truth of divine creation lies in her.

11. "She is the basis of all that is good and beautiful, as she is also the germ of life and death. On her depends the whole existence of man, for she is his natural and moral support.

12. "She gives birth to you in the midst of suffering. By the sweat of her brow she rears you, and until her death you cause her the gravest anxieties. Bless her and worship her, for she is your one friend, your one support on earth.

13. "Respect her, uphold her. In acting thus you will win her love and her heart. You will find favor in the sight of God and many sins shall be forgiven you.

14. "In the same way, love your wives and respect them; for they will be mothers tomorrow, and each later on the ancestress of a race.

15. "Be lenient towards woman. Her love ennobles man, softens his hardened heart, tames the brute in him, and makes of him a lamb.

16. "The wife and the mother are the inappreciable treasures given unto you by God. They are the fairest ornaments of existence, and of them shall be born all inhabitants of the world.

17. "Even as the God of armies separated of old the light from the darkness and the land from the waters, woman possesses the divine faculty of separating in a man good intentions from evil thoughts.

18. "Wherefore I say unto you, after God your best thoughts should belong to the women and the wives, woman being for you the temple wherein you will obtain the most easily perfect happiness.

19. "Imbue yourselves in this temple with moral strength.

Here you will forget your sorrows and your failures, and you will recover the lost energy necessary to enable you to help your neighbor.

20. "Do not expose her to humiliation. In acting thus you would humiliate yourselves and lose the sentiment of love, without which nothing exists here below.

21. "Protect your wife, in order that she may protect you and all your family. All that you do for your wife, your mother, for a widow or another woman in distress, you will have done unto your God."

CHAPTER—XIII

1. Saint Issa taught the people of Israel thus for three years, in every town, in every village, by the waysides and on the plains; and all that he had predicted came to pass.

2. During all this time the disguised servants of Pilate watched him closely without hearing anything said like unto the reports made against Issa in former years by the chiefs of the towns.

3. But the governor Pilate, becoming alarmed at the too great popularity of Saint Issa, who according to his adversaries sought to stir up the people to proclaim him king, ordered one of his spies to accuse him.

4. Then soldiers were commanded to proceed to his arrest, and they imprisoned him in a subterranean cell where they tortured him in various ways in the hope of forcing him to make a confession which should permit of his being put to death.

5. The saint, thinking only of the perfect beatitude of his brethren, supported all his sufferings in the name of his Creator.

6. The servants of Pilate continued to torture him and reduced him to a state of extreme weakness; but God was with him and did not allow him to die.

7. Learning of the sufferings and the tortures which their saint was enduring, the high priests and the wise elders went to pray the governor to set Issa at liberty in honour of an approaching festival.

8. But the governor straightway refused them this. They then prayed him to allow Issa to appear before the tribunal of the ancients so that he might be condemned or acquitted before the festival, and to this Pilate consented.

9. The next day the governor assembled together the chief captains, priests, wise elders, and lawyers so that they might

judge Issa.

10. They brought him from his prison and seated him before the governor between two thieves to be judged at the same time as he, in order to show unto the crowd that he was not the only one to be condemned.

11. And Pilate, addressing himself to Issa, said unto him : "O man ! is it true that thou incitest the people against the authorities with the intent of thyself becoming king of Israel?"

12. "One becomes not king at one's own will," replied Issa, "and they have lied who have told thee that I stir up the people to rebellion. I have never spoken of other than the King of Heaven, and it is he I teach the people to worship.

13. "For the sons of Israel have lost their original purity; and if they have not recourse to the true God, they will be sacrificed and their temple shall fall into ruins.

14. "As temporal power maintains order in a country, I teach them accordingly not to forget it, I say unto them : 'Live conformably to your station and your fortune, so as not to disturb the public order.' And I have exhorted them also to remember that disorder reigns in their hearts and in their minds.

15. "Wherefore the King of Heaven has punished them and suppressed their national kings. Nevertheless, I have said unto them, 'If you become resigned to your destinies, as a reward the kingdom of heaven shall be reserved for you'."

16. At this moment, the witnesses were brought forward, one of whom made the following deposition : "Thou has said to the people that the temporal power is as naught against that of the king who shall soon deliver the Israelites from the pagan yoke."

17. "Blessed art thou," said Issa, "for having spoken the truth. The King of Heaven is greater and more powerful than the terrestrial law, and his kingdom surpasses all the kingdoms of the earth.

18. "And the time is not far off when, conforming to the divine will, the people of Israel shall purify them of their sins; for it has been said that a forerunner will come to proclaim the deliverance of the people, gathering them into one fold."

19. And the governor, addressing himself to the judges, said : "Dost hear? The Israelite Issa confesses to the crime of which he is accused. Judge him, then, according to your laws, and pronounce against him capital punishment."

20. "We cannot condemn him," replied the priests and the

elders. "Thou hast just heard thyself that his allusions were made regarding the King of Heaven and that he has preached naught to the sons of Israel which could constitute an offense against the law."

21. The governor Pilate then sent for the witness who, at his instigation, had betrayed Issa. The man came and addressed Issa thus : "Didst thou not pass thyself off as the king of Israel when thou saidest that he who reigns in the heavens had sent thee to prepare his people?"

22. And Issa, having blessed him, said : "Thou shalt be pardoned, for what thou sayest does not come from thee !" Then, addressing himself to the governor : "Why humiliate thy dignity, and why teach thy inferiors to live in falsehood, as without doing so thou has power to condemn the innocent?"

23. At these words the governor became exceeding wroth, ordering the sentence of death to be passed upon Issa and the acquittal of the two thieves.

24. The judges, having consulted together, said unto Pilate : "We will not take upon our heads the great sin of condemning an innocent man and acquitting thieves. That would be against the law.

25. "Do then as thou wilt." Saying which the priests and the wise elders went out and washed their hands in a sacred vessel, saying : "We are innocent of the death of this just man."

CHAPTER — XIV

1. By the order of the governor, the soldiers then seized Issa and the two thieves, whom they led to the place of execution, where they nailed them to crosses erected on the ground.

2. All the day the bodies of Issa and the two thieves remained suspended, terrible to behold, under the guard of the soldiers; the people standing all around, the relations of the sufferers praying and weeping.

3. At sunset the sufferings of Issa came to an end. He lost consciousness, and the soul of this just man left his body to become absorbed in the Divinity.

4. Thus ended the earthly existence of the reflection of the Eternal Spirit under the form of a man who had saved hardened sinners and endured many sufferings.

5. Meanwhile, Pilate became afraid of his action and gave the body of the saint to his parents, who buried it near the spot of his execution. The crowd came to pray over his tomb,

and the air was filled with groans and lamentations.

6. Three days after, the governor sent his soldiers to carry away the body of Issa to bury it elsewhere, fearing otherwise a popular insurrection.

7. The next day the crowd found the tomb open and empty. At once the rumor spread that the supreme Judge had sent his angels to carry away the mortal remains of the saint in whom dwelt on earth a part of the Divine Spirit.

8. When this rumor reached the knowledge of Pilate, he became angered and forbade anyone, under the pain of slavery and death, to pronounce the name of Issa or to pray the Lord for him.

9. But the people continued to weep and to glorify aloud their Master; wherefore many were led into captivity, subjected to torture, and put to death.

10. And the disciples of Saint Issa abandoned the land of Israel and scattered themselves among the heathen, preaching that they should renounce their errors, bethink them of the salvation of their souls and of the perfect felicity awaiting humanity in that immaterial world of light where, in repose and in all his purity, the Great Creator dwells in perfect majesty.

11. The pagans, their kings, and their warriors listened to the preachers, abandoned their absurd beliefs, and forsook their priests and their idols to celebrate the praise of the all-wise Creator of the universe, the King of kings, whose heart is filled with infinite mercy.